THE GREAT DEPRESSION

ALSO BY JOHN A. GARRATY

Silas Wright (1949)
Henry Cabot Lodge: A Biography (1953)
Woodrow Wilson: A Great Life in Brief (1956)
The Nature of Biography (1957)
From Main Street to the Left Bank: Students and Scholars Abroad (1959)
Right Hand Man: The Life of George W. Perkins (1960)
A Guide to Study Abroad (1962)
The American Nation: A History of the United States (1966)
The New Commonwealth (1968)
Interpreting American History: Conversations with Historians (1970)
Unemployment in History: Economic Thought and Public Policy (1978)
American History (1982)

EDITED WORKS

Quarrels That Have Shaped the Constitution (1964)
Labor and Capital in the Gilded Age (1967)
Historical Viewpoints: Notable Articles from American Heritage (1970)
The Columbia History of the World (with Peter Gay, *1972*)
Encyclopedia of American Biography (with Jerome Sternstein, *1974*)
Dictionary of American Biography: Supplements IV–VII (1974–81)
A Chronological Subject Guide to American Heritage (1985)

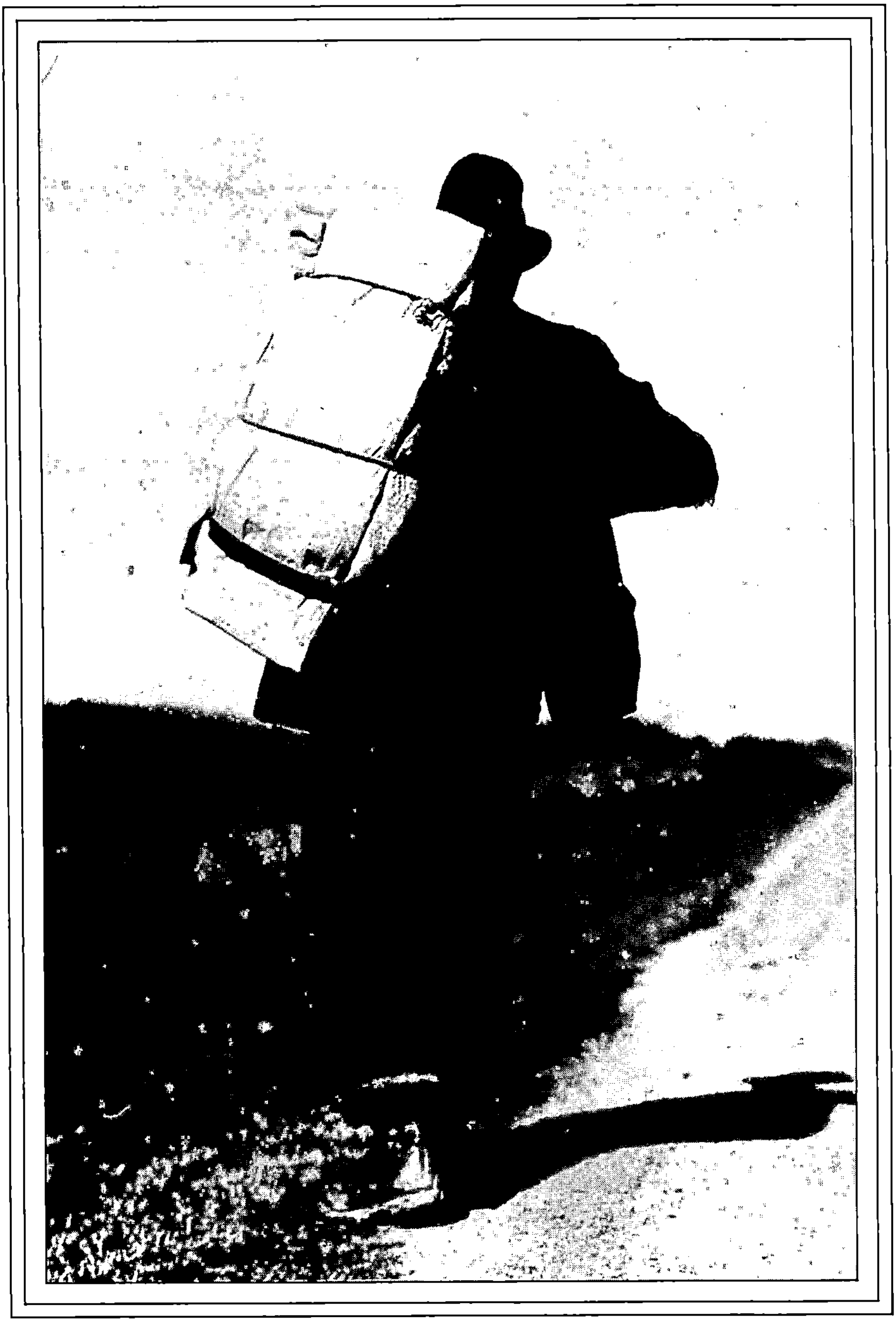

Library of Congress

THE GREAT DEPRESSION

AN INQUIRY into the
causes, course, and *consequences of*
the WORLDWIDE
DEPRESSION
of the *Nineteen-Thirties,*
as seen by contemporaries
and in the
light of HISTORY

JOHN A. GARRATY

HARCOURT BRACE JOVANOVICH
PUBLISHERS
San Diego   New York   London

HBJ

Library of Congress Cataloging-in-Publication Data
Garraty, John Arthur, 1920–
The Great Depression.
Bibliography: p.
Includes index.
1. Depressions, 1929. 2. Economic history—1918–1945.
I. Title.
HB3717 1929.G36   1986   338.5'42   86-3107
ISBN 0-15-136903-8

Designed by Kate Nichols

Printed in the United States of America

First Edition

A B C D E

ACKNOWLEDGMENTS

A s is common when one engages in a scholarly pursuit over a protracted period, persons "too numerous to mention" have helped me in one way or another, and I have tried to show each of them my appreciation at the time. Here I wish only to list a few whose contributions were particularly valuable. Stanley Engerman and Robert Heilbroner read the entire manuscript. Their comments saved me from many errors and led me to ideas and materials that had previously escaped me. The late Carlos Diaz Alejandro and Edward Malefakis made important contributions to my treatment of agriculture. Richard Lowitt brought to my attention a number of obscure sources relevant to the New Deal that he had come across in his own researches, while Knut Borchardt and Ivan T. Berend aided me with key references to European materials. When the book was finished, Patrick Williams checked the manuscript against the sources, catching and correcting many dozens of small errors and a few rather horrendous ones. My editor, Paul McCluskey, has been a constant source of support and encouragement. To these friends and colleagues (and to any I may now be overlooking!) many thanks.

CONTENTS

THE GREAT DEPRESSION

München, 27. September 1922   Preis 15 Mark   27. Jahrgang Nr. 26

SiMPLiCiSSiMUS

Bezugspreis vierteljährlich 120 Mark   Begründet von Albert Langen und Th.Th. Heine   Bezugspreis vierteljährlich 120 Mark
Alle Rechte vorbehalten

Der neue Preis
(siehe Seite 382)

„Sehr aktuell — bloß der Preis ist noch etwas altmodisch!"

CHAPTER I

WHY IT HAPPENED

The Great Depression of the 1930s was a worldwide phenomenon composed of an infinite number of separate but related events. The relationships were often obscure; even today some of the most important of them remain baffling. But it is indisputable that there was a pattern to the trend of events nearly everywhere. After the Great War of 1914–18, both belligerents and neutrals experienced a period of adjustment and reconstruction that lasted until about 1925. By that date, the economies of most countries had gotten back at least to the levels of 1913. There followed a few years of rapid growth, but in 1929 and 1930 the prosperity ended. Then came a precipitous plunge, which lasted until early 1933. This dark period was followed by a gradual, if spotty, recovery. The revival was aborted, however, by the sudden, steep recession of 1937–38. Finally, a still more cataclysmic event, the outbreak of World War II in the summer of 1939, put an end to the depression.

At the time, this developing pattern was not immediately clear. The people of every country were, however, aware that the same forces were at work everywhere and that these forces had caused an economic catastrophe of unprecedented proportions.

Surely if the Great Depression was basically the same everywhere, international cooperation was essential for ending it. That much was recognized almost from the start. But despite the urgings of economists and statesmen, the nations were singularly unsuccessful in coordinating their attempts to overcome the depression. As time passed, most countries adopted narrowly nationalistic policies, some deliberately aimed at benefiting their own people at the expense of the people of other nations. Strangely, none of these divergent attacks appeared to alter the general pattern of the world economy outlined above, except that ultimately, beggar-thy-neighbor economics contributed importantly to the outbreak of World War II.

In retrospect it seems likely that if the nations had cooperated with one another better in dealing with their economic problems, they could have avoided or at least ameliorated the terrible economic losses that all of them suffered during that decade of depression. Certainly the actions that many nations took (as well as some that they could have taken but did not) influenced the course of the depression in observable ways.

Knowledgeable people at the time had a good grasp of the causes of the depression, and modern experts have not added a great deal to what these observers understood. The disagreements—then and now—involve the relative importance of different factors and their interrelationships, not the causes themselves.

During the depression, politicians and businessmen and even supposedly disinterested scholars tended to blame the collapse on events that took place outside their own countries. Many still do. Since the depression was worldwide, and since what happened in one region affected conditions in many others, all such statements, whether well or ill informed, contain at least a germ of truth. But in a sense, the depression was like syphilis, which before its nature was fully understood was referred to in England as the French pox, as the Spanish disease in France, the Italian sickness in Spain, and so on.* As the British civil servant Sir Arthur Salter noted in a

---

* Scholars still argue about the origins of syphilis. Was it imported from America by Columbus's sailors, or was it a suddenly virulent European disease?

1932 speech about the depression, "There is a natural human tendency after any great disaster to search for a single scapegoat, to whom the responsibility that should be shared by others may be diverted."[1]

Many years after it ended, former President Herbert Hoover offered an elaborate explanation of the Great Depression, complete with footnote references to the work of many economists and other experts. "THE DEPRESSION WAS NOT STARTED IN THE UNITED STATES," he insisted. The "primary cause" was the war of 1914–18. In four-fifths of the "economically sensitive" nations of the world, including such remote areas as Bolivia, Bulgaria, and Australia, the downturn was noticeable long before the 1929 collapse of American stock prices.

Hoover blamed America's troubles on an "orgy of speculation" in the late 1920s that resulted from the cheap-money policies that the "mediocrities" who made up the majority of the Federal Reserve Board had adopted in a futile effort to support the value of the British pound and other European currencies. Before he became president, Hoover had warned of the coming danger, but neither the board nor Hoover's predecessor, Calvin Coolidge (whom he detested), had accepted his advice. Coolidge's public statement at the end of his term that stocks were "cheap at current prices" was, Hoover believed, particularly unfortunate, since it undermined his efforts to check the speculative mania on Wall Street after his inauguration.

Hoover could not use this argument to explain the further decline that occurred in the United States in 1930, 1931, and 1932, when he was running the country. He blamed that on foreign developments. European statesmen "did not have the courage to meet the real issues," he claimed. Their rivalries and their heavy spending on arms and "frantic public works programs to meet unemployment" led to unbalanced budgets and inflation that "tore their systems asunder." The ultimate result of these unsound policies was the collapse of the German banking system in 1931; that turned what would have been no more than a minor economic downturn into the Great Depression. "The hurricane that swept our shores," wrote Hoover, "was of European origin."[2]

The Prime Minister of Great Britain during the depression was Ramsay MacDonald, a socialist. He blamed capitalism for the debacle. "We are not on trial," he said in 1930; "it is the system under which we live. It has broken down, not only in this little island . . . it has broken down everywhere, as it was bound to break down." The Germans argued that the depression was political in origin. The harsh terms imposed on them by the Versailles Treaty and especially the reparations payments that, they claimed, sapped the economic vitality of their country, had caused it. One conservative German economist, Hero Moeller, blamed the World War naval blockade for his country's economic troubles in the 1930s. "The English merchant fleet helped to build up the world economy," he said; "the British Navy helped to destroy it."[3]

France escaped the initial impact of the depression. During its early stages, French leaders attributed this happy circumstance to the particular qualities of their country. "France is a garden," they explained. But when the slump became serious in France in 1932, they accused Great Britain of causing it by adopting irresponsible monetary policies and the United States of "exporting unemployment" by substituting machines for workers. "Mechanization," a writer in the *Revue d'Economie Politique* explained in 1932, "is an essential element in the worsening of the depression."[4]

At the time, a substantial majority of Americans and nearly all foreigners who expressed opinions on the subject believed that the Wall Street stock market crash of October 1929 had triggered the depression, thereby suggesting that the United States was the birthplace of the disaster. The connection seemed too obvious to be a coincidence. Many modern writers have agreed; for example, the French historian Jacques Chastenet says in *Les Années d'Illusions: 1918–1931*, "After the stock market crash on the other side of the Atlantic came an economic crisis. . . . The crisis caused a chain reaction in the entire world."

But there have always been students of the subject who have disagreed—among them, not surprisingly, the president of the New York Stock Exchange in 1929, E. H. H. Simmons. He insisted that the September 1929 failure of the financial empire of the English entrepreneur Clarence Hatry had precipitated the collapse. Nowadays, most historians play down the importance of the crash. Robert Sobel, a careful student of the American stock market in the 1920s, claims that "no causal relationship between the events of late October 1929 and the Great Depression has ever been shown through the use of empirical evidence." Sobel probably goes too far. The Wall Street debacle triggered declines in other securities markets and led bankers to make borrowing more difficult, which caused a further decline of already depressed commodity prices. In any case, most scholars tend to locate a majority of the underlying causes of the depression in American events.[5]

One thing that experts at the time did agree on—without regard for their nationality—was that the depression was the downward phase of a business cycle. Awareness that economic activity went through recurrent if not necessarily periodic ups and downs that were essentially self-generating first emerged in the nineteenth century. These cycles were a product of the Industrial Revolution. Before then the only pattern to bad times was the seasonal decline associated with winter, when bad weather made road building, construction, and other outdoor activities extremely difficult. There were periods of economic growth and relative prosperity, others of stagnation and decline. Demographic trends, the opening of new lands, and climatic changes produced these shifts. Random events such as wars, droughts, and pestilences could also alter economic conditions in dramatic fashion. But there was no particular rhythm to these changes.

By the 1860s, economists were pointing out that contemporary economic activity was moving in an irregular wavelike pattern. Most early investigators assumed that periods of hard times were deviations from normality, but they were beginning to understand that in some way good times *caused* bad and that in turn, bad times contained the seeds of recovery. That a boom could go too far had been demonstrated in the past by such speculative excesses as the Dutch tulip mania of the seventeenth century and the South Sea Bubble of 1720. Now, economists agreed, capitalism itself was causing the ups and downs. Cycles, wrote the Russian authority Michael Tugan-Baranowsky in 1894, "were rooted in the very essence of the capitalist economic system."[6]

6

In the early twentieth century, dozens of economists analyzed the dynamics of business cycles. They disagreed about some of the labyrinthine complexities of the process but did not challenge Tugan-Baranowsky's conclusion. The myriad activities of profit-seeking farmers, manufacturers, and merchants; the hunches of speculators; and the shifting tastes of consumers led to imbalances in the supply of and the demand for all kinds of goods and services. The imbalances influenced prices, investment, and popular expectations. High prices tempted producers to increase output; favorable crop reports discouraged speculators from buying current production; and so on. The imbalances were, however, apparently self-correcting; if manufacturers made too much of anything, its price would fall, profits would disappear, and the producers would cut back on output. Hence the cyclical character of economic activity. In 1932 the American writer Stuart Chase described cycles as "the spree and hangover of an undisciplined economy."[7]

Economists divided business cycles into four stages: expansion; crisis (or panic); recession or contraction; and recovery. The definitive description was made shortly before the Great War by Wesley Clair Mitchell of the University of California. A cycle, Mitchell explained in *Business Cycles* (1913), was "the process of cumulative change by which a renewal of [economic] activity develops into intense prosperity, by which the prosperity engenders a crisis, by which crisis turns into depression, and by which depression finally leads to . . . a revival of activity."[8]

Although all economists claimed to know what business cycles looked like, they did not entirely agree about what caused them. Some attributed cycles to the effects of the weather on agriculture: when conditions were good, farmers prospered, and the rest of the economy was carried along. In its most abstruse form, the weather explanation was based on rhythmic variations in sunspot activity. These were thought to alter climate and thus to affect the production of crops. Some economists also claimed that climatic changes had subtle psychological effects on masses of people, at times causing them to be optimistic, at other times to be depressed, with corresponding effects on their economic behavior.

Most economists, however, saw a more direct connection between economic activity and the cycles. Some located the source of change in banking practices. These experts reasoned as follows: When banks had large reserves, they lowered interest rates. Cheaper loans encouraged manufacturers to invest in new equipment and hire additional workers. The resulting expansion of production caused an upswing of the cycle. But the increased borrowing eventually reduced the banks' reserves, causing them to raise interest rates. That discouraged investment and slowed the economy down.

Another explanation blamed maldistribution of wealth for the cycles. During prosperous times, the rich were unable to spend all of their income. They saved more, which resulted in increased investment, more production, and eventually in more goods than the rest of society had the money to consume. Then goods piled up on shelves and in warehouses, prices fell, production was cut back, and workers were discharged. As a result, the economy entered the depression phase of the cycle.

Still another variant focused on profits as the dynamic of business cycles. When producers increased output, their unit costs declined. Profits rose. They were therefore encouraged to expand still more. Their demands for bank loans to do so caused a credit squeeze. Interest rates went up, discouraging investment. Expansion also led to inefficiency by increasing the demand for labor, which forced employers to pay higher wages and employ less-efficient workers. The prosperity associated with expansion also made managers less careful about costs. As the efficiency of the producers who were expanding declined, new producers were able to compete with them successfully. Output rose still more. When the credit squeeze stage was reached, bankruptcies, declining production, unemployment, and other aspects of the depression phase of the cycle resulted.

These many explanations of business cycles differed mainly in emphasis. They complemented rather than contradicted one another. All involved the existence of a critical point—a crisis that occurred not when expansion stopped but when a shift occurred in popular expectations about economic trends. The central importance of crises in the eyes of economists was reflected in the use of the French and German words *la crise* and *die Krise* to denote depressions and the fact that American depressions before the 1930s were commonly called panics. (The so-called Great Depression of 1873–96 was not a cyclical depression at all but a long period of price deflation accompanied by general, if somewhat erratic, economic growth.)

The crisis stage of the cycle was marked by bank failures and by panic selling on stock markets. The crisis precipitated the depression phase, which was marked by falling prices, rising unemployment, a slowing of production, business failures, and pessimism about the future.

In the beginning, the Great Depression appeared to be a typical cyclical downswing, the precipitating crisis being the Wall Street stock market crash of October 1929. By September 1930, however, it was severe enough to cause the League of Nations to commission the economist Gottfried Haberler to make a study of the theories that had been advanced to explain "the recurrence of periods of economic depression." The League authorities hoped that from such a study of past cycles, "measures can be designed to prevent them."[9] But Haberler's book, *Prosperity and Depression: A Theoretical Analysis of Cyclical Movements*, was not published until 1937.

Meanwhile, as month after month passed without signs of recovery, the terms *crisis* and *cycle* seemed less and less adequate as an explanation of what was going on. The French business cycle theorist Jean Lescure, who had been commissioned to prepare an article on "crisis" for the *Encyclopedia of the Social Sciences* (1930–35), wrote in his essay, "A crisis may be defined as a grave and sudden disturbance of economic equilibrium. . . . It would seem that for the term crisis one may henceforth substitute that of depression; it is reasonable to speak today of a world depression rather than of a world crisis."

Other experts went still further. "We may no longer be in a 'cycle', but in a 'chute'," an English economist said in 1932. German authorities of varying schools spoke of a "permanent depression"; the "automatic" corrections were not occurring. "What we are now experiencing," said the German banker Dr. Karl Melchior as early as 1931, "is the destruction of the rules of the game of the capitalist system."[10]

Economists labored to find explanations for the stubborn refusal of the business cycle to correct itself. In 1931 Bertil Ohlin of the University of Stockholm claimed in another study sponsored by the League of Nations that the cyclical downturn had been exacerbated by "structural changes and maladjustments" in the economy. A French economist, Gaëtan Pirou, made the same point. The depression, wrote Pirou, was a *"crise de conjoncture et de structure"*—that is, both a cyclical and a structural one.[11]

Ohlin described these structural elements in detail. Some were financial. The major world currencies fluctuated widely in value. Huge short-term loans had been made to politically unstable nations. The chief international creditor, the United States, was "inexperienced," and less careful about its lending because it was less dependent on this business than the chief prewar lender, Great Britain.

Other elements were related to production. Too many farmers were raising too much food. Manufacturers were turning out more tractors and harvesters than the farmers were able to buy. Lower transportation costs enabled more producers to compete in distant markets. Technological advances had resulted in the invention of new products, such as synthetic textiles, that cut into the market for cloth made from natural fibers. In addition, the growth of installment plan purchasing during the 1920s had encouraged manufacturers to expand output; when consumers cut back on such purchases because of the hard times, the manufacturers were left with large inventories and excess capacity.[12]

The economist Paul Einzig argued in 1931 that the depression was "largely due to inadequate co-operation between various economic interests," national and international. "There is nothing mysterious about the crisis," Einzig claimed. The financial disruptions that followed the collapse of the Austrian *Kreditanstalt* bank in May 1931, culminating in the abandonment of the gold standard by Great Britain, only strengthened Einzig's opinion. "But for inadequate international co-operation," he wrote in 1932, "the calamity of 1931 would never have occurred."[13]

In *Economics of a Changing World* (1933), which he described as a layman's economic text, H. V. Hodson stressed agricultural overproduction as the chief cause of the depression. When crop prices fell, farmers tried to produce more, and new farm machinery made it easy for them to do so. Therefore agricultural prices fell relatively further than other prices. This trend was strengthened when consumer spending on raw materials declined. "Hence," Hodson predicted darkly, "we may expect the economic system not merely to remain liable to industrial fluctuations but to become susceptible to progressively more violent disturbances."[14]

Lionel Robbins, a youthful professor at the London School of Economics, offered what was probably the most influential contemporary explanation of the length of the downturn in *The Great Depression* (1934). The World War had destroyed much property and stimulated nationalistic sentiments that resulted in restrictions on international trade, Robbins wrote. Like Ohlin he believed that the depression was dragging on because of structural weaknesses. For example, monetary confusion and rampant inflation after the war had hampered trade.

But Robbins insisted that the main reason why the depression had not ended was that monopolistic corporations and cartels, labor unions, and government controls were interfering with the free functioning of market forces. Rigid prices, rigid wages, and government regulations such as tariffs (which Robbins called "fusty relics of medieval trade regulation, discredited through five hundred years of theory and hard experience") had stifled new investment, kept inefficient producers from going bankrupt, and prevented prices from falling low enough to stimulate demand. By their very efforts to end the depression, people were preventing the self-correcting adjustments that normally brought about economic recovery. "Intervening to prop up unsound positions . . . must cease," Robbins wrote. Although he admitted that the draconian policies he thought necessary would cause much suffering, he insisted that however well meaning, the policies he was criticizing were causing even more suffering. This was a powerful argument. Then and now, many economists far less enthusiastic about laissez-faire than Robbins have blamed the "administered prices" that existed in highly concentrated industries for the length of the depression.[15]

Robbins was an excellent economist; his reasoning was logically impeccable, though based on premises that were quite unrealistic. The leading Marxist analyst of the time, Eugen Varga, a Hungarian resident in Moscow, used essentially the same argument but interpreted the situation differently. Depressions were of course caused by the capitalist system, he explained in *The Great Crisis* (1933). More specifically, the war had produced a pent-up demand for consumer goods and for capital to replace worn-out equipment. Postwar reconstruction, financed by American loans, had caused production to increase enormously. Because of the maldistribution of wealth resulting from capitalist exploitation of the working class, supply had outstripped demand—the depression was a typical cyclical crisis of overproduction.

Like Robbins, Varga arued that structural factors were responsible for prolonging the depression phase of the cycle. Nationalism resulted in policies that restricted international trade. Government support of industrial monopolies enabled manufacturers to exploit their workers and gobble up a disproportionate share of wealth. Monopolists were keeping prices artificially high, which along with the chronic surplus of agricultural produce and of capital, and the massive unemployment of the era, were prolonging the depression.[16]

These many explanations of the Great Depression, like the theorists' explanations of the basic nature of cycles, had much in common. After his detailed analysis of cycles for the League of Nations, Gottfried Haberler concluded that "the real differences of opinion have been frequently exaggerated," being more matters of emphasis than basic disagreements. Some differed only in the terminology employed. "Most writers," said Haberler, "are inclined rather to dwell on the controversial issues than to stress the points of general agreement."[17]

In a sense, the economists, both conservative ones like Robbins and radicals like Varga, were correct in blaming government regulatory measures for prolonging the depression. A world economy did indeed exist in the 1930s. Efficient transportation and regional specialization had progressed to a point where national restrictions and measures designed to favor local interests were bound to affect the whole system in unforeseen and sometimes counterproductive ways. Of course this had been true ever since merchants first sailed the seas and peddlers tramped with their wares from one country to another. But in the twentieth century, the interrelations of production and commerce reached a volume and complexity of a different order. Regulations imposed by individual nations tended to hamper international commerce. Such regulations tended to favor inefficient producers. They fostered international rivalry rather than international cooperation. To those who tried to see the world economy as a whole, they seemed at best futile, at worst dangerous.

Moreover, government rules and regulations were frequently based on insufficient information. The collection of statistics was haphazard and those that were collected were often grossly inaccurate. In no industrial nation, for example, were adequate figures on unemployment available. Some countries depended on labor unions to keep track of the jobless. Others counted only those who qualified for relief of one kind or another. Still others relied on unemployment insurance data.[18] When laws were passed and edicts issued based on incorrect information, it was hardly likely that they would achieve the desired results. Yet the effects of these laws and edicts could be powerful indeed.

As innumerable historians have pointed out, the leaders of most nations were blissfully ignorant of economics (which was not necessarily a handicap) and (far more serious) short on insight, imagination, and political courage. Frequently they seemed almost blindly unaware of the actual state of the economy in their own countries and elsewhere. At the World Economic Conference in 1933, the representatives of each of the great powers often acted at cross-purposes, pressing at one moment for international cooperation, at another for narrowly nationalistic policies. "Bewildered by depression," a student of the conference has written, "most officials adopted parts of both programs, largely unaware of [their] contradictory nature."[19]

The British historian Derek H. Aldcroft takes a charitable view of the inadequacies of the statesmen of the era in *From Versailles to Wall Street*:

> Enlightened government policies rapidly applied could have alleviated the crisis. But it is difficult to believe that a depression could have been avoided altogether. Lag effects would have required the appropriate action to have been taken a few months before the peak; and governments would have needed the foresight, skill and aptitude to do so, which clearly at that time they had not.

Other scholars have been less tolerant. An Australian describes the policies of his country as "deeply influenced by shibboleths conditioned by the events of an earlier period." Alfred Sauvy, the French economic historian, has been particularly caustic. French statesmen, he writes in his *Economic History of France between the Wars*, were "extremely ignorant of economics," but that was excusable because the typical French economist resembled "a doctor, stuffed with theories, who had never seen a sick person." Politicians on the right could not recognize the difference between prices in France and abroad, "the key index of the era." They "practiced a policy of severe deflation without knowing what it would lead to." The left "made a gigantic arithmetical error." It "let itself be guided by public clamor" and instituted the 40-hour work week at a time when France needed more production rather than less.

In their monumental *Monetary History of the United States*, the American economists Milton Friedman and Anna Jacobson Schwartz describe "contemporary economic comment" about the Great Depression as "hardly distinguished by the correctness or profundity of understanding of the economic forces at work." They are scornful of "the lack of understanding and experience" of the men who shaped Federal Reserve policy in the early 1930s. And they write:

The collapse from 1929 to 1933 was neither foreseeable nor inevitable. It could, in fact, have been greatly moderated by policies that there was every reason in advance to expect would be followed.[20]

Many of the policies that governments adopted during the depression hampered recovery. The American Hawley-Smoot Tariff Act of 1930 dealt a crushing blow to European industry, already hurt by the developing depression. By stifling international trade and preventing the Europeans from earning dollars, the law also destroyed the last possibility that the United States would collect the money it had lent its allies during the World War. Great Britain's decision to maintain the pound at its prewar value when it returned to the gold standard in 1925 made British goods uncompetitive in foreign markets, reduced investment, and caused unemployment to soar. Heavy German spending on public works, financed by short-term loans, contributed to the collapse of the German banking system in 1931.

The most nearly universal example of a counterproductive government policy was the effort that nations made to keep their budgets in balance. Doing so proved next to impossible. The depression caused tax revenues to decline at the same time that the governments were being forced to spend more on relief for the unemployed and others in need. With prices falling, unemployment high, and economic activity stagnating, deliberate deficit spending would have provided salutary stimulation to their economies. Yet just about every nation attempted to maintain its income and reduce expenditures to a minimum in order to balance its budget. As H. W. Arndt wrote in *The Economic Lessons of the Nineteen-Thirties*, published in 1944, "Orthodox finance demanded that the budget should be balanced annually, by rigid economies in expenditure and the imposition of additional taxes."[21]

"A well-balanced budget is not a luxury which is to be avoided," British Chancellor of the Exchequer Philip Snowden lectured Winston Churchill in 1930; "it is a necessity which is to be provided for."[22] During a four-month period in 1931–32, Herbert Hoover, whose economic sophistication was far greater than that of most politicians, made no fewer than 21 public statements stressing the need for a balanced federal budget. In February 1933, after his defeat in the 1932 presidential election, he sent a desperate hand-written letter to President-elect Franklin D. Roosevelt, pleading with him to announce "that there will be no tampering or inflation of the currency [and] that the budget will be unquestionably balanced even if further taxation is necessary."[23]

Roosevelt was unmoved by this letter, but his feelings about budget balancing were not much different than Hoover's. In 1928 William Trufant Foster and Waddill Catchings wrote *The Road to Plenty*, a book that attracted considerable attention. Roosevelt read it. After coming across the sentence, "When business begins to look rotten, more public spending," he wrote in the margin, "Too good to be true—you can't get something for nothing." Four years later, while campaigning for the presidency, he criticized Hoover for spending too much. He promised if elected to balance the budget. "Any Government, like any family, can for a year spend a little more than it earns," Roosevelt said. "But you and I know that a continuation of that habit means the poorhouse." One of his first acts as president was to urge Congress to reduce federal expenditures by $500 million, in order, he said, to save the country from bankruptcy.[24]

When Heinrich Brüning became chancellor of Germany in 1932, he promised President Hindenburg "that as long as I had his trust, I would at any price make the government finances safe." In 1933, after France had begun to feel the full effects of the depression, a special commission called for both a cut in government expenditures and a tax increase in order to balance the budget. "What good is it to talk, what good to draw up plans," Premier Joseph Paul-Boncour explained, "if one ends with a budget deficit which . . . wastes away the resources of the country?"[25]

Leaders in countries large and small—in Asia, the Americas, and Europe—echoed these sentiments. Japanese finance minister Junnosuke Inoue insisted in August 1930 that "increased government spending can only work against our goals. It will . . . weaken the financial soundness of the government." In 1932 a committee of Australian businessmen and economists concluded, "No plan to relieve unemployment can be successful unless deficits are being progressively reduced."[26]

Prime Minister William Lyon Mackensie King of Canada, a man who was so parsimonious that he cut new pencils into three pieces and used them until they were tiny stubs, saw, his biographer has recorded, "a direct connection between federal economies and national prosperity. . . . Governments should live within their means." When King's successor, R. B. Bennett, took office in 1931, he urged spending cuts and higher taxes to get rid of a deficit of more than $80 million. The next year, Bennett was still insisting that "we must practice the most rigid economy and not spend a single [unnecessary] cent." A Canadian historian has written of Bennett's position in the early 1930s, "When it came to proposals of inflation and 'unbalancing' the budget he was as the rock of Gibraltar.[27]

No nation was harder hit by the depression than Chile. Income from its principal exports, nitrates and copper, declined from more than 2 billion pesos in 1929 to 282 million in 1932. The government responded to the resulting financial stringency by cutting its expenses and raising the discount rate to 9 percent in a futile effort to attract foreign exchange. When he became president of Brazil as a result of the Revolution of 1930, Getúlio Vargas continued the conservative financial policies of his predecessor, Washington Luís. Vargas had "a high respect for a balanced budget," a biographer notes.[28]

Although engaged throughout the depression in a "struggle for mere economic survival," the Polish government kept its deficits to a minimum by the most heroic economies. When asked by a journalist to describe his priorities, Jaime Carner, one of a succession of like-minded Spanish finance ministers in the early 1930s, replied that his policy could "be reduced to three points, a balanced budget, a balanced buget, and a balanced budget." As late as 1935, the current Spanish finance minister was still making what he described as "heroic" efforts to avoid deficits.

During the early stages of the depression, the Czechs stepped up spending on public works. But the steep decline of their exports and the central European banking crisis of 1931 caused the government to reverse course. Public expenditures were reduced and income and excise taxes raised in a desperate effort to balance the budget. Officials displayed an "irrational fear of the inflationary nature of a budget deficit." Combined with the extremely conservative monetary policy of the Czech central bank, this policy plunged Czechoslovakia into a still deeper depression. Until 1937, when policy changed, Czech statesmen were, according to a recent scholar, of a "conservative disposition." They "attached a great deal of prestige to currency stability" and were "steeped in traditional principles and fears." Such examples could be multiplied almost endlessly.[29]

These budget-balancing efforts only made the depression worse. Some economists at the time recommended expansionist policies. But the weight of opinion was on the other side. "A unique situation obtained," writes the British historian Sidney Pollard. "[Economists'] advice was totally wrong, and dramatically opposed to the real remedies—a circumstance almost as rare as it is for a group of advisers to be totally right."[30] Unique or not, it is not difficult to understand why this was so. In hard times, prudent people reduced their spending and tried to save more than usual in case conditions should get worse. If individuals had to tighten their belts, surely governments should do so too. In 1931 the British *Financial Times* warned its readers, "The man in the street must understand that if none of us can spend more than he earns without going bankrupt, this rule applies as well for the nation, which is only a collection of individuals."[31]

That markets were feedback mechanisms, where fluctuations of supply and demand balanced and compensated for one another, seemed logically beyond dispute. If a government spent more money than it took in, the argument ran, it would either have to borrow the difference or inflate the currency. If it borrowed, its competition for investors' funds would force up interest rates, which would hinder recovery. Inflation would also tend to push interest rates up. It would benefit persons who had borrowed money but unfairly penalize lenders and people with fixed incomes. More important, inflation would damage public confidence in the government, thus undermining all public policy. The result would be to make the depression worse.

"Our private credit structure is inextricably bound to the credit of the United States," Hoover's secretary of the treasury, Ogden Mills, warned in 1932. "Impair that credit today, and the day after thousands of development projects . . . will stop; thousands of businessmen dependent upon credit renewals will get refusals from their bankers. . . . Merchants who would buy on credit will cancel orders; factories . . . will close." Mills's reasoning was shaky, his rhetoric overblown. But since his opinion was widely shared, policymakers could not safely dismiss his conclusions. The American economist Alvin Hansen stated the case against inflation more soberly in *Economic Stabilization in an Unbalanced World* (1932): "We shall not succeed in solving the depression through the soothing and agreeable device of inflation," he wrote. "We shall come out of it only through hard work, and readjustments that are painful. There is no other alternative."[32]

This "common sense" reasoning was challenged by some economic sophisticates. But in the early 1930s, responsible critics recognized that the common view was so widely held that it could not be ignored. In November 1932, a committee of British economists charged with advising the cabinet recommended an expanded public works program. To pay for it by raising taxes or by cutting down on other government expenditures would be "a deflationary influence, adverse to trade activity," the economists warned. But they recognized that "psychological conventions . . . are still attached to the maintenance of the principle of budgetary equilibrium." They therefore limited themselves to urging that the deflation "not be carried further in a time of depression than considerations of [public] confidence really justify."

"Let me say emphatically that I am not in favor of attempting to balance the budget in the midst of depression," said Professor Sumner Slichter of the Harvard Business School in 1933. *"But if the deficit is too large and excites too much alarm, its net effect may be deflationary. . . ."*[33]

Furthermore, both taxation and government spending made

19

up a much smaller percentage of total economic activity in the 1930s than is common today. In most countries, the stimulation provided by any then-conceivable amount of deficit spending would probably not have been enough to turn the economy around. Governments *did* run deficits despite their best intentions, and these had some effect. But if a nation had deliberately run at a deficit, investors and consumers might well have become so alarmed that the ultimate effect on the economy would have been restrictive, as Slichter suggested. The general opinion was that cutbacks in government spending were necessary to break out of the slump and get the business cycle moving again.

Few economists, fewer politicians, and still fewer ordinary citizens opposed all government efforts to end the depression by interfering with the operation of free market forces. However, anyone who believed in the reality of business cycles assumed that each phase of the cycle caused the next and that even this interminable depression somehow contained within itself the seeds of recovery. Before the seeds could sprout, it seemed, the "painful readjustments" that Hansen mentioned had to take place. Production had to lag until surplus stocks had been sold off. Wages had to fall so that goods could be sold profitably at lower prices. Inefficient producers had to go out of business; workers had to endure wage cuts and long periods of unemployment.

This did not keep people of all sorts—businessmen, labor leaders, philosophers, and clerics as well as economists and political leaders—from suggesting things that governments should do to speed recovery and ease the suffering that the depression was causing. As time passed more and more proposals were advanced, and larger numbers of them were put to the test. But the same reasoning that visualized business cycles as the result of the interactions of billions of individual decisions suggested that piecemeal remedies could work well only by chance, and that measures designed to help one group or nation would probably injure some other. Since the depression was worldwide, how could a local "solution" really solve anything?

Repeatedly during the early thirties, the League of Nations organized conferences at which experts discussed one or another aspect of the disaster. Whatever the specific recommendations that emerged from these meetings, the general point was always the same: international cooperation was essential if the problem was to be solved. This cooperation was almost never achieved.

If custom and public opinion limited the scope and effectiveness of government fiscal policies, nations could nevertheless exert powerful influences on economic activity by their monetary policies. Changes in interest rates and in the amount of money in circulation affected everyone and thus influenced the investments of businessmen, the purchases of consumers, and, even more, the ebb and flow of international trade. It is ironic that in this area the great powers did manage a degree of cooperation. Yet at crucial points, their actions made the depression worse and delayed its ending. The weight of scholarly opinion on this point is clear, though different historians have emphasized different aspects of the question. Flaws in the international financial system were a major cause of the collapse, and errors made by bankers and politicians in trying to repair the damage prolonged it.

Before the Great War, Britain had functioned as a stabilizing force in international money markets. The pound was the currency against which others were measured. The Bank of England's willingness to exchange a fixed amount of gold for the pound was the underlying rock on which all values were based. The exigencies of the war, however, forced Great Britain and the rest of the powers to abandon the gold standard.

After the war Britain returned to the gold standard, foolishly fixing the value of the pound at its prewar level, $4.86. But, ravaged by the war, it was no longer financially powerful enough to serve as the world's banker. Moreover, the overvalued pound made British exports difficult to sell. The nation's foreign trade shrank, further crippling much of its already depressed heavy industry.[34]

When France went back on the gold standard in 1928, it valued the franc at about 25 to the dollar, only one-fifth of its prewar worth. With the franc cheap in relation to gold, the Bank of France accumulated large sums in pounds because more French products were sold in Great Britain, fewer British goods in France. This gave the Bank of France "a tremendous capacity to influence the London money market and the position of the Bank of England." By converting pounds into gold, it could drain the Bank of England of reserves and thus reduce the availability of credit in Britain.[35]

Indirectly, the Germans were the cause of much of the irrational behavior of the other powers. The German obligation to pay reparations for the damage caused by the Great War led the Allies to expect more than Germany was willing to try to pay them. It also encouraged the Allies to believe that they could pay their debts to the United States only to the extent that they received reparations from Germany, a belief that was only slightly less irrational.

The runaway German inflation of 1922–23 was a further reason why nearly every nation adopted deflationary policies during the depression; that disastrous destruction of supposedly fixed values seemed to stand as a warning of what could happen when "irresponsible" monetary policies were pursued.

Germany contributed more directly to the depression by relying heavily on short-term loans. Most of these funds were borrowed in the United States. When American sources of money dried up after 1929, Germany had nowhere to turn when its obligations fell due.

As for the United States, the administrations of the 1920s resented the Europeans' reluctance to pay their debts unless they received reparations from Germany and were almost paranoid in their worry lest "wily" Old World diplomats mislead and deceive them. Their fear and resentment hampered international cooperation and made rational discussion of disagreements difficult—this despite the fact that the Federal Reserve Board, dominated by Benjamin Strong of the New York Fed, maintained close and generally cordial relations with the central banks of Great Britain, Germany, and France.*

* In his memoirs, Herbert Hoover called Strong, whose policies he disapproved of, "a mental annex to Europe."[36]

In the late 1920s, the board was torn between its wish to check the stock market boom by raising interest rates and the fear that doing so would discourage "legitimate" borrowers and slow down economic growth. The importance of lowering rates in order to take pressure off the pound, the mark, and other fragile European currencies was another, less controlling reason why the board did not act vigorously to restrain stock market speculation.

The steep slump of the American economy had widening repercussions. In 1929 the United States produced over 40 percent of the world's manufactured goods, twice as much as Great Britain and Germany combined. When American producers cut back on their purchases of raw materials and other supplies, the effect on other countries was devastating. American protectionism made matters worse, for high tariffs hampered all world trade and further complicated the war debt problem. The deflationary policies of the Federal Reserve Board in the early 1930s put added pressure on European currencies. After Great Britain was again forced to leave the gold standard in 1931, many foreign banks withdrew deposits from America in the form of gold; they were afraid that the United States might go off the gold standard too. When the Reserve Board raised the discount rate to discourage these withdrawals, it inadvertently exacerbated the deflationary trend, thus deepening and prolonging the world depression.

Arguments within the American financial community as to whether or not interest rates should be lowered prevented any consistent policy from being developed. Present-day economists disagree about the exact impact on the world economy of American financial policies between the stock market crash and the 1931 devaluations. Some consider these effects to have been disastrous. Others think them unimportant. Nearly all, however, believe that a more inflationary policy by the Federal Reserve would have helped to ease the situation and shortened the depression. The American deflation was probably the cause of much of the deflation that took place elsewhere and thus an important reason why the depression lasted so long.[37]

Charles P. Kindleberger made this argument effectively in *The*

World in Depression (1973). Since Great Britain could no longer supply the international leadership it had provided before the Great War, probably the United States should have stepped into the breach. What was needed was not merely American cooperation but American financial leadership. If the United States had been willing to act as a lender of last resort to economically distressed nations in 1931, when the Austrian, German, and British banks were threatened with collapse, and if it had agreed to keep its own market open to cheap foreign goods even at some cost to American producers, the depression would have been less disastrous for all nations, including the United States. The United States did not lend generously because it feared it would be throwing good money after bad. Yet as Kindleberger has recently remarked, "The only means of recovering bad money is to send good after it." The Hawley-Smoot tariff was a mistake for both economic and psychological reasons, important, according to Kindleberger, "less for its impact on the United States balance of payments, or as conduct unbecoming a creditor nation, than for its irresponsibility." It caused "a headlong stampede to protection and restrictions on imports" all over the world.[38]

Kindleberger does not blame the length of the depression entirely on the United States. He concedes that "intense international interaction produced both the boom and the collapse." And he admits that American public opinion, "bemused by domestic concerns," was unwilling to support the kind of leadership that was needed. He also points out that the necessary financial actions were "perhaps beyond the power of policy . . . in the existing state of knowledge,"[39] which comes close to saying that the depression was unavoidable.

More important, neither Kindleberger nor any other leading student of the subject claims that the United States alone was responsible for the depression. American financial policy had little to do with the underlying imbalances in the world economy of the 1920s, principally the persistent, pervasive slump in the prices of agricultural commodities and of nearly all raw materials. This structural imbalance hampered economic growth in nonindustrial countries and deprived the industrial countries of potential markets. Because of it, the boom of the late twenties was sure to come to an unhappy end, no matter what any government did or did not do. The war debt and reparations tangle, for which the United States was only partially responsible, also had much to do with the severity of the depression. In any case, the Great Depression occurred and ran its course, which we shall now follow.

CHAPTER II

HOW IT STARTED

W hatever may be said about the causes of the Great Depression, it is quite clear that few people expected trouble in 1929, and almost none of those who did had any idea of how serious the trouble would be. The world economy seemed to have recovered fully from the devastation of the Great War. The growth was not uniform, but business had picked up in most countries. Both international trade and industrial production were roughly 20 percent higher in 1929 than in 1925. Conditions were improving even in the Soviet Union, where the economy had been disrupted repeatedly since the 1917 revolution, by the efforts of the leadership to change the entire system. In 1929 the Russians' first Five-Year Plan was well under way. All signs indicated a wide acceptance of the plan by ordinary Russians, and a real effort to modernize the economy in order to increase production, especially of capital goods.

Nearly everywhere, the problems of postwar reconstruction were at least in the process of being worked out. After the war, just about every nation—the United States and Great Britain were the major exceptions—suffered from drastic inflation. The German "hyperinflation" was by far the most extreme, but France, Italy, and the central and eastern European countries were also afflicted. In 1924, however, a committee of the Allied Reparations Commission chaired by the United States director of the budget, Charles G. Dawes, had drafted a plan restructuring Germany's war debts to the Allies. Besides reducing the debts to more manageable size, the commission reorganized the German central bank and arranged for a large loan so that Germany could return to the gold standard.

In the late 1920s, the frightening postwar inflation appeared to have been checked. Despite the booming world economy, the prices of most goods were trending downward. By presumably settling the reparations problem, the Dawes Plan eased the controversies that had vexed relations between Germany and the Allies and between the Allies and the United States. For his work on the plan, Charles Dawes was awarded a Nobel Peace Prize in 1925.

Then, in 1927, all the powers signed the Kellogg-Briand Pact outlawing war as an instrument of national policy. Skeptics described this toothless treaty as an international kiss, but as the decade ended, the future seemed unclouded.

In December 1928, shortly after Herbert Hoover, darling of American business, won a sweeping victory in the presidential election of that year, the retiring president, Calvin Coolidge, delivered his last Annual Message to Congress. Coolidge said:

> No Congress of the United States ever assembled . . . has met with a more pleasing prospect. . . . The great wealth created by our enterprise and industry, and saved by our economy, has had the widest distribution among our own people, and has gone out in a steady stream to serve the charity and the business of the world. The requirements of existence have passed beyond the standard of necessity into the region of luxury. . . . The country can regard the present with satisfaction and anticipate the future with optimism.[1]

In Great Britain a similar mood predominated. The victory of the Labour Party in 1929 alarmed some conservatives, but the Labour government showed no sign of adopting any very radical policies. Prime Minister Ramsay MacDonald made no move to nationalize industry or institute any drastic change. In July 1929, buoyed by reports of rising exports and declining unemployment, he addressed the House of Commons in a confident and expansive mood. The government, he said, was committed to improving the country's transportation network, a still further growth of exports, and a general improvement of the efficiency of the economy. MacDonald scoffed at the possibility of serious trouble. Stressing political harmony, he urged his parliamentary opponents "to consider ourselves more as a council of State and less as arrayed regiments facing each other in battle."[2]

The situation in France was, if possible, even more reassuring. Both industrial and agricultural production had at last surpassed prewar levels, and they were still rising. Exports were at an all-time high. After France returned to the gold standard in 1926, confidence in the much-battered French franc had been restored. With francs cheap relative to the pound and the dollar, France's gold reserves were mounting steadily. The budget was balanced. Work was plentiful—in December 1929, fewer than a thousand people were receiving unemployment relief. Premier André Tardieu announced a "politics of prosperity." By utilizing a huge treasury surplus just reported by his finance minister, he planned to spend 5 billion francs over the next five years on "systematic aid to the vital forces of the country," a "national retooling" of agriculture, industry, commerce, health, and education.[3]

Germany was also riding a wave of prosperity. Industry was in the midst of an expansion and modernization program. Local governments had begun public works projects of many kinds, some financed by loans from American banks. Surveying the situation when he took office in June 1928, Chancellor Hermann Müller spoke with calm assurance. Müller, a socialist, had headed the German government briefly after the war. At that time, he had called for thoroughgoing changes in order to democratize both the political system and the economy. Now he sang a different tune. "The foundations of the republic stand firm and unshakable," he announced. This was no mere self-congratulatory comment by a victorious politician. A more disinterested witness, the historian Leslie Buell, wrote in 1928:

> The outstanding fact in the domestic affairs of the Reich
> . . . has been the real strengthening and entrenchment of
> the Republic. . . . Monarchist sentiment has definitely
> ebbed [and] the moderate parties are in control. . . . Ger-
> many, after years of tribulation and suffering, has staged
> one of the most remarkable come-backs as well as con-
> versions in history and taken her place among the truly
> democratic and liberal states of the world.[4]

Statesmen of other nations made many similar comments in 1928 and 1929. An occasional individual warned of a coming collapse, but such types were dismissed as Cassandras—prophets of gloom who failed to appreciate the expansive force of the world's economy.

The role that the Wall Street stock market crash of October 1929 played in causing the Great Depression has been exaggerated in the popular mind. But that the Great Crash has become a symbol for the depression, the event that one associates with the onset of bad times, is beyond argument. Why this should be is not hard to understand. Black Tuesday, October 29, was, in John Kenneth Galbraith's words, "the most devastating day in the history of the New York stock market"; the securities making up the *New York Times* industrial averages lost all they had gained in a whole year of boom. The market rebounded the next day, but the respite was tempo-rary. By mid-November, stock prices were nearly 40 percent lower than they had been in September.

The financial losses that this swift decline reflected and the panic and despair it generated among investors account for the association that people made between the Great Crash and the long depression of the 1930s. As a matter of fact, the American economy had begun to decline during the early summer, well before the crash. Furthermore, stock prices rebounded between late Novem-ber and the following April. By the end of 1929, the October collapse no longer seemed particularly significant (except to those who had lost their shirts). In November 1929, the left-leaning commentator Stuart Chase expressed the opinion that "we probably have three more years of prosperity ahead of us" before the next cyclical downturn. A month later, the editor-in-chief of the conservative French newspaper *Le Temps* predicted that "the turmoil that has just shaken New York would probably not have deep or lasting repercussions."[5]

The general opinion of supposedly informed people early in 1930 was that the United States had experienced no more than a minor recession, a typical stock market "panic." In June a delegation of American clergymen obtained an interview with President Hoover in order to urge him to undertake an expanded public works program. "You have come sixty days too late," he told them. "The depression is over."

Of course these words were scarcely out of the president's mouth when the bottom fell out of the American economy, along with the economies of most other nations. By the end of 1930, no one doubted any longer that a worldwide depression was in progress. Looking back from that vantage point, the Wall Street crash seemed the place where it had all begun.

Now, these many years later, this no longer seems correct. Scholars generally agree that American stock prices were not unreasonably high in 1929 and that the October collapse had little or no effect on the level of industrial activity in the United States or anywhere else. No effect, that is, except psychological; it is possible, though impossible to demonstrate convincingly, that the shock of the October crash so discouraged investors and consumers that a recession was turned into an economic collapse.[6]

While all the nations experienced the same kinds of economic problems during the depression—industrial stagnation, soaring unemployment, shrinking agricultural prices, financial collapse—these problems manifested themselves in different ways in different places. What attracted the deepest concern at any given time and place appeared less pressing at others.

In the United States, Secretary of the Treasury Andrew Mellon and other conservatives, including many of the most prestigious economists, insisted that the decline should be allowed to bottom out on its own. They reasoned that the depression would eventually have a beneficial sanitizing effect on the economy. The many business bankruptcies would eliminate inefficient producers and open larger markets for efficient ones. Distress sales would get second-rate goods off the shelves and make room for better-quality products. Writing off bad debts would clear the way for fresh starts. Lowering wages would reduce costs, leading to higher profits.

People like Mellon tended to moralize about the depression. Its victims, they implied, were paying for their economic sins, getting what they deserved. Tough, hard-working, efficient types would survive; ultimately, virtue would be rewarded.

President Hoover admired Secretary Mellon, but he rejected this kind of advice. He recognized the danger that the economic slowdown might feed upon itself if nothing was done to stimulate activity. Therefore, early in the depression, he summoned business leaders to Washington and urged them to resist the temptation to cut prices, lay off some workers, and lower the wages of the rest. If manufacturers followed his advice, he predicted, profit margins and consumer demand could both be maintained.

The businessmen seemed to be impressed. Hoover also persuaded Congress to cut personal and corporation income taxes slightly to encourage spending and investment. But he did not believe that the government should intervene directly in most business matters. Doing so, he said, risked creating "a centralized despotism" that "would destroy not only our American system but with it our progress and freedom."

"Progress is born of Co-operation . . . not from governmental restraints," he said in his inaugural address. "Expansion of government in business means that the government, in order to protect itself from the political consequences of its errors, is driven irresistibly . . . to greater and greater control."[7]

Hoover's policies failed to stop the slide. Yet when the depression deepened, he insisted that only state and local agencies and private charities could deal properly with such problems as unemployment and the relief of the destitute. In 1930 the central section of the country was struck by a severe drought. This had nothing to do with the depression. But thousands of farmers found themselves with no harvest and not enough money to buy next year's seed or feed for their livestock. In some cases, they could not even feed their families.

Hoover quickly called a meeting of the governors of the stricken states. He proposed to create a National Drought Relief Committee, and he asked the governors to set up state committees that would in turn create county committees charged with figuring out what help was needed and how to arrange to supply it.

The elaborate structure of this drought relief plan was typical of Hoover's thinking. The federal government could provide know-how and inspiration, but the actual supervision and operation of programs should be local and in the hands of volunteers. Unfortunately, the drought relief machinery did not function properly. The local committees lacked the money needed to handle the problem. The impoverished farmers needed to borrow, but local banks were unable to supply their needs. Hoover expected the Red Cross to provide relief for the destitute, but that organization was reluctant to take on the task; it too lacked sufficient resources and hesitated to commit the limited funds it did have to drought relief.

Hoover's plan did not work. Yet he continued to insist that "mutual self-help through voluntary giving" was the proper way to deal with such situations. Furthermore, when shrinking federal revenues resulting from the depression caused the government to run at a deficit, Hoover forgot about trying to stimulate consumer spending. He called for tax increases and reduced government outlays in order to balance the budget. In 1932, as the depression sounded the depths, Congress *raised* taxes by a larger percentage than ever before in American history.[8] *

By the end of 1930, the American banking system was in serious trouble. Over 1,300 banks had failed during the year, and the number was increasing rapidly. The harm caused by these fail-

* The deficit was nearly $1.5 billion. It can be argued, however, that because government spending made up less than 4 percent of the GNP at this time, even the elimination of all federal taxation would not have had much effect on the economy!

34

ures—both the actual loss of savings and the fear that the failures inspired among depositors with money in other, "sound" banks—was so great that Hoover recognized that something had to be done.

But he did not ask Congress for legislation or order the secretary of the treasury to do anything. Instead he called a secret meeting of the country's leading bankers. They were caught in "a degenerating vicious cycle," he told them. It was essential "to restore confidence in the people at large." At his urging, the bankers reluctantly agreed to form a National Credit Corporation (despite its name, this was not a government body) and provide it with $500 million to lend to shaky banks.

President Hoover took pride in having dealt with the problem in the "American way." But the solution he devised provided too little relief, and it came too late. The bankers who ran the National Credit Corporation hesitated to lend their precious $500 million to the banks that needed it most. They became, in Hoover's own words, "ultraconservative, then fearful" and the corporation finally died. During 1931, while Hoover continued to stress maintaining the sound fiscal position of the federal government, nearly 2,300 more banks failed.[9]

In 1932, with Hoover's somewhat reluctant approval, Congress created the Reconstruction Finance Corporation (RFC). This was a federal agency empowered to lend money to troubled banks, insurance companies, railroads, and state and local governments. The RFC was modeled on the War Finance Corporation, which had lent money for plant expansion to companies engaged in war production in 1917–18. Another measure, the Glass-Steagall Act, authorized the Federal Reserve Banks to make loans on assets not previously permissible under the law. These measures prevented many business bankruptcies and kept hundreds of banks from having to close their doors. But in early 1933, just before Franklin Roosevelt took office, the banking system collapsed, precipitating a crisis that led to more basic financial reforms.

In Great Britain the depression was less traumatic because the country had been going through a period of high unemployment for many years and had developed ways of dealing with that problem, though not of solving it. Idle workers received insurance benefits for a period of time and welfare payments, the dole, when their insurance benefits ran out. In other words, the depression represented a less drastic change.

What inhibited British recovery was the fact that powerful financial interests were determined to preserve their position as the world's bankers. This was a hopeless task in the face of the losses they had sustained in the war and the rising financial power of the United States. They wanted, a caustic British historian has written, "the satisfaction of pretending that the war had not damaged the pound."[10]

The effort was in large measure counterproductive because it involved keeping interest rates high in order to attract gold and relieve pressure on the overvalued pound. The bankers favored this policy. But British industrialists opposed it for two reasons: it made exports more expensive, and England depended on exports more than almost any other nation; and it made borrowing more expensive and thus discouraged investment.

A conflict of interest between those involved in the depressed older industries of the north and west, such as coal and textiles, and those in the new growth industries, such as automobiles, further hampered British recovery. The former needed to reduce costs by wage cuts and to lower prices by deflation. The latter would benefit from the rising consumer demand that high wages and inflation would encourage. Great Britain had a kind of dual economy; what was good for one branch would have a bad effect on the other. This was an important reason, though by no means the only one, why unemployment in Britain was so high.

The situation made budget balancing an obsession with the British; Prime Minister MacDonald's socialists accepted it as dogma. After taking over in 1929, the MacDonald government was under pressure to undertake an expensive, loan-financed public works program in order to reduce Britain's chronic unemployment, which increased when the world depression deepened. Instead it adopted a conservative financial policy. In 1930 Parliament raised taxes by £47 million in an effort to balance the budget.

In August 1930, MacDonald appointed a committee of five top-flight economists to investigate the causes of the depression and "indicate the conditions of recovery." In its lengthy report, this group skirted the budget problem. Restoring business confidence, it suggested, could best be accomplished by avoiding both higher direct taxes and larger government expenditures. It described the advantages of an expanded public works program as a way of reducing unemployment and stimulating the economy. But it stressed the practical difficulties of doing so efficiently on a large scale, and it avoided discussion of the politically touchy subject of how such a program might be financed.

The cabinet had already decided not to increase public works expenditures. When they read the committee's report in November, the politicians expressed disappointment. "It was prolific of suggestions of a general character [but] contained no practical propositions to which immediate effect could be given," they complained.[11]

The next year, despite the economies achieved, declining government revenues threatened further deficits and caused a run on gold that threatened to force Great Britain off the gold standard. It is hard to believe but true that although the prices of all kinds of goods were falling, the possibility of the government spending more than it took in caused people to think that runaway inflation was in the offing. If the Bank of England was unable to convert pound notes into gold on demand and therefore had to "devalue" the currency, the danger of inflation would be still greater.

Veneration (and not only in Great Britain) of the way the British adhered to the gold standard is difficult to understand because tying the money supply to a single commodity seems foolishly restricting.* It was based on a deeply felt but usually unspoken fear of human frailty. The virtue of a gold standard is that it works automatically and inexorably; it is beyond the control of politicians and even of the democratic process. The historian Robert Skidelsky

* For example, United States Secretary of the Treasury Ogden Mills, who replaced Andrew Mellon in 1932, wrote during the waning days of the Hoover administration, "If I were dictator and could write my own ticket, the first two goals which I would reach for would be the balancing of the budget of the United States Government and the return to the gold standard by Great Britain."[12]

has described how the British felt about abandoning the gold standard in the early 1930s:

> Once different groups of men in different countries started making autonomous decisions about the value at which their currencies should be fixed, there would be no hindrance to an accelerating spiral of depreciation as each nation sought to gain the advantage over the other. . . . It was one thing to be forced off the gold standard. But to leave voluntarily when resources still existed for defending it was regarded as unthinkable.[13]

Prime Minister MacDonald had appointed a committee of businessmen (like many politicians, MacDonald enjoyed having committees do his thinking for him) to study the problem and suggest "all possible reductions in National Expenditure." This committee, which was headed by Sir George May, an insurance company executive, calculated (August 1931) that if nothing was done, Great Britain would run a budget deficit of £97 million in the coming year. To prevent this drain and bring the budget into balance, it recommended reduced spending for social services, the military, and education, including such things as lower unemployment benefits and steep pay cuts for teachers, soldiers, and policemen. It also urged the postponement of some public works projects.

The May Committee's proposals aroused a storm of protest, which in turn made foreign holders of pounds even more fearful of a devaluation. They increased their conversion of pounds into gold, further drawing down Britain's reserves. When the government sought to borrow £80 million in New York and Paris, the American and French bankers insisted that the May Committee economies be instituted before making the funds available.

The British trade unions, a powerful force in the Labour Party, opposed cutting back on social services. They suggested instead a special tax on fixed-interest securities, which would fall on the shoulders of the well-to-do and which could be justified on the ground that the decline of all prices had increased the real value of interest income. Lacking the full support of his own party, MacDonald either had to resign or form a coalition with the Conservatives. To stress the seriousness of the crisis and the need to put politics aside, he formed a coalition of the three major parties, which was known as the National Government. Parliament then voted the necessary economies, including a 10 percent reduction in unemployment benefits. This was understandable because of the falling cost of living. But in addition, Parliament raised taxes on incomes, liquor, gasoline, and tobacco.

Despite these heroic measures, Great Britain still had to leave the gold standard. The pay cuts caused a strike (somewhat unfairly called a mutiny) of sailors at the naval base of Invergordon, in Scotland. The strike, together with the continuing economic decline, led to another rush to trade pounds for gold, a rush that the government could not check. The pound fell from a little below $5 to about $3.50.

This much-feared devaluation actually benefited the country by lowering the cost of British goods in foreign markets and thus stimulating sales. Devaluation did not do much for the unemployed, however. The number of jobless remained in the range of 1.5 million.

The situation in France was almost the reverse of what it was in Great Britain. Since France was not as heavily committed to industry to begin with, the worldwide industrial decline that began in 1929 had relatively little effect there for some time. Unemployment had not been a problem in the twenties because of a low birth rate and the manpower shortage resulting from the terrible loss of life in the Great War. The fact that the franc had been undervalued also gave a big advantage to the French in foreign markets.

These circumstances made the French, not a particularly self-critical people to begin with, even more than normally self-satisfied. "We are a government of young men presided over by a new man," Premier Tardieu boasted. The Wall Street crash attracted only passing notice. A typical reaction was that an "abscess" had been "lanced."[14]

Nevertheless, the obsession with budget balancing and "sound" finance was as great in France as in harder-pressed countries. The inordinate influence of the Bank of France on the government had much to do with this. Earlier in the 1920s, when the directors of the bank had lost confidence in the government of Premier Edouard Herriot after it failed to come up with a balanced budget, they had even refused to lend the government money to meet its current expenses.

The Bank of France was a most unusual institution even at a time when central banks tended to be a law unto themselves. French law gave its 200 largest stockholders complete control of its policies. These men made up the "200 Families" that critics said (with considerable justification) ran the entire country. The arrogance of the bank's directors is illustrated by the following statement, which they issued at a time when Pierre-Etienne Flandin was premier in the 1930s:

> M. Flandin's Government has some praiseworthy actions to its credit. The Budget was voted in good time. . . . It has shown a sound instinct. Its economic measures—though a little less certain—still deserve a good mark, in view of the difficulties of the situation. This good mark has been given to M. Flandin in the form of credit facilities. These credit facilities may not prove sufficient. He will ask for more credit. Our reply will then depend on whether we are satisfied with the actions of the Government during the first respite we have given it as a reward for its present determination to defend the currency.[15]

However, the world depression gradually began to affect the French economy. The 1930 budget had been designed to provide for another surplus, though smaller than the 5-billion-franc surplus of 1929. But production tailed off, tax revenues declined, and the expected surplus turned out in fact to be a deficit of more than 5 billion francs. Although the projected 1931 and 1932 budgets were both intended to balance, each of these years also produced deficits of about 5 billion francs when actual revenues and expenses were tabulated.

The tone of political discussion on the French budget is reflected in this statement made by then-premier Pierre Laval during the debate in the National Assembly on the 1932 budget:

> I love the working class. [hoots from the far left] I am mayor of a heavily populated Paris suburb, and I have seen the ravages of unemployment. . . . The government will never refuse to go as far as the resources of the country will permit [to help]. But do not ask it to commit acts that risk to compromise the balance of the budget.[16]

The British abandonment of the gold standard was a blow to the French economy, in part because many countries that competed with France in international markets had devalued their currencies when Great Britain did. Despite this, most French business and political leaders interpreted the devaluation, which they considered a blow to British prestige, as beneficial to France. Remaining on the gold standard seemed proof of the nation's economic strength and moral superiority. "France has become one of the two pillars that sustain the world economy," *Le Temps* editorialized in September 1931. "France is above the crisis," another commentator boasted.[17]

Over the next few months, French industrial output fell 17 percent. The number of workers employed in industry fell 9 percent. Wholesale prices dropped 28 percent. Yet in 1932, a British investigator noticed what he described as "official indifference to the depression" in France. When he asked an important trade union official how many members of his organization were unemployed, the man replied, "French people do not like statistics."

"I gathered that the French working men are not very excited about the greatest trade crisis in history," the Englishman concluded.[18]

German political leaders responded to the depression in similar fashion. The Wall Street stock market crash had a more immediate

41

effect in Germany than anywhere else, including even the United States. This was not because large numbers of Germans owned American securities but because the crash caused American banks to refuse to renew many short-term loans to Germany. The credit contraction squeezed the German economy hard. Between 1924 and 1930, Germany had borrowed heavily from foreign sources, using the money to meet the reparations payments required under the Dawes Plan and for various domestic purposes, not all of them economically useful. Early in 1929, the powers agreed to scale down Germany's reparations payments still further (the Young Plan), but by the time the new schedule went into effect, the depression was under way.

The German government had been operating at a deficit to begin with. Now it sank still deeper into the red. Unemployment rose. Industry languished. As in other countries, income from taxes failed to meet expectations, and spending on social services had to be increased as unemployment increased. Germany's willingness to pay the reparations, always grudging, further slackened.

The coalition government of socialist Hermann Müller accepted the prevailing wisdom that the way to fight the depression was to reduce expenses and raise taxes. But the powerful trade unions vigorously resisted cuts in unemployment benefits and increases in worker contributions to the insurance fund. Müller, a person of unquestioned integrity who had sought repeatedly during the 1920s to bring together left and center political parties in order to give the country a stable government, came close to working out a compromise. But in the end, his own Social Democratic Party balked at what in retrospect seems a trivial increase in worker contributions to the insurance fund. Müller's coalition broke up in March 1930. He resigned and Heinrich Brüning became chancellor.

Brüning belonged to the Center Party. He was intelligent and well informed but a stiff, rather shy person, somewhat similar in personality to his contemporary, Herbert Hoover. His speeches suffered from a "chilling lack of blood," a German newspaper commented.[19] Like virtually every western leader, he was determined to balance the budget by economizing and raising taxes, exactly the policies likely to make things worse. In his case, however, he had the excuse that Germany was committed by treaty with the western powers to maintain the value of its currency at the level established in 1924 after the great inflation. His long-range objective was to "settle" the reparations question, which was the heaviest drain by far on German resources. He was convinced that the way to do this was to win the confidence of the Allies by fulfilling Germany's treaty obligations scrupulously and by keeping the government solvent.

Except for proposing a substantial increase in aid to President Hindenburg's favorite East Prussian farmers, Brüning's economic program did not differ much from that of his predecessor; it called for reducing government expenditures, including the unemployment benefit, and raising taxes. When the Social Democrats in the Reichstag refused to go along with these austerity measures, he ordered new elections. These resulted in a shift of public support toward extremist parties. The Communists increased their delegation in the Reichstag from 54 to 77 and (far more ominous) the National Socialist Party delegation soared from 12 to 107.

Brüning was no fascist, but he hoped to bring the Nazis into a kind of right-center coalition. He did not succeed in doing so. Since he could not put together any legislative majority, he governed thereafter by decree, a tactic legal during emergencies under the Weimar constitution.

Brüning's belt-tightening policies failed either to check the economic slide—unemployment rose from about 2 million to 6 million—or to maintain financial stability. In May 1931, the failure of the Austrian *Kreditanstalt* led to runs on banks throughout central and eastern Europe. In two weeks, the Reichbank lost half its gold.

The possibility that the German banking system might collapse threatened the international financial system. In this emergency, President Hoover proposed a one-year suspension of all international debt payments, both the German reparations and the Allies' obligations to the United States. Although he was now placing the main blame for the depression on the shoulders of the Europeans,

Hoover recognized that they must be helped in this crisis. The way he justified the moratorium is interesting. He said its purpose was "to give the forthcoming year to the economic recovery of the world," but added immediately "and to help free the recuperative forces already in motion in the United States from retarding influences abroad."[20]

The Hoover moratorium did not immediately end the crisis. In July 1931, representatives of the major powers, meeting in London, worked out a "standstill agreement." The idea was to extend for six months some 6.3 billion marks of credit to the German banks. The Hoover moratorium and the standstill agreement were intended to be short-term measures. As it turned out, they marked the end of all significant war debt and reparations payments. As for Germany, additional results of the crisis were the practical nationalization of its banks; exchange controls; and sharp reductions of imports, which eventually caused an increase in food prices.

Economic conditions in Germany continued to worsen. In 1931 people had begun to speak of a "permanent depression."[21] By 1932 unemployment was approaching 40 percent of the work force. Ruling by decree, Brüning cut prices and wages by 10 percent. He lowered interest rates and instituted rent control. He gradually raised the contributions of workers to the unemployment insurance fund from 3 percent to 6.5 percent of their wages. He further reduced the benefits paid to the jobless. Rioting by extremists of the left and the right became steadily worse. After considerable hesitation, the German government banned the Nazi storm troops (SA) and elite guards (SS), whose riotous behavior was causing much of the trouble.

Despite these draconian measures, in May 1932, President Hindenburg forced Brüning to resign, mainly because he was displeased by the chancellor's proposal to break up some of the inefficient Junker estates in East Prussia. Baron Franz von Papen replaced him.

Papen was a wealthy Prussian nobleman. During the early stages of the Great War, he had been a military attaché in Washington. But in December 1915, his violations of American neutrality led President Wilson to order him out of the country.* Like many upper-class German conservatives, he considered Adolf Hitler a barbarian whom he could use for his own purposes. He rescinded the ban on the storm troops and ordered new elections. The Nazis again made large gains. After still another election, Hindenburg discharged Papen and named General Kurt von Schleicher chancellor.

Schleicher, an intimate friend of President Hindenburg, was a shrewd, behind-the-scenes operator. But he presented himself, as he said in a radio speech when he took office, as being above politics, "the impartial trustee of the interests of all in an emergency."[22] Whatever his ultimate purpose (and there were those who thought him far too willing to work with Nazis), he broke the futile pattern of fighting the depression with relentless austerity measures. He restored the most recent cuts in wages and unemployment benefits and talked of an extensive public works program to create jobs and stimulate the economy. He hoped to obtain the support of the Socialists, the trade union leaders, and the center parties, along with the left wing of the National Socialists.

Like his immediate predecessors, Schleicher failed to give Germany a stable government. Nor was he able to turn the ebbing economic tide. Hindenburg soon called Hitler to the chancellorship, and the Nazi seizure of power followed.

Yet to a considerable degree, the political and economic changes associated with the Nazi revolution were already under way when Hitler became chancellor. Government by executive fiat rather than by legislative vote had become routine. Reparations payments had stopped, and the government had taken over the banks. Both exchange controls and measures that limited imports, steps in the direction of autarchy, had been instituted. The idea of stimulating economic acitivity and putting the jobless to work on public projects without regard for budgetary considerations had been proposed in

---

* Among other things, Papen was accused of trying to foment strikes in American munitions plants, surreptitiously sending supplies to German cruisers on the high seas, and providing German officers in the United States with forged American passports so that they could return to Germany by way of neutral nations.

45

official circles. In this sense (though not, of course, in many others), Hitler's rise to power was not as sharp a break with the past as it is often pictured.

By the end of 1932, the Great Depression had been going on (and getting steadily worse) for more than three years. This was an absolutely unprecedented downswing; no earlier cyclical decline had persisted so long. Nothing that any of the regimes in the industrial nations were doing about it seemed to work. Yet at the end of 1932, conservative governments were in power in the United States, Great Britain, France, Italy, Germany, and in most of the smaller western countries as well.

The conservative General Schleicher was soon to be replaced by Hitler, and Germany would descend into fascism. In the United States, President Hoover had been defeated in his bid for a second term by Franklin D. Roosevelt, and the Democrats had won control of Congress. American voters had expressed dissatisfaction and widespread impatience with the Hoover policies. But there was little reason to expect, on the basis of his campaign promises, that President-elect Roosevelt would make any drastic changes. (During the campaign, he had accused Hoover of presiding over the greatest-spending administration in peacetime in American history.)

In Great Britain, Ramsay MacDonald remained prime minister, but cabinet shifts had made his nationalist coalition increasingly conservative in character. Joseph Paul-Boncour was the French premier in December 1932. Paul-Boncour claimed to be a socialist, but he did not belong to the Socialist Party. And he was as devoted to budget balancing as the most conservative banker. Faced with a large deficit, he appointed a commission of experts headed by an official of the Bank of France to make recommendations. The commission proposed a compromise—half of the shortfall should be met by raising taxes, half by reducing government spending on such things as pensions, public works, and the military. When the government, reacting to these suggestions, increased slightly the proposed military cuts and lowered those of public assistance, the conservative *Journal des Débats* accused it of "democratizing" the commission's recommendations.[23] At the same time, the Socialist delegates voted against Paul-Boncour's government because of the way the budget cuts affected government workers. They did so knowing they were causing the government to fall and opening the way for a more conservative one.

What can be made of the failure of any of these supposedly democratic nations to respond more effectively to the economic calamity that all were enduring? The compulsion to balance national budgets and to preserve the value of currencies was at the heart of the problem. These were counterproductive policies, given conditions in the 1930s, but modern experience with huge deficits and galloping inflation should make one regard the attitudes of the people of that time with compassion and indeed with some respect. That they were not able to end the depression testifies to their ignorance but still more to the enormous complications of the world economy.

This does not excuse the nearly universal tendency of political leaders and other so-called experts to place the blame for the depression—and more particularly for their inability to do much about it—on groups and nations other than their own. Nor is there much excuse for the failings of many key individuals. President Hoover's persistent refusal to recognize that his policies, and especially his emphasis on voluntarism and local control, were not working, is a case in point. Was this stubbornness, or pride, or arrogance? Whatever, it was certainly not very wise, though Hoover was an intelligent person.

The smugness of French bankers in the face of British and German financial difficulties in 1931, when more supportive actions might have avoided the crises that led to devaluation, is another example of foolishness. These crises resulted in injuries to the French economy and contributed mightily to the rise of Hitler. Another such example is the lack of fresh ideas on the part of the leaders of the British Labour Party, and their slavish efforts to "save" the pound, despite the fact that few people other than members of the privileged and almost mindlessly antisocialist banking community benefited from preserving the gold standard.

But it is important to keep in mind the fact that these leaders and others like them were members of societies that *were* democ-

47

racies. This surely helps to explain their apparent pusillanimity. Belief in sound money and balanced budgets was widespread. Many of those who favored expanding public works programs and other policies that they believed would stimulate the economy and help people in distress believed at the same time (and usually far more intensely) that belt-tightening and paying the piper were both economically necessary and morally correct.

During the depression, an American economist later recalled, "fear of debt was so deeply ingrained in the public that even the boldest [theorist] hesitated to advocate a policy which would openly increase deficits." Another American economist claims that when he was a young instructor at Harvard in the early thirties, the head of his department "reprimanded" him for discussing the advantages of deficit spending in his classes. As for cheap money, the British historian H. W. Richardson puts it this way: "The government was very hesitant in coming round to the need for credit expansion, primarily because of excessive fears about the likelihood of inflation which might result from it."[24]

Still more important, these were capitalist societies; any policy that business leaders considered dangerous had little chance of succeeding. This was true not so much because such people would sabotage programs they disliked as because, when faced with such policies, they would be afraid to take the kinds of actions that were necessary to increase output. Pump priming and easy money might make it profitable to borrow, but large government deficits made businessmen afraid to borrow at any interest rate.

Conversely, a balanced budget that theoretically exerted a restrictive influence on a nation's economy might in fact cause economic activity to expand. "Sound" government financial policies made people—especially businessmen and investors—feel hopeful about the future. In explaining the causes of Great Britain's recovery from the depression, the economist H. W. Arndt suggested that "even the orthodox budget policy" of the MacDonald government "probably had a favourable psychological influence."[25]

In a free society, the state can prevent businessmen and investors from doing things, and it can encourage them to do things by

48

granting them favors of one kind or another. But it cannot make them act. This helps to explain the apparent contradiction in the 1932 comment of the *Economist*, which in the same article warned that Great Britain's budget deficit might "become unmanageable" and start a "vicious spiral of uncontrollable inflation," but also that such a deficit might "have a positively deflationary effect on enterprise and prices."[26]

"Looking at the world," wrote the French socialist Léon Blum in December 1932, "one has the impression of an audience . . . waiting restlessly for the end of one act and at the same time listening to the stage hands behind the scenes arranging the scenery for the act that is to follow."[27] As 1932 ended, it was clear that the politicians, the economists, and the public at large of every nation needed to learn to look at economic questions in new ways. But what were the ways and who was to teach them how to find them?

CHAPTER III

WHAT IT DID
TO FARMERS

How important the parlous state of agriculture in the late 1920s was in causing the Great Depression is a subject of some debate. But it is beyond dispute that agriculture was generally depressed in those years. Between 1925 and 1929, nearly every agricultural commodity traded in world markets fell in price. Enormous stocks of grain, coffee, tea, cotton, and other crops piled up in warehouses and elevators. As a result, farmers by the millions suffered heavy losses.*

At the time, students of the farm problem had no trouble explaining why agriculture was in such poor shape, and later scholars have not altered that explanation significantly. The Great War, which caused food production to decline in Europe, had encouraged farmers in the United States, Canada, South America, and Aus-

---

* The agricultural depression was an aspect of the larger depression that affected nearly all raw materials. Producers of copper, tin, nitrates, petroleum, and many other mining products found themselves faced with falling prices and huge unsold stockpiles. Gold was an exception. The devaluation that resulted when important nations abandoned the gold standard caused a gold-mining boom. South African output doubled between 1932 and 1940 and Australian tripled during the decade.[1]

tralia to grow more grain and raise more cattle, sheep, and hogs. When European agriculture got back to prewar levels in the 1920s, world surpluses accumulated.

The European nations then protected their farmers by placing tariffs on foreign foodstuffs and establishing import quotas. This was a blow to producers of staple crops in other parts of the world, many of whom, having bought land and machinery at high prices during the war, were burdened with heavy mortgage payments and other fixed costs. These burdens, in turn, restricted their ability to buy manufactured goods, thus adding to the woes of manufacturers and workers in the industrial nations. It has been argued that the wheat glut of 1925–29 was the primary cause of the Great Depression.[2]

Technological developments during the 1920s led to further increases in world output. More efficient farm machinery and potent new chemical fertilizers became available. Botanists bred new plant varieties that yielded larger harvests and were more resistant to drought and disease. At the same time, other technological advances hurt certain farmers by causing the demand for particular crops to decline. The invention of rayon resulted in changes in consumer tastes that reduced the demand for cotton and wool. The replacement of draft animals by tractors and trucks freed land that had been used to grow oats and hay, land on which farmers then grew more wheat and other bread grains. Furthermore, the prosperity that resulted from new industrial technology injured the growers of cereals indirectly. As living standards improved, people tended to eat less bread and more meat, fruits, vegetables, and dairy products.

In most cases these circumstances did not cause farmers to curtail their operations. Quite the contrary—the amount of land devoted to raising grain, cotton, sugar, and other staples rose steadily. Worldwide, between 1923 and 1929, cotton production increased 30 percent, rubber more than 80 percent. The output of wheat and other cereals and of beets, sugar cane, tea, coffee, and cocoa rose by similar proportions.[3]

Between 1925 and 1929, the combined average price of the

leading agricultural commodities fell about 30 percent, yet unsold supplies of these products piled up in ever-larger volume. To contemporaries the farm problem could be summed up in a word—*overproduction*. Too much was being grown, and the glut was causing prices to fall.

That something ought to be done to make farming more profitable was widely recognized. To do so by getting producers to grow less or by some price-fixing device would obviously accomplish this goal. Manufacturers and merchants had been doing such things for centuries. When the demand for manufactured goods declined during the depression, producers cut back on output and tried to hold the line on prices, or at least to minimize price cuts. Farmers seemed unable to do this; organized attempts to limit the output of agricultural commodities usually failed. The prices of most manufactured goods were sticky, those of farm products volatile. As the American economist Gardiner Means explained in 1935, "The whole Depression might be described as a general dropping of prices at the flexible end of the price scale and a dropping of production at the rigid end."[4]*

Rubber provides an excellent example of why agricultural prices were hard to control. More than 90 percent of the world's rubber was grown in Malaya, Ceylon, Indochina, and the Dutch East Indies, all areas dominated by European nations in the 1920s. Immediately after World War I, the price of rubber fluctuated erratically. In 1921 Winston Churchill, then Great Britain's Secretary of State for the Colonies, appointed a committee headed by Sir James Stevenson, his adviser on commercial affairs, to study the problem. The Stevenson committee recommended compulsory restrictions on production. The cabinet then set quotas on rubber exports from British colonies and imposed a heavy tax on exports in excess of the quotas. Many Dutch planters, whose profits were being squeezed as much as those of the British, voluntarily agreed to go along with the Stevenson Plan. For a time the price of rubber rose.

* Between 1929 and 1934, American agricultural prices fell 40 percent on average, industrial prices only 15 percent.

Yet the Stevenson Plan did not work for long. More than half the rubber produced in Southeast Asia came from big estates owned by Europeans. The rest was made by "natives" who tapped wild trees or cultivated rubber on small plots of a few acres. Higher prices resulting from the quota system encouraged a stream of East Indian farmers to begin to make rubber. The British share of the market declined along with the price of rubber. In 1928 the Stevenson Plan was abandoned and the price then plummeted.[5]

Another scheme for boosting agricultural prices had been developed by the French. At the urging of beet farmers and winemakers, the National Assembly passed a law in 1923 that required that alcohol distilled from these crops be added to French gasoline in a ratio of one part to ten. Besides increasing the market for grapes and beets (and presumably their price), the scheme was intended to reduce the amount of gasoline imported by France. The law had loopholes, however, and did not effectively increase the prices received by farmers.[6]

The United States was a major agricultural nation, and its farmers were not prospering. But as the country was oversupplied with gasoline and other petroleum products in the 1920s, there was no point in converting beets or grapes or any other crop into fuel in America. And if the Stevenson Plan could not be enforced in regions where European powers dominated the local populace, how could such a method succeed in the United States, where farmers had a reputation for being individualists who resisted government regulation of their affairs? Moreover, while a mature rubber tree produced approximately the same amount of latex from year to year, yields of wheat, cotton, and the other staples grown in America were subject to so many unpredictable forces that regulating the size of harvests seemed impossible. As the American Council of Agriculture noted in 1925, "No human agency can except by accident, arrive at, or anywhere near, the desired mark in production. . . . There is no possible way of forecasting to what extent drought and flood, hail and freeze, insects and disease . . . would thwart such calculations."[7]

These difficulties did not prevent American farmers from seeking ways and means of raising the prices of their produce. Many pinned their hopes on the farm cooperative movement. With the help of government subsidies, the cooperatives made low-interest loans to many farmers. But they could not persuade their members to grow less and had no significant effect on the prices farmers got for their crops.

The most popular American scheme for raising agricultural prices depended on tariffs. Protective tariffs on manufactured goods made things that farmers bought more expensive. But since American farmers produced more cotton, wheat, tobacco, and other staple crops than were consumed at home, by themselves tariffs on these products would not raise prices. If domestic prices rose above world levels, exporters would offer their holdings to domestic buyers, thus driving the price down.

During the early 1920s, George N. Peek, a manufacturer of agricultural machinery, developed a plan for using tariffs to boost certain farm prices. Peek proposed that the government buy up surplus American wheat and cotton. He argued that because of the additional demand, the domestic prices of these crops would rise to the limit of whatever tariffs were placed on them. The government would then sell the surpluses it had purchased abroad for whatever it could get. To recover its losses on these foreign sales, the government was to levy a tax called an equalization fee on domestic producers. Peek's scheme was presented to Congress and, as the McNary-Haugen bill, it was passed in 1927 and again in 1928, only to be vetoed each time by President Coolidge.

Coolidge considered the McNary-Haugen bill unconstitutional, but the scheme had practical flaws too, the most obvious being that higher prices would encourage farmers to grow more, thus adding to the amount the government would have to buy. The size of the equalization fee would therefore tend to increase until the additional profit of the growers was swallowed up. The same weakness characterized another American proposal known as the export debenture plan.[8]

The basic ideas behind these schemes did not originate in the United States. A similar technique known as "valorization" had been employed by Brazilian coffee growers since early in the twentieth century. In 1906 the coffee-growing states of Brazil (São Paulo, Minas Geraes, and Rio de Janeiro) contracted to buy up part of the crop in years of bountiful harvests. These purchases were financed by foreign loans, interest payments on the debt being covered by an export tax on coffee. After World War I, an Institute for the Permanent Defense of Coffee supported prices by setting limits on shipments of beans to seaport markets, by loans to growers, and by outright purchases.

In the late 1920s, however, the very success of the valorization system was causing it to break down. Growers did so well that they planted more trees; between 1925 and 1929, output nearly doubled. With farmers in other countries also planting more coffee trees every year, the institute had to buy ever-larger amounts of coffee to support the price. From 1927 to 1929, the stock of unsold coffee in Brazilian warehouses increased from 380 million pounds to over 3.8 billion pounds.[9]

Then came the depression. Between 1929 and 1933, the price of coffee and most other agricultural commodities hit rock bottom. In the United States the Hoover administration responded with the Agricultural Marketing Act of 1929. While he was secretary of commerce in Coolidge's Cabinet, Hoover had opposed the McNary-Haugen scheme because of his distaste for government interference in the marketing of goods. He believed that the federal government should help farmers to help themselves, not treat them as some special type of ideal citizen.[10] The new law set up a Federal Farm Board and authorized it to create stabilization corporations to keep prices steady and lend farm cooperatives up to $500 million—a very large sum by the standards of that day—so that they could afford to hold surplus agricultural commodities in storage pending hoped-for increases in prices.

This system resembled a technique that had been developed by Canadian farm organizations in 1923. The Canadians formed what was known as a "wheat pool" so that farmers would not have to sell their wheat immediately after harvesting it, a time when the price was usually depressed. The pool borrowed money from banks and lent it to farmers who deposited their grain in the organization's elevators as security. Then a Central Selling Agency released the grain gradually into the market.* Although the pool was of only limited benefit when the price of wheat remained low throughout the year, it worked reasonably well until 1928.

The bumper 1928 crop left Canadian grain elevators bulging. It was followed by a poor harvest in 1929. This encouraged the pool managers to hold back their stores, but the expected price rise did not materialize. Instead, the world price of wheat fell precipitously, ruining the pool. In 1930 the Canadian provincial governments had to take over the support system to prevent a liquidation of the pool's stocks that would have had a devastating effect on prices. In 1931 wheat farmers were granted a subsidy of 5 cents a bushel, and the Dominion government began purchasing wheat in the market in an effort to stabilize the price.[11]

The next year, as part of the imperial preference system adopted at that time, Great Britain gave Canadian growers what amounted to a 6 cents a bushel advantage in the British market. In exchange Canada agreed to sell wheat to the British "in quantities sufficient to supply the requirements of United Kingdom consumers."[12]†

The falling world price of wheat caused heavy losses wherever the crop was grown. Yet many countries deliberately increased production. The Soviet Union, desperate for foreign capital needed to carry out its ambitious Five-Year Plan, increased its export of wheat from 1 million tons in 1929 to 5.4 million in 1930, though doing so caused severe food shortages in Russia. In Australia Prime Minister James Scullin urged a "Grow More Wheat" campaign on farmers in 1930. (When reminded that in the United States the new Federal Farm Board was recommending cutbacks in wheat production, Scullin answered, "I have noticed the statement, but it has not abated my conviction one iota that Australian farmers should increase their wheat acreage.") The farmers responded en-

* There were three regional pools but one Selling Agency handled all the wheat.
† France, Belgium, and the Netherlands also gave preferential treatment to their dependencies.

thusiastically, with the result that Australian wheat acreage rose by 21 percent and output by 30 percent in a single year.*

When the loans to cooperatives failed to check falling agricultural prices in the United States, the Federal Farm Board began to buy wheat and cotton outright through the stabilization boards in an effort to stop the decline. The effort failed because farmers, despite the recommendations of Farm Board officials and their own cooperatives, were not cutting back on their production. By 1932 both the Grain and Cotton Stabilization corporations had to sell their accumulated stocks at large losses; cotton alone cost the government $129 million in less than a year.[13]

In other parts of the world, different methods were adopted, none with much success. Brazil used $100 million borrowed from American banks to buy up the coffee ripening in 1930, but the crop was huge—more than twice the size of the previous year's. Coffee beans fell from 22 cents a pound to about 13 cents on the world market. In October 1930, Getúlio Vargas came to power in Brazil. Vargas made the coffee institute a subsidiary of a new National Coffee Council. Although he was no friend of the planters, his government put about $11 million into the support program. But the price of beans fell still further, to 8 cents a pound. The government then destroyed about a third of the crop to bring supply more nearly in line with demand. In 1931, 374 million pounds of beans were burned, the next year 1.2 billion pounds.[14]

Attempts to support the prices of other crops fared no better. In 1929 the Egyptian government purchased local cotton futures and then took delivery on the cotton. The price continued downward. In 1931 Egypt set limits on the number of acres that farmers could devote to cotton. The reduction was substantial—and strictly enforced. The cutbacks, however, had little effect on the price that the next crop commanded in the world market and caused much

---

* Scullin promised farmers a guaranteed price for their wheat, and the government put on a big newspaper and radio campaign to sell the program. But after the farmers expanded their wheat acreage, the conservative Australian Senate defeated the bill guaranteeing the price. The result was "a ghastly bungle from start to finish."

public resentment. The next year, the government permitted a large increase in cotton acreage.[15]

The chief exporters of tea were British and Dutch colonies in India and the East Indies. Mounting unsold stocks in the late 1920s caused fierce competition among them. In 1930 British and Dutch growers reached a "voluntary" agreement to reduce production of the cheaper varieties of tea in order to discourage tea merchants from putting more low-quality tea in their blends. But many of the Dutch growers did not stick to the agreement. Tea prices slumped, and more tea piled up in the warehouses.[16]

The already low price of rubber fell still lower as the Great Depression deepened. In 1930 British and Dutch planters declared a "tapping holiday," but the "native" growers ignored the holiday. They increased their output in an effort to make up for lower prices, and the glut continued. The price dropped from 20 cents a pound in 1929 to less than 3 cents in 1932, while indignant European planters complained that the business was "going native."[17]

Sugar growers were also hard hit by falling prices. In 1931 Cuba, Java, and five other countries that exported cane sugar agreed to limit production and accept export quotas. But the agreement, drafted by Thomas L. Chadbourne, a New York lawyer, failed to stop the slide because sugar beet growers continued to produce large surpluses. After a few years, the Chadbourne Agreement was scrapped.[18]

If growers of rubber, tea, and coffee, which could be raised only in limited regions, were unable to control prices, the crops that were grown by tens of thousands of farmers in many parts of the globe seemed totally beyond regulation. Hard hit by falling prices, the winegrowers of France obtained government backing for various relief schemes. Tariffs on foreign wines and a quota on Italian imports proved ineffective because large domestic harvests clogged the market. The *Statut du Vin* of 1930 provided for direct purchases of surpluses by the government, the wine to be turned into alcohol. That law also put limits on new plantings and applied a steeply progressive tax on yields per acre.

The French tried to increase the domestic consumption of wine too. Posters bearing the slogan "A meal without wine is like a day without sunshine" appeared everywhere. The *Chevaliers du Tastevin* and other clubs devoted to the appreciation (and sale) of fine wines were founded. None of these measures had much effect. The 1930 law had loopholes, the most gaping being that small growers were exempt from the controls. Since two-thirds of French wine was produced by small farmers, supplies continued to exceed demand. Prices declined still further.[19]

In December 1932, after the British imperial preference system caused a sharp drop in British purchases of Danish bacon, the Danish producers tried to limit their production by voluntary means. They agreed to suspend hog slaughtering for a week and to slow down the fattening of hogs. Each producer was assigned a quota. But the quotas were not enforceable.

Between January 1930 and May 1931, no fewer than 16 international conferences were held in an effort to find some way to bolster the price of wheat. These conferences produced much vague talk but no concrete results—an American critic remarked that in the debates " 'principles' were unduly emphasized and the 'details' unduly subordinated."[20]

Most Western European countries were net importers of food, but their dependency on foreign sources was shrinking. The world economic crisis was pushing them inexorably toward protectionism. They enacted stiff tariffs on grains and other agricultural imports during the late 1920s and early 1930s. Fascist Italy launched a "battle for wheat" in 1925. The goal was self-sufficiency. The government offered prizes to farmers with high yields and subsidized purchases of farm machinery and fertilizers. By 1931 the Italian tariff on wheat exceeded the price of the imported grain itself. Norway, France, Germany, and Switzerland protected domestic farmers with high tariffs. Beginning with France in 1931, many European governments also adopted quotas limiting the importation of wheat and other locally grown cereals.

Some nations granted direct subsidies to their farmers. The British were so dependent upon foreign food that they were reluctant to put tariffs on any important crop. (British farmers raised only about 15 percent of the wheat consumed in the country.) Instead, the Wheat Act of 1932 assured British farmers a "standard guaranteed price" roughly double the world price, the subsidy being financed by a processing tax paid by flour millers. British growers of barley, oats, and sugar beets also received subsidies.[21]

In Germany the subsidy system meant aiding President Hindenburg's favorites, the hard-pressed Junker landlords of East Prussia. The government bought their rye at one price, dyed it red, and sold it back to them at a lower price to be used as fodder.* In Hungary subsidies benefited poor peasants struggling to survive on "dwarf" holdings. Poland subsidized agricultural exports and taxed agricultural imports. Spain prohibited the importation of wheat except in years of poor harvests, and in 1932 Spanish wheat production was about 25 percent above normal.[22]

In 1927 Norway had passed a law that required bakers to use a fixed percentage of homegrown wheat in their bread. By the early 1930s, France, Germany, Italy, and many other European countries had established similar milling ratios, most of them requiring the use of more than 90 percent local grain.

In Poland large landowners reduced their labor costs by shifting from sugar beets to wheat, a crop requiring less care. Polish wheat production had averaged about 1.6 million tons in the late 1920s, sugar beet production nearly 5 million tons. In the early 1930s, wheat output rose to well over 2 million tons, while beet production dropped to about 2 million tons.[23]

Yugoslavia, Rumania, and Hungary were exporters of foodstuffs and eager to expand output. They also hoped to modernize their agriculture in order to improve the lives of peasants and agricultural laborers. This was a laudable objective. But to the extent that they succeeded, they added to the size of harvests, which further depressed world prices.

All these many regulations caused European grain production

* This policy, combined with restrictions on the importation of foreign grain, drew angry protests from German dairy farmers.

62

to increase. That exacerbated the difficulties of the exporting countries and injured consumers by raising prices, encouraging inefficiency, and stifling potentially beneficial regional specialization. When retail prices rose, consumption declined, and this led to further piling up of unsalable surpluses. Controls became self-perpetuating. In January 1932, a group of experts studying the wheat problem at the Food Research Institute of Stanford University concluded:

> Whatever benefits have been or are being derived from these national policies . . . the net effect of this extensive interference with the operation of economic forces has been to intensify the world wheat crisis and to retard its correction.[24]

The same could be said about other staples.

Two things were happening to agriculture in the early 1930s. Farmers in Asia, Africa, and the Americas, exporters of grain, cotton, coffee, tea, sugar, rubber, and staple crops of lesser importance, were trying to limit production in order to raise prices or at least keep them from falling still further. Few of their efforts succeeded. The Europeans, who imported these products, sought to protect their own farmers, who tended to be relatively inefficient, by means of tariffs, quotas, and subsidies. They did not try to affect the general price level, or alter world supplies. Their approach was narrowly nationalistic, and their methods worked, at least to a degree.

But the jumble of regulations, both those imposed by the producers of staples and those of the Europeans, had the overall effect of crippling international trade and hampering recovery from the depression.

The seriousness of the situation had become clear by 1931, when the League of Nations Economic Committee convened a conference of experts from 24 nations to discuss the "agricultural crisis." An "atmosphere of despondency" clouded the proceedings. Delegate after delegate told the same story: "In Spain, agriculture is passing through a period of acute depression." "Argentine agriculture has been in an unfavourable position since 1921." "Finnish agriculture is encountering great difficulties."

The Cuban delegate spoke of "the gravity of the crisis . . . particularly in respect to sugar." The Bulgarian reported that in his country "the depression is still continuing, spreading misery and discouragement." The Persian delegate described a general decline in agricultural prices in his nation and an exodus of people from the countryside. Even the Persian poppy growers were suffering—"the principal opium-producing districts are . . . undergoing a very severe crisis."

Almost alone among the delegates, the American representative, Loyd V. Steere, took a moderately optimistic view. He admitted that "a sharp, general decline in agricultural prices" had been "a serious setback." Nevertheless, he insisted that there were "substantial grounds for belief" that the bad times "will not endure for long." Like President Hoover, Steere evidently believed that prosperity was just around the corner in 1931.

Most of the other delegates felt differently. They concluded that the problem was beyond the capacity of individual nations to remedy. "Only organization of the market can put an end to the crisis." Alas, no one seemed able to provide the necessary organization. "Can the States force the agriculturalists to restrict their production?" the delegates asked in their final report. "And if so, will the States be prepared to do so?" They were not hopeful. Like the Stanford experts, they believed that wheat presented the most serious problem. "Cereals are produced in practically every part of the globe. The whole effort will be frustrated if a single country of any importance remains outside."[25]

It was against this background that the Congress of the United States passed the Agricultural Adjustment Act of 1933. The law provided a practical way to get farmers to reduce output "voluntarily." Producers of wheat, cotton, corn, tobacco, hogs, and milk—the commodities that were in excess supply—were to be polled. In each case, if a majority agreed to reduce the acreage devoted to the crop by a specified percentage, the government would "rent" that land at a stated price per acre. Processing taxes levied on the middlemen who handled the protected crops (for example, flour millers) would provide the money to finance the program. Ultimately, of course, the cost was passed on to consumers. The object was to raise farmers' incomes to "parity" with the prices of things farmers had to buy. The ratio was based on agricultural and industrial prices in the period 1909–14, when these prices were believed to have been in fair balance.[26]

The scheme was called the domestic allotment plan. The person most responsible for designing it was Milburn Lincoln Wilson, an agricultural economist. Wilson had been deeply involved with agriculture and its problems all his life. He had farmed in several midwestern states, been a county agent, worked for the Bureau of Agricultural Economics in Washington. Wilson spent several months in the Soviet Union in 1929 as an adviser on farm mechanization. He came home impressed (too impressed, it turned out) by Russia's potential as an exporter of grain. Increased Russian wheat exports would soon drive agricultural prices still lower, he predicted. The combination of foreign tariffs and larger world supplies would further shrink the demand for American farm commodities. The only way to raise the prices of staple crops was to cut back on production. His domestic allotment plan was the result of this line of reasoning.[27]

The Agricultural Adjustment Act marked a sharp break with the past for the United States. Paying farmers not to grow crops was unprecedented. Yet the tactic merely reflected the constitutional restrictions of the American political system. The strategy of subsidizing agriculture and trying to reduce output in order to bring supplies down to the level of current demand had already been adopted by many countries. The New Deal response to the farm problem was part of a worldwide response.

In defending his plan before the Agriculture Committee of the House of Representatives, Wilson made passing reference to "all kinds of artificial schemes" that were being tried in other countries. When a congressman asked him specifically about the Egyptian cotton-control plan, he replied that his proposal was "somewhat like

65

the Egypt plan." But he treated the question as an aside. In justifying his proposal, he emphasized the baneful effect of European tariffs on American farm exports.[28]

American agricultural experts like Wilson focused their sights on Europe because so large a proportion of American agricultural exports was sold there. European restrictions struck hard. After Great Britain adopted the imperial preference system in 1932, British imports of American wheat, which had averaged over 100 million bushels a year in the 1920s, practically ended.[29]

If the Agricultural Adjustment Act was not an innovation when seen in world perspective, it was certainly a kind of milestone. The year 1933 saw the triumph nearly everywhere of a simple supply-and-demand kind of thinking that the French called "economic Malthusianism," the belief that the only way to raise prices was to bring production down to the level of current consumption.

In February 1933, representatives of Indian, Ceylonese, and Dutch East Indian tea growers signed the International Tea Agreement. The parties promised to limit exports, and they assigned to each a quota fixed at 85 percent of what was chosen as the "standard" output year, 1929 for the Indian and Ceylonese, 1931 for the Dutch. No new tea plantings were to be permitted for five years. An International Tea Committee was named to manage the system.

The Tea Committee was made up of planters, and their arrangement was a private one. Nevertheless, the Tea Agreement had real force. The governments involved promised not to sell or lease any more land for tea growing and to enforce the limits on exports established by the committee. The agreement marked the abandonment of free trade by the Dutch; they were led to this change by Great Britain's devaluation of the pound, which made Indian and Ceylonese tea cheaper, and the British imperial system, which in a single year reduced the importation of foreign tea into the United Kingdom by about half.[30]

In April the Dutch signed the International Rubber Regulation Agreement with representatives of Great Britain, France, India, and Siam. These countries produced 98 percent of the world's rubber. The goal was what the signatories rather delicately termed "fair and equitable" prices for rubber, the method of achieving it, reduction of output and strict control of exports. As with the tea agreement, a committee of planters assigned the participants annual quotas. Increasing acreage and planting additional rubber trees were prohibited.[31]

In August representatives of nearly all the countries of Europe met in London with delegates of the major wheat exporting nations. The conference produced an International Wheat Agreement designed to "adjust the production of wheat to world demand," and to raise and then stabilize the price at a level that would be both profitable for farmers and "reasonable" for consumers. The exporters (Argentina, Australia, Canada, the United States, the Soviet Union, and several East European nations) agreed to limit their combined exports in 1933–34 to 560 million bushels, the amount the importing countries could be expected to absorb, and to reduce production by 15 percent the following year. A 14-member International Wheat Committee was created to administer the agreement. In September the committee assigned quotas to the exporters, which all except the Russians accepted.[32]

In addition to these international arrangements, many countries established new restrictive policies in 1933. Instead of merely regulating imports and exports, most of these organized and controlled their domestic markets. Here are some examples. Argentina adopted a comprehensive program of exchange controls, limitations on imports, and regulation of the production and sale of wheat and cattle. The government purchased 75 percent of the 1933 wheat crop at a fixed price and sold it abroad for whatever it would bring, incidentally exceeding the quota it had been assigned by the International Wheat Committee by 37 million bushels. "The country should look to itself, with its own resources, for the relief of its present difficulties," the minister of agriculture explained in December 1933. The following year Argentina applied the new controls to milk and wine, the next year to cotton, the next to lumber, petroleum, and coal.

Unlike most of the nations of western Europe, Denmark and

67

Holland were, on balance, exporters of agricultural products. A Danish law of 1933 provided for government purchase and destruction of large numbers of low-quality cattle, the cost being covered by a slaughterhouse tax on all cattle consumed in Denmark. Because of British restrictions on the importation of Danish bacon, the Danes also cut hog production in 1933. Producers were issued specific numbers of "pig cards." Those pigs sent to the bacon factories accompanied by pig cards were purchased at one price, those without cards at a lower one.

The Netherlands, having abandoned laissez-faire by accepting limitations on the tea and rubber produced in its East Indian colonies, regulated nearly every aspect of its agriculture in 1933. It had already created special bureaus to control the output of pork and dairy products; now it set up a Central Cattle Office, which ordered the slaughtering of part of the nation's cattle herd. An Agricultural Crisis Law giving the state the right to regulate the production and sale of any agricultural commodity the government considered a "crisis product" was also passed.[33]

In 1933 Switzerland began to regulate the importation of feed grains and to reduce the production of milk. Great Britain created marketing boards that guaranteed processors of milk a minimum price and limited the importation of foreign beef and bacon. Sweden set minimum prices for homegrown wheat and rye, subsidized butter exports, and put import quotas on all cereals. The French stiffened the 1930 wine statute by applying the ban on new plantings to small vineyards.

Another French law (April 1933) provided for government purchase of surplus wheat, which like surplus wine was to be converted into alcohol. At the same time, the use of *any* foreign wheat in French bread was prohibited. A few months later, responding to pressure from farm organizations, the National Assembly fixed a minimum price for French wheat. A cynical member of the Senate remarked that the law was "absolutely fatal and necessary," and his judgment proved sound. Faced with bumper crops—wheat acreage was not restricted—French farmers were soon selling what became known as "gangster wheat" at prices far below the legal minimum.[34]*

After they came to power in Germany in 1933, the Nazis regulated the production, distribution, and sale of all foodstuffs. Every link in the food chain from farmer to consumer was controlled. There were marketing associations for each product and regional groupings to deal with local issues. When the unusually large 1933 wheat and rye harvests threatened further to depress prices, the government compelled flour millers to purchase and store the excess. Special boards controlled food imports, fixing the amounts admitted and the prices at which they could be sold, the object being to hold imports to a minimum so that Germany would be as nearly self-sufficient agriculturally as possible.[35]

National Socialist agricultural policy differed from the policies already discussed. It aimed at raising output as well as prices, both goals being theoretically possible in a rigidly controlled economy. Like the rest of the world, however, the Germans disregarded the effects of their actions on other nations.

Looking at the situation more broadly, the producers of staple crops for export were trying to raise prices by reducing supplies, ignoring the fact that higher prices were likely to reduce demand still further. At the same time, the agricultural policies of the European industrial nations were making a bad situation worse. By reducing imports (and in some cases increasing domestic production), they were simultaneously injuring the major food-producing countries and adding to the costs of their own consumers. It was, as the British historian Sidney Pollard has written, "a world of rising tariffs, international commodity schemes, bilateral trade agreements and managed currencies."

Everyone blamed somebody else. This is perfectly illustrated by the collapse of the London Economic Conference in the summer of 1933. The conference had been called by the League of Nations in 1932, and President Hoover had agreed to allow American experts to participate in the planning sessions. By the time the del-

* When the official price was 115 francs per 100 kilograms, farmers were selling wheat at 80 francs.

egates gathered in London in June 1933, however, Roosevelt had been president for several months, and the New Deal was in full swing. Roosevelt's secretary of state, Cordell Hull, who headed the American delegation, was a firm believer in free trade and international cooperation. When he was boarding the liner that took him to London, Hull stressed to reporters the importance of reaching "an agreement between countries to lower trade barriers and stabilize the currency exchange."

Roosevelt had sent Hull and the other American delegates off to London with instructions to seek international agreements regarding tariffs, "the control of production and distribution of world commodities," and "an adequate and enduring monetary standard." But unlike the secretary, he was not committed to any particular approach. One historian has said that in his usual way, FDR was "oscillating between opposed policies, attempting to juggle them together." When the Americans worked out a scheme for international currency stabilization with British and French delegates, he rejected it as "untimely." He said he was unwilling "to permit limitation of our action . . . by any other nation."

The trend of Roosevelt's thinking since his inauguration had been in the direction of economic nationalism. Besides the Agricultural Adjustment Act, Congress had passed the National Industrial Recovery Act, encouraging manufacturers to agree to restrict output and fix prices, and the president had taken the country off the gold standard. Moreover, the great powers attending the conference, along with dozens of other countries not represented, had enacted many similar restrictive, narrowly nationalistic laws. Secretary Hull knew this as well as anyone. "The entire world is in a state of bitter economic war," he admitted.

In any case, after the conference opened, Roosevelt fired his "bombshell message" to the American delegation. His cable informed them of his decision to put "the sound internal economic system of [the] nation" above dealing with the depression by means of international agreements.

Hull was "benumbed" by Roosevelt's announcement, and everyone involved in the conference was surprised. French and

British leaders were downcast; obviously they were all hoping that the president would somehow force them to be better than themselves, or at least that by taking a strong stand for international cooperation he would make it politically possible for them to do so too. But they should not have felt betrayed. As Herbert Feis, a participant in and close student of the London Conference, remarked, early New Deal economic policy consisted of "national efforts to which our foreign economic relations were left to adjust themselves."

By 1933 "Save your own neck" had become the motto of policymakers everywhere. Both during the preparatory discussions and at the conference itself, the Europeans were as parochial and inconsistent in dealing with questions relating to international trade and finance as President Roosevelt was. Despite his supposed inability to understand the complexities of economic theory, Roosevelt understood this. "England left the gold standard nearly two years ago," he reminded one of the American delegates who objected to his policy.[36]

However self-centered, narrow, nationalistic policies appeared to work in the mid-1930s. Once the rubber growers accepted export quotas, the price of rubber experienced a spectacular improvement. Industrial recovery put further upward pressure on prices, and by 1937 rubber was selling at 26 cents a pound, well above the predepression price. The International Rubber Regulation Agreement was then extended, and the quotas were gradually increased.

Tea, which had fallen below 8 pence a pound in 1932, ranged in price between 11 and 14 pence under the International Tea Agreement and touched 16 pence in 1937. In 1934 four British colonies in East Africa were taken into the system. Although efforts to persuade China, Japan, and other tea-growing countries to join failed, these nations produced well below 20 percent of world exports, and they did not increase their share during the 1930s. In 1938 the International Tea Agreement was extended for another five years.[37]

American cotton doubled in price after the domestic allotment

71

plan went into effect. What is more, the cutback in American production benefited other cotton-growing countries as well. What Secretary of Agriculture Henry Wallace called the "artificial disparity" between the price of American and foreign cotton caused a sharp reduction of American cotton exports. As a result, Egyptian exports jumped by more than 40 percent. In 1934 the Egyptian Cotton Year Book reported that "our country has been very materially helped by the policy of the American government, so that whilst marketing an enormous (for us) supply we have been able to obtain very satisfactory prices." Less important cotton-producing countries also benefited from the slackening of American competition. Brazil's exports soared; those of Peru doubled.

Brazil's coffee valorization plan had a similar effect on other coffee producers. The price of coffee did not rise much, but after 1933 it ceased to fall. Over the next few years, Brazil's share of the world market declined, while the coffee exports of Colombia, Peru, El Salvador, and Guatemala increased substantially.[38]

There were so many national restrictions on the production and sale of wheat that the British economist Lionel Robbins wrote in 1934 that "to speak of a world price for wheat has become an absurdity." Yet the number and variety of wheat farmers made the kinds of restrictions on output that were developed by growers of coffee, tea, and similar crops impossible to apply. The International Wheat Agreement of 1933 was a failure. It was imprecise to begin with, and since it lacked sanctions, many of the signers evaded its restrictions when it suited their interests to do so. As one expert explained, the influence of the agreement on "trade, prices, acreage, and production was negligible, and it broke down within a year."

The United States domestic allotment plan did not work well where wheat was concerned. Only about half of the eligible farmers participated. Those who had grown very little wheat before 1933 and who therefore could not profit from the program often increased their wheat plantings on the assumption that the cutbacks of participating farmers would cause the price of wheat to rise. Participating farmers frequently planted grass where their wheat had grown and used the crop to feed dairy cattle, thus undermining the milk program. Wheat acreage in 1934 fell only 8.5 percent, although even without the allotment scheme, the United States was committed by the International Wheat Agreement to reduce planting by 15 percent.[39]

The world price of wheat did rise somewhat in the fall of 1933 but chiefly because of crop failures. In North America, a prolonged drought had produced dust storms that devastated the plains from Texas to Saskatchewan. The drought began in Canada in 1929. By 1931 powdered soil was piling up in ditches like "snow drifts in winter" in parts of Saskatchewan. One Canadian farmer wrote with only slight exaggeration that there was not a grain of wheat to be had in his part of the country. "Even the Russian Thistle will not grow," he added. By 1932 the wheat belt in the United States was also parched. In 1934 the country produced only 526 million bushels, the smallest crop since 1896. Americans imported a small amount of wheat in 1934 and again in 1935.

Higher wheat prices could not help farmers who had little or no wheat to sell. In Haskell County, Kansas, in the heart of the American wheat belt, farmers had harvested more than 3.4 million bushels in 1931. They produced only 89,000 bushels in 1933, but not because of the Agricultural Adjustment Act. Lack of rain had already cut the 1932 crop to 333,000 bushels. In 1934, under AAA "limitations," the crop reached 395,000 bushels, and output remained in this range until 1940, when the dry cycle ended. In 1942 ideal growing conditions prevailed in Kansas, and more than 2 million bushels were harvested in Haskell County. Despite New Deal restrictions, wheat acreage in the United States increased from about 42 million acres in 1934 to 53 million in 1939.

The Canadians did not try to reduce wheat acreage; instead they continued to rely on their wheat pool to stabilize prices. In 1934 the Canadian Parliament passed a Natural Products Marketing Act and the next year set up a Wheat Board to market Canadian wheat. As in the United States, however, lack of rainfall had far more effect on the fortunes of Canadian farmers than any government policy.[40]

When the Socialists came to power in France in 1936, they set up a Wheat Office to control the buying and selling of wheat. The Wheat Office resembled the Agricultural Adjustment Administration in that the votes of farmers organized in cooperatives influenced the program, and its purpose was to establish a relationship between the price of wheat and the cost of manufactured goods similar to that which had existed on the eve of World War I. With its elaborate system of weighted representation for growers, middlemen, consumers, and the government, the French system also bore a superficial resemblance to Italian corporatism. It differed from the Italian, however, by regulating the price of wheat directly—the Italians subsidized wheat by means of high tariffs.

Unlike the Americans, the French did not attempt to control the amount of wheat that farmers planted. Instead the Wheat Office set the price each year, basing it on crop estimates and the parity concept. The office purchased all the wheat grown in France at that price. The grain was then offered at another fixed price to processors. Any excess beyond domestic demand was to be exported by the office if a favorable price could be obtained. If not, it was held in storage.[41]

In 1936 poor harvests throughout Europe and the almost total failure of the Argentine crop made the job of the Wheat Office relatively simple—the world price of wheat more than doubled between 1935 and 1937. However, weather conditions improved in 1938, and by the summer of 1939, the office found itself with so much wheat on hand that it had to stop paying for grain beyond what could be sold domestically. The excess was held in storage pending an improvement in the market. The improvement, of course, came quickly once World War II erupted.[42]

Attempts to deal with the agricultural depression in individual countries, and efforts to raise prices by cutting back on production, combined to stifle international trade. Quotas on imports did so directly. Protective tariffs, exchange controls, and subsidies granted to domestic producers achieved the same result indirectly. Many countries devalued their currencies to make their exports more attractive to foreign buyers. But the widespread use of this device reduced its effectiveness.

The slump in trade hit nations with surpluses of agricultural goods especially hard, because the prices of raw materials fell further during the depression than the prices of most manufactured goods. It became extremely difficult for unindustrialized countries to pay for the manufactures they customarily imported. The economist Carlos F. Diaz Alejandro calculated that by 1933 the purchasing power of eight important Latin American nations (Argentina, Brazil, Cuba, Chile, Ecuador, Mexico, Peru, and Venezuela) had fallen between 40 and 75 percent below 1929 levels. The declining price of wool had a similar effect on New Zealand, as did that of jute on India and that of silk on Japan.[43]

The effect that unfavorable "terms of trade" during the depression had on unindustrialized nations was not always unfortunate. Quite the contrary, in many instances it caused beneficial structural changes in their economies. When they ran out of foreign exchange to pay for manufactures, they shifted capital and labor from agriculture and mining to the production of cement, paper, soap, textiles, and other previously imported necessities. The process, called "import substitution," was often carried out without plan by large numbers of small entrepreneurs. Nevertheless, it resulted in better-balanced economies and improved standards of living.

Governments contributed to the trend, sometimes consciously, sometimes inadvertently. Revenue tariffs on imported manufactured products had been a major source of income for most unindustrialized countries. With the collapse of foreign trade, this income shrank. Such nations had to devalue their currencies and resort to deficit spending. Willy-nilly, this stimulated internal economic activity and provided a favorable climate for industrial development. Domestic raw materials were available at bargain prices, and unemployed agricultural laborers were willing to work for low wages. When further buttressed by new protective tariffs, this new local manufacturing flourished.

No country suffered a more catastrophic loss of foreign markets than Chile, whose prosperity had depended on the export of copper

75

and nitrates. When foreign demand slackened, the plummeting prices of these products caused the value of Chile's exports to fall from about 2.3 billion pesos in 1929 to only 282 million pesos in 1932. Unemployment soared.

Shrinking incomes and a shortage of foreign exchange forced Chileans to cut their foreign purchases to the bone. The government tried to deal with the stagnating economy by reducing its expenditures, but it was compelled to unbalance the budget. As one historian explained, "No matter how drastically expenses were cut, revenue fell even more rapidly." Although the government put 32,000 unemployed copper miners to work panning for gold in mountain streams, it had to abandon the gold standard. But the resulting inflation and the availability of thousands of unemployed workers soon led to economic recovery. With foreign goods out of reach, dozens of small manufacturing enterprises sprang up. By 1935 the Chilean economy was back at pre-depression levels.[44]

Elsewhere in the world, other countries that had relied on foreign manufactures went through similar changes. India's economy was in desperate straits in 1931. Jute, one of its most important exports, was selling at a fifth of the 1926 price, and tea, cotton, and other agricultural exports were also depressed. Yet India's very desperation encouraged domestic industry. The output of cotton textiles expanded. Cement production doubled between 1931 and 1937. In much the same manner, the declining demand for raw silk, particularly in the United States, forced Japan to shift resources from agriculture to industry. By 1937 Japan was almost self-sufficient in textiles, railroad equipment, electrical machinery, and many other manufactures.[45]

Similar examples abound. In Mexico "the industrial sector became the engine of growth" during the 1930s, in large measure because of the prohibitive cost of foreign manufactures. In Spain the loss of markets resulting from the decline of world trade was particularly severe. Great Britain's imperial preference system, for example, dealt a terrible blow to Spanish growers of citrus fruits, rice, and spring vegetables. But the low world price of cotton in the early 1930s was a boon to Spanish textile manufacturers. Between 1928 and 1932, they increased their foreign purchases of cotton by about a third, but the larger volume cost them barely half as much as the foreign cotton they bought in 1928. Australian output of textiles, light metals, paper, and chemicals soared in the mid-1930s, all, the historian C. B. Schedvin notes, because of the "near elimination of import competition." In Argentina new textile manufacturers could rely on cheap locally grown cotton and wool and an adequate supply of low-wage labor. The government helped by putting high tariffs on yarn and cloth while allowing textile machinery to enter the country duty-free.

In Brazil the troubles that beset the coffee growers were a powerful stimulus to industrial development. When it purchased and destroyed surplus coffee, the government injected money into the economy. At the same time, imports of manufactured goods were falling sharply because of the shortage of foreign exchange. The demand for manufactures remained, and soon capital and labor were moving into the production of everything from steel and cement to paper and glass. By 1939 Brazil was making more than 90 percent of its own cloth and clothing, leather goods, furniture, and many other commodities in everyday use.

Most of the new Brazilian shops and factories were inefficient, and nearly all were labor intensive. The development took place without pattern or overall plan. Government deficits had a good deal to do with the expansion, but these were not merely unplanned but undesired; shrinking revenues and unavoidable expenses caused by having to put down an insurrection in the state of São Paulo in 1932 compelled the government to run in the red. It was, the Brazilian historian Celso Furtado writes, a "pump-priming policy unconsciously adopted as a by-product of the protection of the coffee interests." Another historian has characterized the dictatorial Vargas regime as "government by improvisation." Furthermore, most of the coffee planters, who were the direct recipients of government payments, did not take advantage of the new industrial opportunities. Much of the capital diverted from growing coffee went into real estate, banking, and cotton speculation. Nevertheless, by the end of 1932 industrial production in Brazil had far

77

surpassed the 1929 level. More important, over the rest of the decade it increased at an annual rate of more than 8 percent.[46]

Industrialization was not a cure-all for nations that had been heavily dependent on agricultural exports before the depression. Most of the Caribbean countries, for example, were too small and too undeveloped economically to do more than wait for foreign demand for their coffee or bananas or sugar to improve. The Cuban economy, which was perhaps large enough to change, remained a satellite of that of the United States: Cuba signed a reciprocity treaty in 1934 that made it more dependent than ever on American products and American markets. Territories or outright colonies often fared better than small "independent" countries because of their favored positions in the markets of the controlling power. The sugar exports of Puerto Rico and the Philippines to the United States increased, while Cuba's declined. Great Britain imported more bananas from its colony of Jamaica, fewer from the independent "banana republics" of Central America.[47]

Nor did industrial development necessarily benefit the agricultural sector in countries where the shift did occur. Many American farmers claimed that the New Deal industrial recovery program had caused the prices of things they bought to go up faster than the agricultural program was causing farm prices to rise. Banks and other creditors had taken their pants, rural wits quipped, now NRA was taking their shirts.

The jokesters may or may not have been correct, but there is no doubt that in the United States, as elsewhere, the higher farm prices that crop controls brought about did not always improve the lot of the people who grew the crops. The workings of the AAA cotton program harmed many tenants and sharecroppers because when landowners took fields out of production in order to qualify for government subsidies, they often needed fewer laborers to cultivate their remaining acres. Benefit payments were supposed to be shared fairly with tenants. All too frequently they were not. Under the act, landlords were supposed to try "in good faith" to maintain "in so far as possible . . . the normal number of tenants" on their plantations. But that requirement was obviously unenforceable and frequently ignored. The combination of higher prices for their cotton and the rent paid by the government for the land kept out of production enabled many landowners to buy tractors and trucks and reduce the number of laborers they needed. Others employed displaced tenants and sharecroppers as hired hands.

Italian tariff and price-support policies favored large producers and forced many tenants to become sharecroppers. In the cases of rubber and tea, the large planters who controlled the administration of the restrictive schemes tended to favor their own interests to the disadvantage of small growers.[48]

Although in general, agricultural interests suffered heavier losses than industrial interests during the depression, the idea that farming could be a refuge in hard times flourished in many parts of the world. In predominantly rural countries with a few large industrial centers—France, Poland, Canada, and Colombia, for example—urban workers frequently did return to family farms when they lost their jobs. There they could find food and shelter without seriously inconveniencing their rural relatives. Governments encouraged such movements, which reduced the cost of unemployment relief. They offered no solution, however, to the problem of mass unemployment.

But relieving *rural* poverty in a time of agricultural depression by giving land to the landless made good sense. In 1931 the new socialist government that took over in Spain after the abdication of Alfonso XIII set out to place at least 60,000 landless peasant families a year on small farms. An Agrarian Reform Act was passed in 1932. But landowner resistance proved too powerful. Fewer than 5,000 families were placed in 1933, and the program was soon abandoned.

In Latin America, however, similar efforts proved more successful. The president of Mexico in the middle and late thirties, Lázaro Cárdenas, sought to check the flow of poor peons to the cities. During his presidency, he expanded the *ejido* (homestead) program under which farms of 15 or 20 acres were turned over to poor rural families. "For the [Mexican] Indian, *land is life*,"

Cárdenas told the journalist John Gunther. Cárdenas believed in modernization. He created an Ejido Bank to help small farmers obtain machinery, and he sent agricultural experts into the countryside to introduce improved plant varieties and to otherwise help raise agricultural efficiency. Far from opposing manufacturing, he encouraged the development of village industries and cooperative projects such as sugar mills. In a similar vein, President Alfonso López of Colombia obtained legislation in 1936 enabling large numbers of squatters to get title to land.[49]

People like Cárdenas and López were looking forward rather than backward. In technologically advanced societies, however, the idea of resettlement—putting idle industrial workers and their families on small farms as a way of coping with the depression—was profoundly reactionary. The so-called "back to the soil" movement reflected disillusionment with industrial capitalism, but it was a conservative critique, made by people who harked back to a simpler, supposedly idyllic era when most people lived on the land, self-reliant and secure.

It had no necessary relation to the depression. Its best-known manifestation in the United States was the book of essays written by twelve southerners called *I'll Take My Stand*. These writers opposed industrialism because they believed that it was destroying the way of life they loved, not because they thought industrial society was breaking down. The South "should dread industrialism like a pizen snake," wrote Andrew Nelson Lytle. The southern farmer "is swapping his culture for machine-made bric-à-brac." Instead "he must deny himself the articles the industrialists offer for sale," exchange his radio for a fiddle, give up the movies and go back to square dancing, and "diversify so that he may live rather than that he may grow rich."

This agrarian philosophy was a basic element in Gandhi's movement in India, where it made at least political, if not economic, sense. It was also popular in France, where it made little sense of any kind. No one advanced it more passionately than the essayist and novelist Jean Giono. Before the Great War, "everyone had enough of everything, and no one wanted more," Giono insisted.

Life then was better by far. "I have a thousand times more money than my father had," he wrote, but "in my youth I ate more and better fruit than my daughters now can."

Giono carried this reasoning to extremes. "I have 90,000 kilograms of unsalable wheat to my credit at the cooperative," he wrote. "If by bad luck the next harvest is as big as the last, what do you want me to do with it? . . . There will be nothing to do but set fire to the farm, lie down on the ground, and die." Giono was not particularly concerned about urban unemployment. He disliked the entire modern system of economic organization—money, he insisted, was "inane," and "an absurdity." Only the self-sufficient peasant proprietor could be truly free.[50]

Few went so far as Giono in praising rural simplicity, but throughout the western world many people saw in small-scale farming a refuge from the depression. The simplest form of this idea was the perfectly reasonable one that if given small plots, unemployed people could grow some of their own food. In *Middletown in Transition*, Robert and Helen Lynd described "a six-month wave of farm enthusiasm" that swept over the city of Muncie, Indiana, in 1930. In Germany wartime food shortages and the runaway postwar inflation had caused millions of urban dwellers to cultivate small plots on the outskirts of cities long before the depression. Owning a patch of land meant security of a sort in uncertain times.

The depression greatly strengthened the appeal of resettlement. In Germany both the socialist government of Hermann Müller and the conservative government of Heinrich Brüning that followed it strongly supported the idea, and this did not change after Hitler came to power. Indeed, glorification of the small farmer, his life rooted in the soil, was a fundamental Nazi social attitude. Walther Darré, the ideologue of National Socialist agricultural policy, praised peasant life and so-called rural values as enthusiastically as Jean Giono. According to Darré, farmers were the "life source" of the German nation both in the sense that they raised food and in the sense that, as another Nazi agricultural authority put it, they had "the biological strength to . . . compensate for population losses resulting from migration to cities and from war." To preserve this "life source," a law was enacted in September 1933 making family-sized farms (about a third of all German agricultural units) entailed properties. These *Erbhöfe* could not be sold or mortgaged and were to pass on the death of an owner to his principal heir.[51]*

President Franklin Roosevelt had less grandiose expectations for agriculturalists in the United States, but he too idealized small-farm life. While governor of New York he published an article entitled "Back to the Land" in the *Saturday Evening Post*. He also initiated a small state program for settling unemployed city families on farms. Before and after he became president, Roosevelt's speeches and writings on the subject were full of remarks drawing unfavorable comparisons between "over-crowded cities" and life in the country.

Roosevelt's expressions on this subject undoubtedly came from the heart. It is sometimes difficult to estimate the sincerity of other politicians who praised the virtues of small-scale agriculture in the 1930s. When one finds André Tardieu, Paris born and "a bourgeois to his finger tips," telling French farmers that "the land is your nobility," and "you teach city people the grandeur of continuity," and "whoever defends you, defends the future," one is tempted to suspect his motives. The same doubts are raised by the French communists' pledge to come to the defense of *"la petite propriété paysanne."*[52]

Everywhere and for generations, the flow of population had been from country to city and from small farm to large. The depression slowed these movements somewhat, as it slowed so many other things. But efforts to reverse their direction failed because the forces that had set them in motion had not changed. Advocates of the shift either managed somehow to ignore the desperate plight of so many existing farmers or, like Giono, wished to discard the whole economic system.

The unemployed were hungry and idle and the state lacked the resources to support them. On farms they would be less "visible"

---

* The Japanese had a similar attitude, believing farmers to be "the backbone of the nation, the source of its military strength and the guardian of traditional virtues against alien influences."

statistically and less likely to cause trouble. In any case, their idleness was wasteful and character eroding. Therefore let the jobless have bits of land so that they may work to feed themselves, thus achieving both sustenance and independence. A writer describing the back-to-the-land movement in the journal *Land Economics* in 1935 predicted that it would "create vast strongholds and immeasurable reserves against future depressions." This view was narrow and short-sighted. That well-meaning people could find it heartening shows how stultifying the impact of the depression was on human expectations.

The depression made people grasp at straws. The back-to-the-soil concept was quite impracticable. Most city people either rejected suggestions that they become subsistence farmers or, if they made the move, found that they lacked the skills and physical endurance that farm work required. Farmers either resented efforts to introduce new "competitors" into their ranks or, if they took in the city people as laborers, frequently complained that they were poor workers. In France a private organization, *Le Circle François-Villon*, specialized in placing jobless intellectuals in the country. It reported many cases of "exploitation," including one where a young doctor, after an 11-hour day of "repulsive" labor, was fed bad food and forced to sleep on straw in the barn. One would need to hear the farmer's side of this story before condemning him as an exploiter of labor.[53]

Few realists had ever expected the back-to-the-soil movement to succeed. As an American agricultural economist explained in 1933, "There are already too many farmers eking out a miserable existence. City people without capital and without farming experience have an even smaller chance to make a decent living in agriculture." The Canadian socialist J. S. Woodsworth, who was deeply concerned with the troubles of both western farmers and the urban unemployed, put it this way: "In the old days we could send people from the cities to the country. If they went out today they would meet another army of unemployed coming back from the country to the city; that outlet is closed."

The self-sufficient farm was rapidly disappearing, at least in

Europe and North America. The prewar French peasants whose lifestyle Giono admired so much had gotten "in the habit of buying." Louis Salleron, the principal theoretician of an important French farm organization, said, "Agriculture is the peasantry, but it is also production. The condition of peasant becomes the *métier* of producer the moment the product is sold, and there is born the drama."[54]

Yet the hope that the jobless might find refuge on the land persisted. In 1936 the economist Wladimir Woytinsky called attention to a difference in the reactions of industrial workers and farmers to adversity that may explain why this was so. "The depression tended to produce discord within the ranks of wage earners in industry," Woytinsky wrote in *Social Consequences of the Economic Depression*. "On the other hand, the depression united the farmers."[55]

While perhaps overstated, Woytinsky's generalization was essentially sound. Agriculture was hard hit by the depression, but there was relatively little agricultural unemployment. Most farmers appeared (to themselves as well as to outsiders) to be more or less in the same boat. Industrial losses were distributed less equitably. Those who kept their jobs suffered little, many not at all. Others— the unemployed—lost everything. To economists this was easily explained: industrial prices did not fall as rapidly or as far as agricultural ones. Their "stickiness" further curtailed demand, thus exacerbating the depression and leading to more unemployment. For workers this made for feast or famine, and as Woytinsky noted, it caused "discord within the ranks." For some persons who were concerned with helping the losers in the industrial conflict, the apparent harmony among farmers obscured the actual condition of the agricultural sector.

CHAPTER IV

WORKERS AND UNIONS

I t is important to keep in mind that during the Great Depression, people who had full-time jobs were usually better off, at least economically, than they had been before 1929. This was true because in nearly every nation, the cost of living fell faster and further than wages fell. It is also worth noting that at all times, a large majority of the work force was employed. Put the other way around, the unemployed, although unprecedentedly numerous, were always a minority.

Another important fact to remember is that unemployment, for a majority of those who suffered the experience, tended to be a temporary condition. Relatively few of the draftees who served in what Karl Marx called "the industrial reserve army" of the unemployed were enlisted for the duration. This fact blurs all the generalizations that we tend to make about how people were affected by the loss of work. Consider, for example, these statistics: in 1930, 16,500 Belgian workers were unemployed; in 1931 the number rose to 41,100; and by 1934 it had reached 72,300.[1] These are official figures, as accurate as any at the time, but they conceal as much as they reveal—in a way, more. Many, perhaps most, of the Belgians who were out of work in 1930 had jobs in 1931. Still more were idle only part of any of the years in question.

On the other hand, during any year, the number of Belgian workers who were unemployed at some time was much larger than any of the annual figures. To cite another example, in Great Britain in the 1920s, a 10 percent unemployment rate meant that about 1.2 million workers were idle. But at that rate, about 4 million layoffs were involved each year.[2] In addition, in all countries, the hours of many workers were severely reduced. People on short time were not counted as being out of work, although in some cases they were idle for more time than workers who were without any job for substantial periods.

In the middle and late twenties, real wages were rising and working conditions improving in most industrial regions. The percentage of white-collar and service industry jobs was increasing, which meant (among other things) that more workers had adopted middle class values and expectations. When workers moved up the economic and social ladder, places opened for others to take the jobs they had vacated; the movement of Poles to French mines and of American blacks from southern farms to factory jobs in northern cities were examples of this. As early as 1923, about 5,000 blacks were employed in the Detroit area by the Ford Motor Company.[3]

Thus, the onset of the depression brought to an end what had been a period of relatively good times for most workers. Even those who continued to work steadily after 1929 were bound to find the change in the economic climate unsettling. The social and economic mobility characteristic of the previous decade slowed to a halt. Few workers could feel safe when ever-larger numbers of their colleagues were out of work, and no end to the hard times was in sight. "A clear divergence of interest emerged," writes a British historian, "between those in employment who benefited by cheap food and cheap services, and those eking out an existence on the dole or perhaps without any income whatever."

The depression caused labor unions, which had been losing members even in the 1920s, to suffer still further declines. In Great

Britain and Germany, where unions were large and influential, membership in 1932 was down to roughly half of what it had been in 1920. The decline in France and the United States was smaller, mainly because the number of unionized workers had not been been very large to begin with.[4]

Workers tended to drop out of unions when they lost their jobs because they could not afford to pay dues, but also because the attitude of most unions was less than fully supportive of the jobless. Especially in countries that had government insurance and relief systems, the help that unions provided for their idle members was chiefly rhetorical.

Important differences existed, however, in the condition and attitudes of workers in the different nations, and these differences influenced the way they reacted when the depression struck. Industrial workers in the United States had a far higher standard of living than their counterparts in Europe. They ate better, and had better housing and far more of the amenities and small luxuries of life. The better off among them lived as well as many petit-bourgeois Europeans. By the end of the decade, nearly every American worker owned an automobile—at a time when a new Ford could be bought for a few hundred dollars, the average annual wage of workers in manufacturing was more than $1,500. Serviceable used cars cost almost nothing, and gasoline was cheap and relatively untaxed compared to Europe.

This helps explain why most American workers were unorganized; out of a nonagricultural labor force of some 37 million, only about 3.5 million belonged to unions, and few of these were employed in the mass production industries.

As for the unions, most adopted extremely conservative policies. The largest, the American Federation of Labor, was determinedly apolitical. Its branches were organized on trade rather than industrial lines and consequently had done almost nothing in the 1920s about organizing unskilled workers in the expanding mass production industries such as electrical appliances, chemicals, and automobiles.

Nearly all the AFL locals discriminated against blacks. (In

1928, for example, only 81,000 of the 3 million-odd AFL members were black.) Most AFL leaders concentrated on bread-and-butter issues in the style recommended by their long-time leader Samuel Gompers. They made little use of professional economists or of any kind of research. They distrusted government officials, whom they thought tended to side with employers in labor disputes. The one kind of labor legislation that the AFL supported in the 1920s was workmen's compensation laws. Even in 1932, when unemployment exceeded 10 million, it opposed government relief for the jobless on the ground that relief "instills in those cared for a sense of irresponsibility and dependence that is harmful to society." It did come out for an unemployment insurance law in 1932, however. Other issues on which it began to express opinions during the early years of the depression were public works projects and balanced budgets, both of which it favored, although the adoption of one almost inevitably would have excluded the other.[5]

Ordinary British workers were as much given to copying bourgeois values as their American counterparts, but their expectations were less ambitious. (Automobile ownership among wage earners lagged 30 years behind what it was in the United States.)[6] Most of them were not enthusiastic socialists, despite the fact that they supported the Labour Party, which was nominally committed to Marxist ideas and goals.

The British trade union movement, however, differed from the American in almost every respect. Union membership in Britain was down to about 3.7 million in 1929 from 6.5 million right after the war, but this was more than in the United States, with its far larger population. Although British workers had the highest standard of living among European workers, they suffered throughout the twenties from high unemployment—the "intractable million" who had no work was the phrase used to describe the situation. The unemployment was concentrated in the northern and western parts of the nation. Industries that had been the driving force of British economic growth in the nineteenth century—coal mining, iron and steel, and ship building—were the hardest hit, with rates roughly double the national average.[7]

89

The British unions were, unlike the American, socialist in orientation and politically active. The Trades Union Council (TUC) was a powerful force in the British Labour Party. Union leaders were more interested in economic theory and more in contact with professional economists and other intellectuals than their American counterparts. Ernest Bevin, founder of the Transport and General Workers' Union and later head of the Trades Union Council, served on various government commissions with important economists and was much influenced by their ideas.

The policies of the TUC, however, were far from being radical. Until well into the depression, the unions followed the Labour Party lead in insisting that the government balance the budget. They also pursued conservative and essentially short-sighted policies designed to protect their members against possible competition from the unemployed. The high unemployment of the 1920s, particularly in the depressed industries, which were the backbone of union strength, tended to make union leaders cautious.

In 1926 the TUC did call a general strike in support of the coal miners, who walked out in response to a wage cut. The general strike paralyzed the country. All public transport stopped; the government had to take over utility plants to keep the lights burning; conservatives accused the unions of holding a pistol to the nation's head. But after a little over a week, the TUC called off the strike, leaving the miners to fend for themselves.

Actually, the general strike had a further chastening effect on the unions (and on most employers as well). "Never again!" was a common reaction. The TUC and the leading employers' organizations formed a National Industrial Council to discuss future problems. Thereafter the unions accepted the idea that industrial modernization would result in a certain amount of technological unemployment. For their part, the employers agreed to maintain current wage levels. Between 1923 and 1937, British wages remained almost constant, but prices fell about 15 percent. In effect, the unions traded jobs for wages.[8]

In France a most unusual situation developed during the 1920s. Despite the relative shortage of labor, workers were poorly paid and, in general, badly treated by their employers. French industry was divided into a modern, mechanized sector, and an old-fashioned, handicraft one made up of hundreds of small firms that produced high-quality products made by skilled workers. In neither case were many of the workers organized. Only about 10 percent of the French labor force belonged to unions, approximately the same percentage as in the United States.

French workers retained preindustrial attitudes more than workers in other industrial societies. Because they were in short supply, unemployment was seldom a problem. But they tended to be suspicious of their employers (more often than not with good reason) and of politicians too. They preferred to leave to foreigners unpleasant tasks, such as were common in chemical plants and mines. Small shops, which were not labor efficient, persisted in many fields. Even some automobile carburetors were assembled under the putting-out system in individual homes.

About 3 million laborers, most of them from Poland, Spain, Portugal, and Italy, immigrated to France during the postwar decade. They brought with them low standards of living, and they were extremely dependent on their employers. Most were unable to speak French, at least when they arrived in the country.

Many French peasants also worked in factories part time. Since they lived on and drew sustenance from their land, they were not entirely dependent on wages for their survival. But because of their attachment to their farms, they lacked mobility in the labor market and were relatively easy for employers to exploit. In general, factory workers were alienated but not politically sophisticated, a further reason why they were low paid. Many voted socialist.[9]

The small French labor movement was badly divided. The most important union was the *Confédération Générale du Travail* (CGT), which was allied with the Socialist Party. It appealed mainly to skilled workers. (Even more than elsewhere, the wage gap between skilled and unskilled labor was wide in France.) Next in importance was the communist union, the *Confédération Générale du Travail Unitaire* (CGTU). There was also a smaller Catholic union, the *Confédération Française des Travailleurs Crétiens* (CFTC), which was conservative in outlook. Many French workers were put off by the

91

Marxist rhetoric of the CGT and the CGTU and by the constant squabbling and political infighting of the two organizations.

The CGTU claimed to be waiting for the revolution that would result in the establishment of a Marxist utopia. Its leaders predicted that the depression signaled the beginning of the end of capitalism. They envisaged marshaling the unemployed as the shock troops of the uprising that would end it. Unemployment insurance and other kinds of labor and social legislation were at best worthless, the communists claimed. Probably such laws would do harm because they would delay the revolution by easing some of the pain caused by capitalist exploitation. In any case,

> the workers will be the only ones to pay. . . . You cannot collect contributions from workers when their wages are insufficient. Social insurance is an inalienable *right* of the worker. The *bourgeoisie*, as the privileged class, should pay the cost.[10]

The CGT employed an almost equally radical rhetoric but acted "in perpetual contradiction to what it said." Its leaders talked confidently of a future socialist state but acknowledged that capitalism was still very much alive. Unlike the communists, who abjured cooperation with the political establishment, the CGT favored *"la politique de la présence,"* which meant being willing to serve on government commissions and participate in other government functions. They did so in hopes of having some influence on policy, and in order to "educate" workers so that they would know what to do when the socialists took over at some future date.[11]

The CGT supported all kinds of labor legislation, demanded improvements in public education, and campaigned for high tariffs on foreign manufactures. It opposed efforts to rationalize antiquated industries on the ground that mechanization would lead to wage cuts and the elimination of jobs, and it tried to get the government to stop the influx of foreign workers. It made frequent use of strikes to obtain what it wanted, but usually the immediate object was to get the government to intervene as arbitrator.[12]

In this sense, the Marxist CGT was even less militant than the conservative AFL in the United States. One reason was that French employers were both well organized and vehemently antiunion. Their organization, the *Confédération Générale de la Production Française*, was adamantly opposed to collective bargaining and to all types of social legislation. The members did adopt some paternalistic labor policies. For example, they commonly paid workers with large families extra money. But they resisted having anything *imposed* on them, either by unions or by the government. In this they resembled many American corporate officials.

When the depression began to affect France seriously in 1931, employers reduced wages. They demanded (along with nearly everyone else) that the government economize in order to balance the budget. But they opposed every proposal for government intervention in their affairs. The CGT responded to the wage cuts with a traditional Marxist argument, not very different from the communists':

Wage cuts are iniquitous because they place on the workers the effects of an economic crisis they had nothing to do with. Their poverty should not be the ransom of the disorder of capitalism.[13]

The steep decline in the cost of living the union leaders simply ignored.

CGT leaders were quite interested in economic theory. They located the main cause of the depression in the disproportion between business profits and workers' wages. Union spokesmen insisted that the disproportion explained why production had outrun consumption. Only international cooperation would end the depression. Among other things, they suggested creating vast international public works projects, including driving a tunnel under the English Channel.[14] Meanwhile, the French government should assist municipalities in caring for the unemployed. The National Assembly should enact laws that would increase the purchasing power of consumers (read "workers"). But French union leaders showed

93

little understanding of either the costs or the other effects of their proposals.

Germany, like Great Britain, was plagued by considerable unemployment during the otherwise prosperous late twenties. An additional problem, one that had a great deal to do with the rise of the Nazis, was the fact that white-collar workers and professionals were badly paid and often unable to find any job at all.

On the other hand, German industrial workers were better organized than workers in France and the United States and even more influential in politics than their British counterparts. The General German Trade Union Federation (*Allgemeiner Deutscher Gewerkschaftsbund,* or ADGB) was a major force in German politics. There was also an organization of Catholic unions, conservative in outlook, but nearly all the leaders of the Trade Union Federation were socialists. And rank-and-file German workers were more deeply committed to socialist ideas and ideals than any other workers in the western world.

Union officials were very political and gave the backing of the ADGB to the Socialist Party (SPD). This meant not only the support of the federation newspapers, which reached about 6 million readers, but also substantial campaign contributions. This was possible because of the large union membership and the commitment of the rank-and-filers to socialism. The federation had an income of about 250 million marks in 1929, roughly $60 million. (The AFL took in $432,000 in 1929, though of course AFL locals also collected dues.)

About 20 percent of the Socialist deputies in the Reichstag were ADGB officers, and nearly all of the others were members of some union. "The party and the government are two," the slogan ran. "The party and the unions are one." In short, organized labor was a powerful force in Germany. Like their French counterparts, German union leaders were intellectually oriented and had a more sophisticated understanding of economics than most unionists. Unlike French socialists, they were not rigidly uncompromising. They believed that the capitalist system was still evolving and that it could be directed in ways that would benefit the working class. "We

94

must recognize," wrote Fritz Tarnow, the president of the carpenters' union in 1929, "that although the economic system cannot be changed overnight, it *can* be changed. We do not have to wait until political power is a hundred percent in our hands to begin to change it."[15]

Some excellent economists and statisticians were employed by the federation. Among these was Wladimir Woytinsky. Before the depression, Woytinsky had written a huge seven-volume statistical reference work, *Die Welt in Zahlen* (The World in Figures). He improved the federation's method of estimating the amount of unemployment in the country, and when the full force of the depression struck, he developed a plan for stimulating the German economy through a combination of public works projects and easy money. This proposal got little support because of the widespread German fear of inflation. But soon thereafter Woytinsky and two other union officials worked out a modification of the scheme that attracted much favorable comment. (A more radical federation idea was one that included nationalizing basic industries and carving up large estates into small farms. This would have amounted to a modified form of state socialism, with the unions becoming part of the government administrative system.)

No union antidepression proposal stood much chance of being put into practice. The point is that more than any other western labor organization, the German Federation had interesting things to say and made significant intellectual contributions to the fight against the depression.

This fact makes what happened to the German labor movement in 1933 ironic as well as tragic. Few industrial workers joined the Nazi Party. Some socialist and communist workers wanted to oppose the Nazi takeover by force. But the Socialist Party was against this, and the federation went along. Its leaders, mostly old men, could not believe that their federation could be seriously harmed, let alone wiped out, by Hitler. In any case, it seems probable that a majority of the workers, despite their fear and hatred of fascism, which was evident, were unwilling to start a civil war.[16]

When Hitler became chancellor, federation leaders were prepared to cooperate with the new government to save their organization. They agreed to cease all political activity. They even marched in the Nazis' huge Day of German Labor parade on April 19. This was Hitler's substitute for May Day, the traditional socialist labor holiday. The next morning Hitler outlawed all unions, seized their assets, and arrested their leaders.

Wladimir Woytinsky resigned from the federation when the leaders decided not to resist the Nazis. (They went along with Hitler, he later recalled, "like a group of captives dragged behind the chariot of the conqueror.") He then fled to Switzerland, escaping arrest by a matter of hours. After spending some time working for the International Labor Organization, he emigrated to the United States, where he was eventually employed by the Social Security Board and other New Deal organizations. Like so many refugees of that generation, he became a fervent American patriot, referring to the country as "the promised land I discovered at the end of my stormy passage."[17]

Throughout the Great Depression, people with jobs tended to view the unemployed with mixed feelings. They sympathized with them on humane grounds and because awareness of their plight was a reminder of their own vulnerability—"there but for the grace of God go I." Yet they also feared the unemployed as possible competitors. In the case of unions and their leaders, this ambivalence amounted almost to hypocrisy. The recent statement of two English historians that the British unions "tended to ignore the unemployed" is something of an exaggeration, but it contains more than one grain of truth.[18]

Rhetorically the unions were "for" the unemployed all-out. But *doing* something for the unemployed was more often than not another matter entirely. Most unions outside the United States favored government relief programs and unemployment insurance systems. They opposed cuts in benefits and in welfare payments to workers whose insurance benefits had been exhausted. But the unions did so in large part out of self-interest. Welfare and unemployment insurance took some of the pressure off union members in the sense that without this kind of assistance, unemployed people would be forced to seek work at any wage at all. And the unions resisted government proposals to increase worker contributions to the insurance funds. They did so without regard for the steady decline in the cost of living, which was causing the real wages of full-time workers to rise.

During the depression, job security was obviously of enormous importance to workers. When layoffs occurred, last hired, first fired was an almost universal union policy. The stress on seniority discriminated against younger workers and in most instances against women.

Work sharing might have helped to spread the burden of unemployment, but work sharing never had much appeal in the labor movement. When the 1937 recession struck the United States, the United Electrical Workers union at one Westinghouse Company plant tried first to deal with reductions in the work force by obtaining a work-sharing agreement. Instead of layoffs, everyone would work shorter hours. But what the union newspaper called a "tremendous sharing of misery" soon got to be more than the majority would stomach. The union went back to the seniority principle. If the average work week fell below 36 hours, as many as necessary with less than a year's seniority would be let go. If it fell below 34 hours, as many as necessary with less than five years on the job would be released.[19]

The British unions were equally opposed to work sharing. The steelworkers' union refused to put such a scheme into effect despite the fact that since steelworkers were paid on a tonnage basis and output per worker was rising, their earnings were going up. Other British unions even objected when the sponsors of clubs for the unemployed gave idle workers a chance to keep busy and earn a few shillings by tailoring, carpentry, and other handicraft work.[20]

During the depression, unions tended to tighten rules governing the admission and training of apprentices. They also advocated keeping young people in school longer and lowering the retirement age, both socially desirable policies but ones that if adopted would put some people out of work for the benefit of others. In a way, they attacked the unemployment problem by redefining who was unemployed, not by finding new jobs for the idle. Unions also favored getting married women out of the work force, which was not socially desirable at all, and strictly selfish national policies such as high protective tariffs, "buy American" (or whatever), and measures aimed at sending foreign workers "back where they came from."

What can be made of the sad history of labor organizations during the Great Depression? Probably no more than the truism that hard times are tough on unions, indeed on nearly all working people. That, and the fact, already stated, that since no one really knew what to do to end the depression, forceful group action did not make much sense either to responsible labor leaders or to their constituents.

CHAPTER V

WHAT IT DID TO
THE JOBLESS

To contemporaries, persistent, unprecedentedly high unemployment was the most alarming aspect of the Great Depression. In every industrial nation, more people were out of work than in any period in the past. It has been estimated that in 1933 about 30 million workers were jobless, about two-thirds of these in three countries—the United States, Germany, and Great Britain. If anything, this estimate is low.

But little can be gained by citing numbers. No accurate counts were made either before or during the depression. Furthermore, the estimates that were made were arrived at by different methods in different countries. B. R. Mitchell's authoritative *European Historical Statistics: 1750–1970* (1976) ends six pages of statistics on unemployment in nineteen nations with this caution: "The variety of different indicators of unemployment used is clear from the footnotes [25 in number]. This should serve as a warning against incautious comparisons."

Modern American economists have gone to great lengths in the effort to estimate the number of people unemployed in the

United States in the twenties and thirties. They have used frag-
mentary contemporary evidence, much of it derived from labor
union records. One recent student of the problem, Gene Smiley,
has characterized the best of these records as "strikingly different
and contradictory." A League of Nations publication, the *International Labour Review*, put the problem this way back in 1936:

> In view of the great diversity which exists in the scope
> and methods of compilation . . . international comparisons
> [of unemployment] are extremely difficult and only pos-
> sible with considerable reservations. . . . Figures relate
> to persons recorded as *wholly* unemployed, and in most
> cases fall far short of the reality.

The most useful way to express numerically the extent of unemployment during the Great Depression is to use the index of the
International Labor Organization. According to the ILO index, if
the world's unemployed population is taken as 100 in 1929, it was
235 by 1931, 291 in the autumn of 1932, and still about 200 as late
as 1935.[1]

Investigators repeatedly found government unemployment figures far off the mark. In Poland, for example, between 1929 and
1933, the number of registered unemployed workers rose from 185,000
to 343,000, an increase of 158,000. But in that period, the official
number of people employed (a figure much easier to estimate accurately) declined by 300,000. A Polish researcher located about
400,000 "invisible" unemployed, mostly city people who had lost
their jobs and gone to live with relatives on farms. He concluded
that there were actually a million idle workers in Poland and an
additional million peasants who were eager to leave the land for
industrial jobs if jobs ever became available. According to official
statistics, French unemployment reached a peak in 1935, when
503,500 people were out of work. But other government figures
showed that the number of people working in 1935 was 1.88 million
below the 1929 level. Similar examples abound.[2]

Beyond the difficulty in counting the unemployed, there are all sorts of variations to be considered that affected the significance of unemployment to the unemployed and to the societies they inhabited. It made a great difference whether a person was unemployed for a few weeks or months or for a longer period. Unemployment affected men differently in most cases than women, old people differently than the young, married people differently than single. Such obvious matters as the number of children in a breadwinner's family and the existence and amount of unemployment insurance or welfare also affected the meaning of joblessness for its victims. So did the amount of unemployment in the community.

Investigators, government and private, did a much better job of studying the effects of unemployment than of counting the number of people without work. Studies of the impact of unemployment on living conditions, school attendance, health, and other topics were carried out in many lands. The records of relief agencies were combed, and questionnaires were administered by the hundreds to social workers and their idle clients. In 1931 the New York City Welfare Council obtained the views of social workers who were handling 100,000 poor families about the physical and mental effects of unemployment. It did so by circulating a questionnaire among them. In Europe the Polish Institute of Social Economy sponsored a prize essay contest among the unemployed. The contestants were asked to write autobiographies describing the kind of work they had done, the reasons why they had been discharged, the length of time they had been idle, the amount of welfare they had received, and similar matters.

Much valuable information was gathered in these ways, but by far the most interesting and useful investigations were those conducted by field workers who studied the jobless directly. Two now-classic examples were those of the sociologists E. Wight Bakke, an American, and Paul F. Lazarsfeld, an Austrian.*

Bakke, at the time a Yale graduate student, spent six months in 1931 in the London suburb of Greenwich. He lived with a work-

* Both of these men went on to distinguished academic careers, Bakke at Yale and Lazarsfeld at Columbia.

ing-class family and spent many hours observing people in local pubs and employment offices. He went with jobless men as they made the rounds looking for work. In these ways, he got to know many unemployed people well. Some he interviewed repeatedly, recording carefully their changing moods—their attitudes toward themselves and English society, toward politics, and so on. He persuaded some of them to write day-by-day accounts of their activities and feelings. He published his conclusions in *The Unemployed Man* (1933), his doctoral dissertation.[3]

Lazarsfeld was the head of a team of social scientists from the University of Vienna who spent the winter of 1931–32 in the village of Marienthal, not far from Vienna. Marienthal was a one-factory town. The factory, a textile mill, had gone bankrupt and closed down, so that just about everyone in the village of about 1,500 people was unemployed. For most the tiny relief payments supplied by the Austrian government were the only source of income.

The Lazarsfeld team used two kinds of data—what they called "natural" evidence obtained by observing the subjects, and "experimental" material designed by the team, such as questionnaires. The investigators lived among the villagers and followed their activities closely. They kept a file on each of the 478 families in Marienthal.

They studied town records, election results, and the activities of various businesses, including the village tavern. They organized an essay contest for the schoolchildren, assigning topics designed to get them to reveal their expectations and values. Eighty Marienthalers kept hour-by-hour records of their routine movements for the team. Forty families kept track of exactly what they ate at each meal for a week. In one project, a researcher sat in an upstairs window overlooking the main street and recorded how many times each passer-by stopped while walking a certain distance. The object of this elaborate study was to better understand the condition, unemployment, rather than merely to discover what was happening to the people of Marienthal.[4]

Bakke's and Lazarsfeld's painstaking research projects were only the most original of many such investigations. Important studies were made by field workers in Italy, Czechoslovakia, Poland, France, England, and the United States. In America such analyses were almost without number. After completing his dissertation, Bakke became head of Yale's Institute for Human Relations, where he directed an elaborate study of unemployment in New Haven. He published the results in two books, *The Unemployed Worker* and *Citizens Without Work* (1940). Lazarsfeld emigrated to the United States in 1933, where he was soon engaged in a number of projects related to the unemployment problem.

The unemployment studies of the 1930s varied a great deal in scope and quality—they were indeed a mixed bag. Jobless people and their families were subjected to batteries of tests. Some investigators sought to plumb the psyches of idle workers, hoping to isolate traits that might explain why they could not find work or why they reacted in the ways they did to their unfortunate condition. Some compared the unemployed with people in their trades and professions who were still working. There were studies of tramps and vagrants, of people on relief, of those employed on public works projects.

No single pattern or explanation emerged from these investigations. But an enormous amount was learned. It is surely correct to say that the people of that era knew more about the effects of unemployment than they did about the extent of unemployment or its causes.

Despite the physical and mental suffering that often resulted from prolonged joblessness, there is no evidence that the general health of society was affected by the depression.[5] In the United States, the trend toward increased longevity (one that fortunately still continues) proceeded unchecked during the depression. Life expectancy was 57.1 years in 1929, 63.7 years in 1939. The death rate fell from 11.9 per thousand to 10.6 in those years. Trends in the European industrial countries were similar.

The trends of course obscure what was happening to many individuals. After all, the unemployed were a relatively small minority of the population. Furthermore, the steep decline of food prices, a result of the agricultural depression, meant that most people with jobs could improve their diets during the depression years. In some places the per capita consumption of fruit, milk, and meat increased. In France meat consumption rose by more than 10 percent between 1928 and 1936, milk consumption by 20 percent. This much conceded, it is certain that many unemployed people did not get enough to eat and that the quality of the food that the jobless and their dependents consumed was often poorer than what was necessary to maintain good health.

There were 20 known cases of starvation in New York City in 1931, though how many of these were related to unemployment is not clear. Such deaths could occur in places where there were no well-organized welfare systems. Starvation was everywhere rare, however. Highly colored accounts of mass malnutrition do not stand up to close investigation.

Field studies in a number of countries of what unemployed families actually ate show that in nearly all cases, people were getting enough calories to maintain body weight. Consumption ranged from about 2,600 to 2,900 calories per day for adult males, no more than 200 or 300 fewer than what working people were getting.

But in order to obtain *enough* to eat, unemployed people had to cut down on relatively expensive items like meat and fresh fruit. Even milk and other dairy products cost more than many could afford to buy in adequate amounts. In New York City, by December 1930, milk consumption was down by a million quarts a day. Meat consumption plummeted in Vienna in 1931–32. In Budapest, where relief agencies were swamped by hordes of rural people who had crowded in looking for jobs, conditions were even worse. An Australian doctor with a large practice among the unemployed reported in 1935 that many of the children he treated were undernourished. "None will complain of insufficient bread and meat, and in some cases they will admit that they have more bread than necessary," he reported. But they were not obtaining milk, vegetables, or fruit "in sufficient quantities."[6]

The failure of many poor people to manage their meager resources efficiently complicated the problem. Lazarsfeld reported that nearly half the residents of Marienthal had nothing to eat at their evening meal but bread and coffee—the coffee of course had no nutritional value whatsoever. In the depths of the depression, George Orwell made a trip through the northern part of England, where unemployment was especially high. He reported his impressions in a fascinating book, *The Road to Wigan Pier.* Orwell was appalled by how much money unemployed people were spending on sweets, fried potatoes, and tea. (He called tea "the Englishman's opium.") Numbers of unemployed Belgians spent money raising pigeons—not to eat but in hopes of winning a worthless prize. Students of French unemployment complained that the jobless continued to spend a large part of their food budgets on coffee and wine.

It is probably true that some of this "inefficient" consumption was due to ignorance. But as George Orwell noted, it was also an understandable reaction on the part of people in straitened circumstances who had few other ways to relieve the tedium of day-to-day existence. "When you are unemployed," Orwell wrote, "you don't *want* to eat dull, wholesome food. You want something a little bit 'tasty.' " The German sociologist Siegfried Kracauer made a related observation in commenting on the tendency of idle German workers to spend money on movie tickets. They were doing so, he surmised, "less for pleasure than to drive away the ghost of bad times."[7]

Furthermore, the margin for poor people was so thin that it was difficult even with the best management to provide a good diet. A study of 869 German families revealed that they were spending 45 percent of their incomes on food. A French estimate of a similar group reported the food percentage at 60, which is perhaps a comment on the French value system as much as on the limited resources of the subjects.

Routine medical and dental care tended to be neglected by the unemployed in favor of more pressing needs. A report of the German Welfare Ministry issued in 1931 noted that doctors were complaining about parents who were not bringing in their children soon enough when they were sick. According to a dentist in Muncie, Indiana, "working-class patients have tended to delay about two years longer in coming in, and then the tooth has become so bad that there is nothing left to do but to extract it." Orwell mentioned in *The Road to Wigan Pier* that people told him that to avoid toothaches "it is best to 'get shut of' your teeth as early in life as possible."[8]

Many of the unemployed suffered from a lack of proper clothing and from poor housing. Social workers often reported that children of their clients could not go to school because they had no shoes. Many families suffered cruelly in winter because they had no money for coal or wood. It is true that landlords frequently allowed destitute families to remain in their flats out of pity or, the chance of finding another tenant being small, because they preferred having the places occupied in order to prevent them from being vandalized. But the press was full of stories of people evicted for nonpayment of rent or forced to part with their homes because they could not meet mortgage payments.

There was a big increase in vagrancy as people lost their homes and as the jobless took to the road in search of work. Lodging houses operated by local governments and by charitable organizations such as the Salvation Army took care of many of these unfortunates. On the borders of cities from Adelaide and Sydney in Australia to Buenos Aires in Argentina, shantytowns sprang up as groups of homeless people constructed ramshackle shelters on vacant land. One of the most elaborate of these places was the Village of Misery on the northwest outskirts of Vienna, with its shacks made of broken bricks, rusting stovepipes, and other discarded building materials.

The Australians gave these settlements names ranging from Hungry Mile to the sardonic Happy Valley; they called the shacks, constructed of packing cases, scrap lumber, and sheets of rusting metal, "humpies." At first Americans gave their shantytowns similar names—Hardluck-on-the-River for example, and Prosperity Park. But they soon began to call them Hoovervilles, an indication of what the result of the 1932 election was likely to be. In France the shantytowns received a more politically neutral name, *bidonvilles* or tin can cities.[9]

The social and psychological effects of unemployment were studied at least as thoroughly as the material effects, and the results of these investigations make interesting reading. In few areas was there so much agreement; it did not seem to matter what the geographical, political, social, or cultural background—people who lost their jobs reacted in similar ways. Not every individual responded in exactly the same manner. But the patterns of the responses were few in number and not very different from one country to the next.

Statistics show that birth rates declined during the depression. In the United States, the rate went down by 10 percent, which was typical. Marriage rates were less uniformly affected. That rate fell by about 20 percent in the United States and France, still further, for example, in South Australia. But it remained unaffected in Great Britain, and in Germany the birth rate rose after the Nazis came to power. Divorce rates declined, most probably because of the high cost of divorce in most nations.

At least in America, the suicide rate rose during the depression, though as John Kenneth Galbraith demonstrated in *The Great Crash*, ruined investors did not jump out of the windows of skyscrapers in droves after Black Tuesday or at any time during the depression. The suicide rate also went up in Germany. Crime statistics show no clear trend, though it is obvious that many unemployed people stole things they needed but could not afford and committed crimes of many kinds because of the emotional strains they were enduring.

As for the psychological impact of unemployment on its victims, the number of studies of this subject made during the depression was almost infinite. The Lazarsfeld and Bakke projects and the Polish prize essay contest have already been mentioned. One of the most ambitious investigations was carried out in six English industrial towns. Agents of a foundation, the Pilgrim Trust, interviewed more than a thousand families where the head of the household had been idle for more than a year.[10]

These and other studies varied widely in scope, method, and scientific objectivity. (The Polish essay contest obviously only sampled the reactions of relatively intelligent and well-educated people.) But their conclusions were remarkably uniform. The intelligence, nationality, and work experience of unemployed persons had little effect on how they reacted. In brief, when people lost their jobs, they responded first by searching energetically for new ones. If nothing turned up, they gradually became discouraged, perhaps emotionally distraught. But after some months of idleness, they either sank into apathy or adjusted to doing nothing, in either case leading extremely circumscribed existences in apparent calm.

One of the first to describe this pattern was E. Wight Bakke. The behavior of one of his informants, whom he called "A," is worth describing in some detail. A was a truck driver whom Bakke met at a political rally in Greenwich a few days after he was laid off. "There's plenty of jobs for a man with my experience," A told Bakke on that occasion. "I've never been out more than a week or so before. I'll soon be back."

But it did not work out that way. A answered want ads without success. To save money, he moved in with his parents. When Bakke saw him again a few weeks later, he had not given up hope, but he was getting discouraged. And after another five weeks, he told Bakke, "I'm beginning to wonder what is wrong with me." Three more weeks passed, and he said, "Either I'm no good, or there is something wrong with business around here. . . . Even my family is beginning to think I'm not trying." Finally A became despondent, complaining to Bakke of "the hopelessness of every step you take."[11]

After his later work with unemployed people in New Haven, Bakke produced a description of the process couched in typical social science jargon. The unemployed pass through several stages, he wrote. The first is *momentum stability*. The worker expects to be recalled and feels little concern. Perhaps he cuts out a few "luxuries." Next comes *unstable equilibrium* (a most unfortunate expression). This stage is marked by a feverish search for a job. The person cuts out unnecessary expenditures but tries not to skimp on his children's needs. He buys on credit when he can. He blames his being out of work on bad luck.

This stage is followed by *disorganization*. He gives up looking for work and no longer maintains appearances. He withdraws from contact with other people and stops looking ahead or making plans. Then comes *experimental readjustment*. The victim may look for work from time to time but without any sense of urgency. He spends money when he has it, accepts relief and charity when available. He devotes time to hobbies and other relatively aimless, low-keyed activities. The final stage, according to Bakke, is *permanent readjustment*. The person has learned to live with unemployment.

An investigator connected with the Pilgrim Trust study described a subject who had reached this stage as follows:

> He is coming to accept unemployment as something which is natural and inevitable. . . . His life is switched down to a lower economic plane. . . . He ultimately settles down to a new routine.[12]

Lazarsfeld's generalizations, reached after his work in Marienthal, dealt of necessity with how people reacted after long periods of idleness more than with the evolution of their reactions. He focused on the hundred poorest families in the village. He found four types.

Those least affected he called *unbroken*. They continued to seek work, made plans for the future, and had an optimistic outlook. Though poor by any standard, these people had a little more money than the others in the group. Next came those Lazarsfeld called the *resigned* (by far the largest segment, nearly half those studied). They had adjusted to a limited existence, made no plans, had few expectations. (These people would fall into Bakke's "permanent readjustment" category). Another quarter of the group Lazarsfeld called *despairing*. They were gloomy and full of undirected rage and given to frequent bouts of drunkenness. Finally there were the *apathetic*. These were the poorest of the poor. They had given up completely, apparently uninterested even in the present moment.

In a town such as Marienthal, the percentage of the people who were crushed by unemployment may have been higher than in less blighted communities. Lazarsfeld called Marienthal *"die müde*

Gemeinschaft," the tired community. "For hours on end," he wrote, "the men stand around in the street, alone or in small groups, leaning against the wall of a house or the parapet of the bridge. . . . They have forgotten how to hurry."[13]

A mountain of other evidence demonstrates that apathy and despair were widespread among the unemployed. "You see that corner?" a Welsh miner asked an investigator. "My time is spent between here and that corner."

"I was one of a gang," a young Englishman explained. "We used to stay in bed late . . . so as not to need breakfast. . . . Then we would all go down to the library and read the papers. Then we went home for a bit of lunch, and then we met again at a billiard hall where you could watch the play for nothing. . . . In the evening we all used to go to the pictures. That was how we spent the dole money." This man added, showing that he had not completely surrendered to apathy, "In the end I thought I'd go mad if I went on like that."

"Another day!" a jobless Australian wrote in 1931. "The routine continues, in dread and anxiety and tears. . . . To stay at home seems effortless; to walk the streets without definite purpose is futile."

Unemployment, says a character in the English novel *Love on the Dole*, "got you slowly, with the slippered stealth of an unsuspected malignant disease. You fell into the habit of slouching, of putting your hands into your pockets and keeping them there; of glancing at people furtively, ashamed of your secret, until you fancied that everybody eyed you with suspicion." A German novelist made the same point somewhat differently. "If [the unemployed] speak of the future, they mean tomorrow or the next day. They do not think of anything beyond that. And if a year passes, that time becomes yesterday, the next year, tomorrow."[14]

Siegfried Kracauer reported that the men at a German employment office scarcely listened to the announcements of jobs. They were "too numbed to believe in their chance of being chosen." The reports of American social workers who dealt with the unemployed are full of words like depression, indifference, lethargy, submission, and apathy. In Boston, one wrote, people on relief seemed emotionally flat. They expressed neither resentment at their condition nor gratitude for the government benefits they were receiving. As Lillian Wald of the Henry Street settlement house explained, the jobless lost "self-respect . . . ambition and pride."[15]

Of course personal differences, the degree of suffering, and the kind of emotional support available from friends and relatives influenced how people reacted to long-term joblessness. Observers noted that people who had experienced periodic unemployment in the past could handle the inevitable psychological depression better than those for whom unemployment was a new experience. Hard-driving, ambitious types seemed less able than more relaxed people to resist the debilitating effect of being out of work for long periods.

Much discussion occurred during the depression as to whether or not being on relief or accepting charity of any kind encouraged idleness or undermined the recipient's eagerness to work. This was almost certainly not the case for most people. The sociologist Mirra Komarovsky studied 59 unemployed New York City men during the depression; of all, she wrote, work was apparently the sole organizing principle in their lives. Bakke found that about half the unemployed people that he studied in New Haven *never* applied for help, no matter how desperate their situations. The autobiographies of the Polish workers reveal "a deep-seated love of work." Social workers were almost unanimous in arguing that work relief programs were preferable to direct grants of money to the jobless. But the reason was their belief that work sustained people, not that a dole would make them lazy.

In the United States, people were supposed to be individualistic, self-reliant pioneer types. Accepting any kind of aid was thought to be an especially painful experience, what two sociologists called "a severe mental jolt." Dependency was indeed hard for most Americans to take, but all the evidence demonstrates that it was equally hard for the jobless of other industrial nations.[16]

Observers everywhere were amazed by evidence that the jobless, despite the extent and duration of mass unemployment, tended to blame themselves for their inability to find work. "When for the first time I held out my hand for my 9 *zloty* of benefit I was filled with disgust for the whole of my previous existence," one of the Polish autobiographers wrote.

"The way I was brought up" an Australian explained to an interviewer many years later, "it wasn't the right thing to do to accept this sort of thing."

Even in England, where chronic unemployment had plagued certain districts since the mid-1920s, this attitude was common among the jobless. "Many of them were *ashamed* of being unemployed," George Orwell wrote.[17]

How, then, to explain the tendency of observers to claim that many of the unemployed were deadbeats who should be compelled to work for any aid they received? Partly by the fact that some *were* lazy and happy to live off the labor of others. Partly also because some of the unemployed were true unemployables: the physical and mental misfits who exist in any community even in prosperous times. But mostly because many unemployed people suffered from the debilitating effects of long-term joblessness.

Besides studying the unemployed, social scientists paid a great deal of attention to the effects of unemployment on the families of the jobless. Lazarsfeld wrote an important book on this subject with the Harvard sociologist Samuel Stouffer. Many years later the sociologist Glenn Elder, Jr., made use of data collected by two researchers who had followed the development of a group of adolescents in Oakland, California, during and after the depression, in order to investigate the effects of deprivation on all kinds of family relationships.*

The conclusions reached by the many investigators of family life during the depression were much less clearcut than those reached by students of the unemployed themselves, mostly because with more complex human relationships involved, the number of possible

---

* The original investigators had not been particularly concerned about unemployment, but since their data included material on the occupations and home life of the children's parents, Elder was able to use it for this purpose in his book *Children of the Depression: Social Change in Life Experience* (1974).

reactions increased enormously. Members of families that suffered serious financial setbacks substituted their own labor for goods and services previously obtained with money—the changes might range from baking a cake instead of buying one to discharging a servant and doing one's own housework. Boys who found jobs after school tended to become more appreciative of the value of money and be more "adult oriented."

Most patterns mentioned by investigators were as unsurprising as these. Here is another and still more obvious response:

Perception of a substantial disparity between family income and needs frequently led to . . . a general reduction in the level of consumption, a shift in consumption priorities to food, shelter, and safety needs, etc.

It should be noted however, that even in this instance the researcher qualified the generalization with the word "frequently." In some cases, unemployment caused trouble within families. In other instances, it brought family members closer together. Some men enjoyed having more time to be with their children. Others found that being around the children for prolonged periods drove them up the wall. Some men became absorbed in doing chores around the house; some took up new hobbies. Some took to drink. Others sulked.

One of the few general effects of unemployment on family life was its strong tendency to increase the influence of women, both as wives and as mothers. Elder, for example, writes of "mother's centrality as decision maker and emotional resource . . . among deprived households" in the Oakland study.

What form this influence took and its impact on husband-wife and mother-child relationships varied considerably. Some wives were very supportive of their jobless spouses, others scornful. Some found jobs, leaving their husbands to take care of home and children. All kinds of role reversals could occur, with unpredictable results. Much depended on the basic relationships between family members. When these were shaky to begin with, unemployment was likely to make them worse. Lazarsfeld published the following entries from a diary kept by a resident of Marienthal, the first written soon after the man lost his job:

"Going into the forest with Martha [his wife] to collect some wood. The best, the only real friend one has in life is a good wife."

"Martha, that most faithful life companion, has just accomplished a feat worth recommending to all for imitation; she has managed to prepare an evening meal for three adults and four children for only sixty-five groschen."

"I am condemned to silence but Martha is beginning to waver. . . . Icy silence at home, petty things disrupt the harmony. She did not say good night."

"What strangers we are to each other; we are getting visibly harder. Is it my fault that times are bad, do I have to take all the blame in silence?"[18]

Here are a few examples of the kinds of difficulties other investigators reported:

1. Male resentment at loss of dominance, especially if the woman became the breadwinner.
2. Loss of prestige (and the power to control by the dispensing of allowance money) in the eyes of children.
3. Social isolation, caused by lack of money to entertain, by shame, and eventually by apathy.
4. Sexual problems, caused by such things as decline in physical energy, apathy again, and fear of pregnancy.

Worldwide, in 1929 about one-third of all workers were women. Many of these women lost their jobs during the depression. But the statistics suggest (though like other unemployment figures of the period, they are not very reliable) that proportionately fewer women were laid off than men. This was true partly because most women were paid lower wages than men for the same work. Employers tended to keep them on when it was necessary to cut back. Also, the kinds of work that most women did were not as hard hit during the depression as the heavy industry and building trade work that was done by males.

On the other hand, many women workers were domestics, and unemployment among domestics was seldom recorded. Furthermore, the tendency of married women to look for work if their husbands were laid off meant that more of them found jobs. (Today this would raise the female unemployment rate because of the way joblessness is measured, but this was not the case in the 1930s.)

The question of whether they suffered the ravages of unemployment more or less frequently than men aside, the depression had many bad effects upon women. Massive efforts were made to get married women, especially those whose husbands were employed, out of the work force. Even before 1929, many countries had passed laws restricting the employment of married women. In some, women civil servants were expected to retire when they married. If their husbands were also employed by the government, in some countries laws against nepotism required that one or the other be discharged. In nearly every instance, the wife was the one to go.

The depression increased this pressure on women workers. A 1932 American antinepotism law for government workers did not stipulate which spouse must be discharged, but three out of every four who were let go under the law were females. An Austrian law stated specifically that the woman had to retire.

An editorial in a German newspaper, the *Vossische Zeitung*, displayed this attitude in its most extreme form:

Germany has 4 million unemployed. But the number of women workers is growing. . . . Now 6 million of them have full-time jobs. More than 20,000 young male teachers are unemployed but the number of women teachers, even married women teachers, grows ever larger. . . . Germany will perish if the women are working and the men are unemployed.[19]

Restrictions on women workers took extreme forms in Nazi Germany. To the Nazi way of thinking, women were supposed to concentrate their energies on household tasks and child raising. "A job will not bring happiness near. The home alone is your proper sphere" a Nazi slogan ran. Women were barred from certain professions. A quota of only 10 percent was placed on women entering the universities. Marriage loans provided to encourage population growth and stimulate industry were made conditional on the bride giving up work.

All these antifemale policies made little sense. In Germany before the depression, only about 30 percent of women workers were married. Three-quarters of these were helpers in family-run businesses, such as grocery stores and small craft enterprises. Many of the few who held true second jobs worked because their husbands were not earning enough money to support the family. Many of the rest were engaged in professions that men traditionally avoided, such as domestic service and nursing. As a study made by the United States Women's Bureau put it, most women worked "because they have to."[20]

What to do about unemployment was part of the larger question of how to end the economic collapse that had caused so many workers to be laid off. Everyone agreed that ending the depression would solve the unemployment problem or at least bring unemployment down to manageable levels. There was also, however, the more immediate problem of what to do about the unemployed people who needed help merely to survive. Whether efforts to aid the unemployed would help to end the depression or make it worse was a matter of bitter controversy.

The established wisdom of how to deal with the unemployed in bad times was to reduce wage rates enough so that employers could afford to hire more people with the same amount of money. The reasoning went back to the nineteenth-century classical economists, who had insisted that the law of supply and demand made mass unemployment impossible. People had to work or starve. If they chose the latter course, they would no longer be unemployed. On the other hand, if employers failed to pay workers a living wage, the workers would also starve. In either case, the supply of workers would shrink, a shortage would develop, and competition for labor would force employers to raise wages. There was, the classical writers argued, a *wages fund* that was divided among the members of the work force. The existence of substantial numbers of unemployed workers meant that wages were too high—too few people were getting too large a share of the fund.

John Stuart Mill described the process succinctly in *Principles of Political Economy* (1848). In bad times, manufacturers lay off unneeded workers. The labor market becomes "overstocked." Competition for jobs then causes wages to fall, reducing the cost of production and therefore the price of goods. Increased consumption results from the lower prices, and the manufacturers rehire the idle workers in order to supply this new demand. "The rate of wages which results from competition," Mill explained, "distributes the whole existing wages-fund among the whole labouring population."[21]

As time passed, other economists challenged the classical analysis in various ways. The most influential of these by far was Karl Marx. In *Das Kapital* (1871) Marx argued that capitalism *caused* unemployment. When manufacturers expanded output, he reasoned, the demand for labor increased, causing wages to rise. Employers then invested more capital in machinery and discharged some of their workers. The workers thus idled made up "a disposable industrial reserve army."

In ordinary times, the existence of this jobless army acted as as check on wage rates. But far more important according to Marx, its existence was essential if economic growth was to take place. How, for example, could the railroads have been built if large numbers of idle men were not on hand to grade rights-of-way and lay track? Because of the industrial reserve army, capitalists could throw "great masses of men suddenly on the decisive points without injury to the scale of production in other spheres." Capitalist economies grow "by fits and starts." This, said Marx, explains why business cycles exist.[22]

Although most economists rejected Marx's argument that the industrial reserve army was reason enough for doing away with capitalism, the idea that a pool of unemployed workers was necessary for economic growth to occur was soon widely accepted. (The modern idea that economic growth is necessary if we are to have full employment is the Marxian argument put the other way around.) In practice Marx's explanation led most people of that time to tolerate unemployment as a natural phenomenon and to settle for trying to help the jobless to survive, thus helping to preserve the system Marx wanted to abolish.

But the classical position remained the dominant view. The puzzle for members of this school in the thirties was that high unemployment existed and that it persisted for so long. Their explanation of this unprecedented development was presented in crystal-clear form by Lionel Robbins in his book on the depression.

The blame, according to Robbins, was widespread. It rested on the shoulders of employers, labor unions, and governments. By maintaining high prices by means of cartel agreements, producers were further stifling the already reduced demand for goods. By resisting wage cuts, unions were preventing producers from making the profits that would encourage them to expand output and rehire unemployed workers. "A policy which holds wage rates rigid . . . creates unemployment."

Governments were fostering inefficiency by extending aid to industry through such means as tariffs, subsidies, and tax breaks. These policies prevented the bankruptcies that would clear the market of excess stocks and reduce cutthroat competition. "Property must be left to stand on its own legs," Robbins insisted. All three interests—capital, labor, the state—were preventing the free market from functioning as it should. In trying to restore prosperity, they were making the depression worse.[23]

This argument was advanced by many economists in the early 1930s. According to Professor Jacques Rueff of the Sorbonne, mass unemployment could only occur when wages were "higher than the level that would be established spontaneously." Both Karl Pribram of the University of Frankfurt and the Austrian economist Ludwig von Mises echoed this belief. "Persistent mass unemployment is an unavoidable result of the effort to keep wages above the level they would find in a free market," Mises wrote. A Swiss economist characterized the attempts of governments to save failing businesses as a "hopeless effort to bring cadavers back to life."[24]

Whether or not this reasoning was correct, political, social, and humanitarian pressures prevented it from being applied as single-mindedly as these economists recommended. Money wages did go down, for example, though usually not as rapidly as prices. In any case, mass unemployment did not go away. And the longer it lasted, the greater the temptation to experiment with other means of dealing with it.

In broad terms, this meant trying to increase the demand for goods instead of trying to reduce the cost of making them. This could be done by government spending on roads and other public works (which would employ people directly and also encourage the production of tools, machinery, and building materials by private companies), or simply by giving money to the jobless and other poor people. Critics argued that if financed by taxation, such policies would merely transfer money from one group of pockets to another. Borrowing the money would reduce the amount of capital available to private investors. An English financial expert called the idea "charwoman" economics—the belief that people could earn their living by taking in one another's washing.

Those who favored public works responded by arguing that the recipients, being in need, would spend the money promptly, thus stimulating new production. If financed by inflation, the stimulating effect of government spending would be even greater. The British economist John Maynard Keynes stressed the importance of inflation as a way of increasing investment to a point where it was slightly in excess of savings—a little inflation would make people optimistic and (this is his word) "enterprising."

In 1931 a student of Keynes, Richard Kahn, developed the

concept of the *multiplier*—the theory that employing the idle on public works would start a kind of chain reaction: those hired would spend their wages on goods, the producers of which would have to hire other unemployed workers, who would in turn spend their wages on other goods, and so on. The true cost of the public works would be quite small, Kahn claimed, because the government would no longer have to support so many unemployed people and because the new workers would be paying taxes on their earnings. The projects, Kahn added, would not cause inflation when the economy was running far below its productive capacity.[25]

A number of American and German economists agreed at least with the general thrust of the reasoning of Keynes and Kahn. Few important political leaders did so until late in the depression. Nevertheless, public works programs were expanded in some countries, most notably in the United States, in Germany, in Australia, and in Sweden, where government policies were much influenced by a number of economists of this school. Even in financially conservative France, the government subsidized borrowing for public works by municipal authorities.

No government, however, accepted the responsibility of creating jobs for all its unemployed citizens, though eventually, one way or another, most did provide some support for those in need. The last holdouts were France and the United States. It was not until the passage of the Social Security Act in 1935 that the United States created a national unemployment insurance system, and even then the law failed to cover a large percentage of the working population.

Another way to "solve" the unemployment problem was to export the jobless. There was nothing new about this technique; a substantial percentage of the white settlers of the New World were people who at the time were considered surplus in their native lands. In 1922 Great Britain sought to reduce unemployment by subsidizing the migration of "suitable" British subjects to Canada, Australia, and the other dominions. The number assisted was relatively modest—only about 345,000 in nearly a decade. Most of these were domestic servants and agricultural laborers, since the dominions were reluctant to admit industrial workers. The Canadians, for example, opposed "letting industrial workers in unless they have an absolute job to come to." And once the world depression struck, the program had to be abandoned. The "absorptive capacity" of the dominions no longer justified it, a cabinet committee noted in 1930.[26]

The French government, responding to demands that it "get rid of those who . . . come from who knows where to take bread from the mouths of our unemployed," made work permits so difficult for foreigners to renew that half a million Poles, Spaniards, and Italians in France had to return to their native lands.[27] American authorities disposed of thousands of Mexican workers in the southwestern states in a similar manner.

What reduced the number of jobless people in one country only increased it in another; agricultural workers expelled from France caused Spanish unemployment to rise in the mid-thirties. The heartless refusal of many nations to admit Jewish refugees from Germany after Hitler came to power in 1933 was related to unemployment; the fear that the newcomers would either take jobs away from native workers or that they would become public charges overcame humanitarian sentiments.

Still another way of dealing with unemployment was to ship the urban unemployed to rural areas, where presumably they could at least grow their own food. In discussing the problems of agriculture during the depression, I pointed out that many governments encouraged such movement, which reduced the cost of unemployment relief. As early as 1930, Brazil settled 40,000 unemployed urban workers in rural districts. In 1932 a special commission on unemployment in Argentina helped jobless workers in Buenos Aires to return to their native provinces. Beginning in 1935, France offered registered unemployed workers who would agree to move with their families to the country half-fare railroad tickets and a sum equal to several months of relief payments. The French also set up a government agency to place urban adolescents in farm jobs.[28]

Late in the depression, the Canadian government began to pay western farmers five dollars a month to take in unemployed workers for the winter. If a worker stuck it out for the entire winter on one of these bleak farms in the grain belt, the government paid him a bonus as well. Both the central government and most of the provincial governments of the dominion also had programs during the 1930s for settling idle workers and their families permanently on undeveloped land.

The Austrian government developed an interesting program for reducing the cost of supporting the unemployed. Jobless men were set to work building houses in the suburbs of Vienna. The theory was that they would move their families into the houses and raise their own food on the surrounding land. More than 6,700 units were completed before the *Anschluss* with Germany in 1938.

Even in highly industrialized Great Britain, efforts were made to resettle idle city people on the land. In 1930 former Prime Minister David Lloyd George suggested placing 100,000 families on small farms. Nothing came of his grandiose proposal, but the following year Parliament passed a Land Utilisation Act, under which long-term unemployed industrial workers were to be trained to raise pigs, poultry, and garden vegetables.

In the United States, both President Roosevelt and the father of the Agricultural Adjustment Act, M. L. Wilson, favored settling unemployed workers on land on the outskirts of cities. They were to be part-time farmers, holding down jobs in new suburban factories and raising most of their own food in off hours. There was a distinct anticity tone to this concept. In addition to the economic benefits, Wilson claimed, the relocated workers would develop the "psychological and philosophical values which attach to the soil."[29] The practice of allotting small plots on the edge of town to the jobless was a modest variation of this approach. By enabling idle people to engage in productive labor, it provided psychological as well as material benefits.

These programs met varying fates; those that merely tried to help people do what they already wanted to do succeeded fairly well; the more complicated and ambitious ones were mostly failures.

Despite the large sums the British spent training prospective farmers under the Land Utilisation Act, a third of the thousand-odd men in the program dropped out because, a former British minister of agriculture explained, "they, or their wives, did not like the work and life, or were not suitable for it." Nine out of ten of the young people that the French government sent to rural regions returned to the cities after one year.[30]

So much for the general impact of unemployment during the Great Depression. There were, however, certain national differences that merit discussion. In the United States, where unemployment was extremely high, the absence of any national system of unemployment insurance or welfare when the depression began made solving the problem especially difficult. The long American experience of more or less automatic economic expansion made adjusting to depression conditions harder still for many unemployed people.

On the other hand, the American tradition of voluntarism that Herbert Hoover made so much of did mean that there were strong charitable organizations and a community commitment to aiding unfortunates that helped to make up for the lack of government assistance for the jobless. Before the New Deal, city governments and private charitable organizations bore the brunt of the work. Aside from the millions of dollars dispensed in the form of food, clothing, and cash grants by charities, organizations in some cities created jobs for thousands of the unemployed. In 1930 a New York City group employed about 25,000 people, and the next year another committee put 32,000 New Yorkers to work at tasks ranging from planting trees and maintaining public buildings to jobs as librarians and musicians. A similar organizatioin in Philadelphia was equally imaginative, even finding suitable employment for architects, dieticians, artists, and other professionals as well as for laborers and artisans.

The relatively high American standard of living meant that people, individually and collectively, had more to fall back upon when hard times struck. And its basically harmonious society enabled the nation to get through the time of troubles with less social discord than many other countries experienced.

124

The situation in Great Britain was both different and similar to that in the United States. Because unemployment had become serious so much sooner, the country had effective unemployment insurance and a welfare system well before 1929. This meant that during the depression, no drastic break with the past was necessary. The dole in particular was controversial and the cause of a great deal of debate, but no significant effort was made to do away with it.

The employer class in Great Britain was fairly enlightened where social welfare issues were concerned, and organized labor was a powerful political force. Both these conditions helped to minimize social conflict in hard times. Since unemployment was a chronic problem, however, many people had already been beaten down by it. And the geographical concentration of the unemployed in the northern and western parts of Great Britain was a further cause of difficulty.

Germany also had a functioning system of unemployment insurance and a politically powerful labor movement when the depression struck. But there the similarity with Great Britain ended. The German insurance system, being new, lacked the reserves needed to meet the increased demands that resulted from soaring unemployment in the early 1930s. Many important German employers were reactionaries of the most unreconstructed sort. The country was torn by social and political conflicts that made compromise difficult.

As for France, having a less industrialized economy meant that unemployment was lower than elsewhere. When urban workers were laid off, many had relatives in the countryside who could take them in. By expelling no-longer-needed immigrant workers, the French, in effect, put the burden of dealing with the unemployed on the shoulders of other nations.

Still, unemployment was a serious problem for France, in part because the French governments of the period were weak. Frequent changes of ministries made continuity of policy hard to maintain. Furthermore, the conservative character of French economic thought discouraged the bureaucrats who administered policy from trying to do much about the problem. The official position of the

Ministry of Labor was, "The state cannot pretend to eliminate or reduce unemployment, since its intervention does not affect the cause of the trouble." The French government made unemployment relief both difficult to get and demeaning to accept. People on relief had to report to a local relief office twice a week, those in some categories daily, and always at a particular hour. Much government effort went into making sure that "unqualified" persons did not receive any aid. In 1935 some 323,000 francs were extracted from people found to have obtained relief improperly.[31]

These comments apply to the major industrial nations in the early stages of the depression. Conditions in other countries were not significantly different. These conditions often changed after 1933, a key year for industry as it was for agriculture.

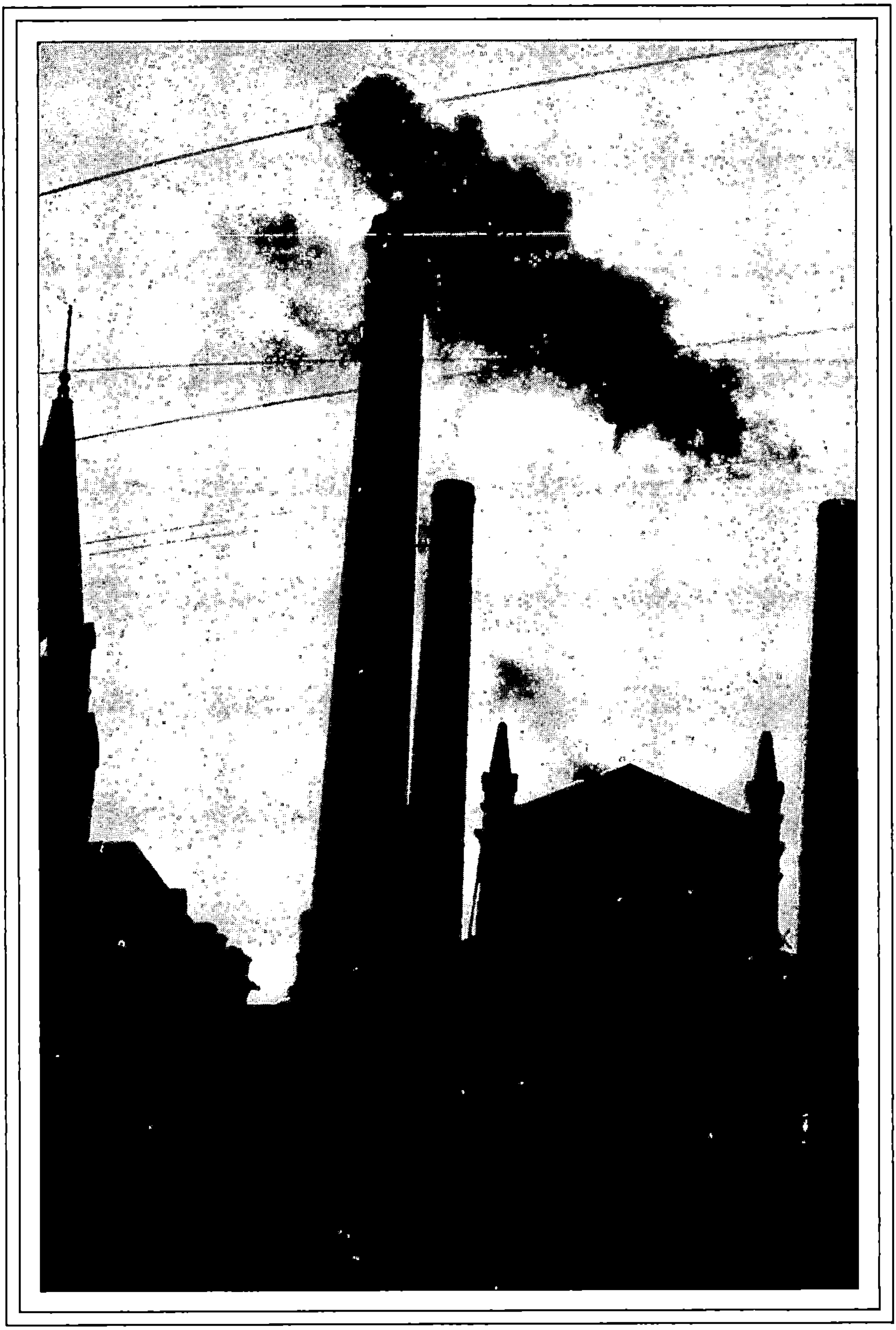

The Bettmann Archive

CHAPTER VI

WHAT TO DO
ABOUT IT

The longer the Great Depression lasted, the more ideas about what could and should be done to end it were put forward by people of all sorts. In 1934 George Soule, editor of the *New Republic*, wrote a book, *The Coming American Revolution*. In it he said, "As an editor of a magazine which dealt with public problems, I can testify that if . . . I had conscientiously analzyed every scheme which came to me I could have done nothing else." The competition of schemes for ending the depression was as intense as the competition for work among the jobless. Soule compared it to the "ferment of religious ideas which accompanied the Puritan revolution in England." After surveying the relatively small part of this vast outpouring written by professional American economists, the economist Joseph Dorfman concluded that the depression had "made 'amateur economists' of most thinking citizens."[1]

The result of all this intellectual effort was more often confusion than enlightenment. No one could possibly understand all the forces that collectively were paralyzing the world economy. The depression was ubiquitous, but conditions varied from country to country and from one field of activity to another. Those who attempted to solve the problems of the day had to generalize from limited information. Professional economists lived in one world, politicians in another, business leaders, social workers, labor union officials in still others. Those who knew most were often so baffled by the complexities and contradictions of what they were studying that they threw up their hands in despair. Those whose minds were less encumbered tended to seize upon those relationships they did understand and attribute to them influences on the economy as a whole far greater than the relationships possessed in fact. Lacking deep understanding and thus true confidence in their beliefs, would-be purveyors of economic salvation often substituted rhetoric for reason and unsupported assertiveness for logical demonstration.

Most of these proposals were, in George Soule's words, "fancy panaceas and economic gadgets."[2] The majority now seem simple-minded. Only some of these, however, seemed simple-minded to informed persons at the time. The fact that the world was in desperate straits encouraged grasping at straws.

Since the language of most economists is not easily accessible to laymen, many of the most widely read analyses of the depression were the work of popularizers whose knowledge of economics was superficial and whose estimation of the public's intellectual capacity and attention span was low. Yet it would be a mistake to dismiss the popular writings of the time, even that part of the literature produced by crackpots and fanatics, as either uninfluential or, from the point of view of history, uninstructive.

Before the 1930s, the most common response of conservatives to depressions was to urge everyone to stand by while the inscrutable forces of the marketplace worked their way to recovery. "The law of supply and demand cannot be violated with impunity," a French civil engineer explained in 1934. According to this line of reasoning, prosperity had led producers to tolerate wasteful business practices and to make overly optimistic estimates of demand that had resulted in their piling up heavy inventories. The economy must be "purged" of all such "maladjustments." In other words, depressions performed vital therapeutic functions. Unemployment, bankruptcies, and general belt-tightening might be unpleasant, but they were essential. A government could serve society best by keeping its own affairs in order, by maintaining a sound currency, and by seeing to it that the laws of honest business practices were fairly enforced. Everything was sure to work out well in the long run.

In the long run. Economists of this persuasion used the phrase repeatedly. They also specialized in shooting holes in the suggestions of less-patient observers. Providing unemployment relief might seem the humane thing to do, but it encouraged laziness and prevented wage reductions that were essential to the revival of production. Public works projects might appear to reduce unemployment, but in reality they absorbed funds that would otherwise be available to private businesses. If financed by borrowing rather than by taxation at a time when governments were already running in the red, government projects would further reduce public confidence. Tariffs, price supports, and other "abusive privileges" granted to special interests by the state drove up the cost of living to consumers and fostered inefficiency. In general, any tampering with specific parts of the economy, no matter how well intentioned, was certain to produce unpredictable side effects and might well do more harm than good. "The world will be cured when it . . . stops interfering with the natural laws of the economy," a French editorialist wrote in 1933.[3]

Those who took this position were pessimists in the short run but optimistic about the future of the economic system. They were conservatives but not reactionaries. Reactionaries, however, existed in large numbers. The devastation caused by the depression was most obvious in industrial districts. There were located the breadlines; the rootless, ragged derelicts; the silent factories that marked the collapse of the economy. To a certain type of person, the depression could best be dealt with by rejecting industrialization and going back to a simpler system, a less complicated but more emotionally rewarding way of life that was said to have existed before the invention of the steam engine and the factory system of production.

This attitude of mind long antedated the depression, but the collapse caused it to spread rapidly. I have already treated its relation to the agricultural depression. No matter that farmers all over the world were burdened with huge stocks of unsold wheat and corn and coffee and tea and rubber and cotton—settling idle city people on farms where they could grow their own food would greatly improve their lot. So the argument ran.

The impracticality of turning factory workers and bookkeepers into farmers did not prevent many intelligent persons from succumbing to the temptations of this idea. Before he was elected President of the United States, Franklin D. Roosevelt dreamed of putting a million families into subsistence farming. Although he liked to think of himself as a gentleman farmer, Roosevelt knew relatively little about agriculture and less about what the life of a subsistence farmer was like. But Henry A. Wallace, who was later to become Roosevelt's secretary of agriculture and who was thoroughly familiar with that way of life, claimed that "self-subsistence homesteads . . . will eventually lead us a long way toward a new and finer world."[4]

How seriously such remarks were meant to be taken is not always easy to determine; they surely indicate, however, that politicians were aware that the idea appealed to thousands of depressed, baffled people who did not seem to realize that running even a small farm required capital and skills that unemployed city dwellers did not possess.

The American novelist Upton Sinclair won the Democratic nomination for governor of California in 1934 on a platform that had as its principal plank a scheme for the state to take over idle land and allow the unemployed to grow their own food on it. Sinclair's program was known as End Poverty in California (EPIC). He also proposed having the state government buy or rent unused factories and put unemployed people back to work making such things as shoes and clothing for their own use. Sinclair favored issuing scrip to facilitate the exchange of goods and services among the idle who had no money.[5]

Sinclair was not an economic sophisticate, but the well-known German economist Emil Lederer, an authority on business cycles, who had written widely on the causes and cures of depressions, had made a similar proposal in 1930. Lederer's interest in such simple self-help ideas was greeted by German critics more with amusement than with serious discussion. But it is an indication of the discouragement that was causing so many people to give up on the existing system and try to return to a simpler world.

In Europe, where the peasant way of life still existed, this reactionary longing to return to a lost golden age, was more fully developed and more earnestly espoused than in the United States. "The return to the earth must lead to the replacement of the pro-letarian working class with a class of peasant artisans," an Italian wrote in 1933. "It will lead to the decentralization of cities, the breaking up of big industries and great estates, the triumph of individual skilled labor in the city and country, among workers and intellectuals."[6]

As a close reading of this passage indicates, there was no nec-essary relation between this attitude and the depression. Denun-ciations of industrial society, and particularly the argument that machine production destroyed the independence and self-respect of workers and indeed of all citizens, were not unusual even in good times. The German economist and social philosopher Werner Som-bart was among the best known and most influential of these critics. Sombart had been a Marxist, but the revolutionary violence and the severe inflation that had vexed so much of postwar Europe caused him to change his mind. He still claimed to be a socialist in the sense of anticapitalist. But he now rejected Marxism because, he said, it accepted modern industrialism as the preferred means of producing goods.

The depression added to his contempt for what he called "*das Maschinensystem*" and the materialistic culture it fostered. In *Deutscher Sozialismus* (1934), Sombart claimed that machines de-stroyed the independence of small craftsmen, blurred individual differences of all kinds, and indeed undermined the dignity of human labor. Mechanization and urbanization were the source of all modern social problems. It was, he insisted, "beyond doubt" that because of mechanization the average human being was less intelligent than the typical person in preindustrial times.[7]

132

This kind of thinking was widespread among conservatives in the twenties, as the already mentioned southern *cri de coeur*, *I'll Take My Stand*, indicates. At about the same time, a group of New York intellectuals denounced what they saw as the "joyless and colorless" character of industrial society, with its "worship of wealth and machinery." The French novelist Georges Duhamel's widely read *Scènes de la vie future* (1930), written after a visit to the United States, is an example of the genre in its most extreme form. The United States was addicted to all the excesses of industrialization, Duhamel wrote. Material values had overwhelmed human ones. American colleges had more buildings than books. Sensitive souls—poets and novelists—were fleeing the country in disgust. American industrial cities were disasters. Duhamel called Chicago a "hell without a Dante" and peppered his description of that city with such words as *cancer, monstrous,* and *fetid.*[8]*

According to Duhamel, industrialization had destroyed American individualism and made the people of the United States slaves to bureaucracy and dupes of mass advertisers. Total materialists, they clamored for such things as phonographs, radios, movies, illustrated magazines, electric refrigerators, and "autos, autos, still more autos." In addition, mechanization meant the sacrifice of quality to quantity—shirts that wore out after two washings, socks too sleazy to be worth darning—and at the same time the loss of variety—only a couple of kinds of apples, for example—whereas in France farmers cultivated "with love" 50 kinds of grapes and, "from that simple food, milk," made more than a hundred kinds of cheese.[10]

Duhamel and people like him who focused their sights on the United States really objected to industrial society per se. The depression only deepened their dislike. Having already rejected the goals of that society—economic growth, the glorification of creature comforts, and the like—they took its failure to achieve these goals as proof of the soundness of their reasoning.

Other critics of the existing industrial system believed it could

* The English novelist Aldous Huxley, who traveled across the United States in the mid-twenties, described Los Angeles as the "City of Dreadful Joy," the "'joy of rushing about, of always being busy, of having no time to think, of being too rich to doubt, . . . of being always in a crowd, never alone."[9]

be reformed. These tended to concentrate their fire on big, "soul-less" corporations. They pointed out that in industries dominated by large corporations, prices tended to fall more slowly than they did in highly competitive fields with lots of small producers. Instead of cutting prices when demand fell off, the giants tried to hold the line on prices. To counter falling demand, they reduced output, laying off large numbers of workers in the process. According to many economists, then and now, this policy prolonged and deepened the collapse.

Some economists believed that the kind of price control exercised by large corporations was inevitable. They concluded that government regulation was the best way to deal with the problem. Others called for breaking up the giants in order to counteract the "unwholesome" lack of buying power that was hampering recovery. Both schools assumed that the problem of industrial concentration could be solved. Not all economists were so optimistic. Some went so far as to change their expectations about the future of industrial society. Suddenly the era of economic expansion that had begun in eighteenth century England seemed to have ended. The industrial system had "matured." New lands and new markets were no longer being opened up. It seemed possible, one American analyst said, that the Industrial Revolution had "come to a natural breathing place," a "plateau in its rate of growth."[11]

In *Das Ende des Kapitalismus* (1931), Ferdinand Fried, a German journalist, presented this argument in considerable detail. Fried described what he called a "rhythm of inventions" that had powered economic growth throughout the "modern capitalistic era." First had come the "cotton era," the birth of the factory system in the eighteenth century. Then in swift succession came the steam engine and the age of iron and steel; then the steamboat and the railroad; then the age of electricity; and finally the age of the gasoline engine. Now the stimulus provided by this last invention had spent itself. A new stimulus was needed, but "no decisive invention had appeared." So, Fried concluded, "the age of inventions, the mechanical and industrial revolution, is over."

For some observers, declining birth rates contributed to and

134

also reflected the economic decline. The English eugenicist Enid Charles predicted in 1934 that unless the trend was reversed, the population of England and Wales, about 45 million at that time, would fall within 200 years to a mere 6 million. The reason, she explained in *The Twilight of Parenthood*, was that "the number of new and profitable markets has become limited." Industrialism, she added, "is a biological failure. . . . Children have now come to be regarded as a form of capital expenditure which brings the parent no return commensurate with its investment value to society."[12]

Charles was uninterested in economics per se. Fried was a publicist, not a scholar. But many professional economists adopted equally pessimistic views. A leading American expert, Alvin Hansen of the University of Minnesota, argued in *Economic Stabilization in an Unbalanced World* (1932) that the world economy was leaving "the great era of growth and expansion" and passing "over a divide." Only the development of new technology could end the stagnation.

Hansen and other stagnationists saw little indication that such a development would be forthcoming. A period of technological advance comparable to that of the nineteenth century was "scarcely to be hoped for," the English economist Joan Robinson wrote in 1937. The next year, Hansen expressed concern about "the possibility of a slowing down in capital-consuming technological innovations." Hansen and Robinson were among the leading economists of their generation; their pessimism is a reflection of the psychological effects that the deep and long-lasting slump had on so many intelligent people who were trying to fathom its causes and devise means of ending it.

People of this persuasion found some virtue in the more constricted world they envisioned. After a visit to Mexico early in the Great Depression, Stuart Chase praised the cautious way that Mexican leaders were seeking to build up industry. "The machine is admitted only on good behavior," he wrote. In this way Mexico might avoid "the mad plunges of the business cycle."[13]

Pessimism about the likelihood of economic growth was responsible for the widespread adoption of price-fixing and output-restricting policies by producers and governments. The early New Deal agricultural and industrial recovery schemes are only the most famous examples of legislation that was based on the belief that since supply had outstripped demand, prosperity could best be restored by reducing supply. There were too many workers in the world, not too few jobs; too much food, not too few people with enough money to be able to afford to eat well. This attitude caused France to restrict the admission of foreigners to the medical and legal professions, Brazil to burn "surplus" coffee, Egypt to limit the acreage farmers could devote to growing cotton. It led many countries to try to get women out of the work force in order to make places for men and to raise the school-leaving age, not to improve the general level of public education but as a device for reducing unemployment.

It was, however, possible to accept the predictions of stagnationists like Hansen and Robinson that further technological advance was unlikely and at the same time believe that a world of plenty, vexed neither by unemployment nor by the need for incessant labor, lay within reach. No new inventions or discoveries were necessary, this argument ran. Society already possessed the means to make everyone rich—all that was lacking was efficient organization.

In a widely read French work, *Le grand relève des hommes par la machine* (1932), Jacques Duboin explained how this could be the case. Duboin's explanation took the form of supposed conversations between one "Dr. Hermondan," a sage, and an industrialist, a merchant, a farmer, an engineer, an architect, and a druggist. One by one these types advanced economic theories, which the wise doctor demolished as easily and as definitively as a champion bowler knocks over tenpins. Hermondan preached the doctrine of abundance. Workers were indeed being replaced by machines because "mechanization makes possible the multiplication of output without any increase in labor." But this kind of unemployment was a boon to humanity, not a curse. The way to correct it was to have everyone work shorter hours and permit workers to retire while still in their fifties.

Turn the marvelous machinery of modern production loose, Hermondan recommended. During their working years, people will have more time each day for such pleasurable pursuits as gardening. Early retirement will enable them to devote their mature years to "study, the arts, science, sport, in brief, everything that makes life worth living." Inefficient distribution, not overproduction, had caused the depression, Hermondan insisted. The present "disorder" must give way to "the new situation made possible by science."

Duboin's book has a naive quality that, along with its glorification of mechanization, reminds one of Edward Bellamy's nineteenth-century novel, *Looking Backward*. It failed to explain how the necessary adjustments in both economic thinking and personal attitudes and values were to be achieved. Although many people read it, economists (and probably most sophisticated readers) did not take it seriously. But the argument that technological unemployment was a liberating rather than an oppressive force in human life was made by far more profound analysts than Duboin, among them Lewis Mumford, whose *Technics and Civilization* (1934) was particularly influential in the United States.[14]

Professional economists admitted that past improvements in industrial efficiency had made it possible to increase output and at the same time make life easier for workers. Further improvements were certainly conceivable. As H.V. Hodson wrote in *Economics of a Changing World* (1933), "Economic progress . . . has enabled us to make things more cheaply and to work less; in the depths of a depression . . . it seems good to us to make things more dearly and to work harder, but doubtless the time will come when we shall be both able and content to be rich."[15]

This attitude explains why Technocracy, another proposal for ending the depression that was based on a similar veneration of technology, attracted wide attention in the United States. Technocracy was the brain child of a group of American engineers who called themselves the Continental Committee on Technocracy. The committee claimed to be making an Energy Survey of North America. With the help of a group of unemployed draughtsmen and engineers who were supported by the Architects' Emergency Relief

Committee of New York, the committee by early 1933 had produced several hundred charts "drawn from the statistics of industrial history." A founder of the group, Professor Walter Rautenstrauch, chairman of the Department of Industrial Engineering at Columbia University, explained that when complete, "some 3,000 charts will have been prepared and every field of human enterprise brought under review."

According to the Technocrats, these charts demonstrated that modern methods of mass production were causing mechanical energy to be substituted for human labor. This was producing mass unemployment. "If present trends continue," Howard Scott, the "consulting technologist" who was director of the survey, announced in January 1933, "we say that unemployment in the United States in eighteen months . . . will exceed 20,000,000."

Scott insisted that the shift from human to machine power made it necessary to get rid of "all the riffraff of social institutions carried over from yesterday's seven thousand static years." Production for use, not for profit, should be the purpose of every economic enterprise. The use of gold or any other commodity to measure the value of goods and services should be ended. Money was obsolete. Instead, everything should be valued according to the units of energy (called ergs or calories or kilowatts or whatever) that were needed to make it. If this was done, Scott claimed, such was the productive power of modern industry that even if the work day was reduced to four hours and the retirement age lowered to 45, so much would be produced that everyone could be given nonnegotiable "energy certificates" sufficient to buy what an annual income of $20,000 would currently purchase.

The depression had occurred, the Technocrats explained, because society had become too complicated for mere politicians to manage. None of our leaders, said Scott, "is equipped with knowledge adequate to cope with the present dilemma." Therefore (these words were Rautenstrauch's) "control should be placed in the hands of engineers and scientists." They would apply "sound scientific judgment to the solution of the industrial problems of our national life."

Neither Rautenstrauch nor Scott nor any other member of the Technocracy inner circle ever explained how this political transformation was to be accomplished. Although they implied that capitalism and democracy were outmoded institutions, they do not appear to have given much thought to how their ideas might be put into practice. "Technocracy proposes no solution," said Scott. "It merely poses the problem." Scott talked of distributing energy certificates on a share-and-share-alike basis, but he did not think like a communist or describe himself as one. Technocracy was apolitical; its leaders had no intention either of seeking political power in the usual way or of attempting to seize it by coup d'état or revolution. Scott dismissed fascism as "a process of consolidating all the minor rackets into one major monopoly" and "an attempt to maintain an unbroken front against oncoming social change."

Technocracy soon proved to be something of a fraud; its promised "rigorous quantitative analysis of social phenomena" never got beyond such sententious generalities as "production as a whole varies with the cube of time" and "man-hours in manufacturing are decreasing inversely with time." Investigators soon discovered that many of the figures the Technocrats had used in describing the increases in production resulting from efficient engineering were grossly exaggerated.

Professor Rautenstrauch began to back away from the movement, alarmed by some of Scott's more extreme statements. After it came out that Scott had made false claims about his professional training and engineering experience, Rautenstrauch and some of the other founders withdrew from the Continental Committee, which was then forced to give up its quarters at Columbia. The Technocracy movement, however, continued to flourish for a year or more, especially in the Far West.

The popularity of Technocracy resulted from the fact that its inventors explained the causes of the depression with impressive, scientific-sounding mumbo jumbo and described their cure for the depression in simplistic terms. Where the stagnationists had bemoaned the lack of further technological advances, the Technocrats claimed that all that was needed was a more efficient organization of existing productive techniques. Like the marvelous system described by Duboin's Dr. Hermondan, the society envisioned by the Technocrats resembled the world of the future pictured by Edward Bellamy in *Looking Backward*. Indeed, the Technocrats consciously drew some of their ideas from Bellamy's work. Technocracy was also another example of the growing disillusionment with laissez-faire, its popularity evidence, as one economist noted, that "people are beginning to believe that human destinies need not be left to the blind working of natural forces."[16]

In other words, the need for planning and the rational organizing and control of economic activity was becoming more apparent. Long before the depression, people concerned with economic questions had demonstrated that more rational, carefully thought out methods of producing and distributing goods could have great material benefits. Some, such as most Marxists, argued that planning would produce moral and spiritual benefits too, because it would make possible a more equitable distribution of the material benefits.

The Marxists, of course, were thinking of planning in broad social terms. Less ambitious devotees of planning concentrated on trying to improve the way goods were made and distributed. Well before the Great Depression began, American manufacturing methods, especially the moving assembly line developed by Henry Ford, and Frederick W. Taylor's scientific management techniques, were being studied closely by manufacturers, labor leaders, economists, and others all over the world. In 1927 the International Labor Organization published *The Scientific Organization of Labor in Europe*, a study financed by the Twentieth Century Fund. The book, written by Paul Devinat, summarized developments in 14 countries. Devinat concluded that despite widespread resistance to "American methods of work" and to the standardized products they created, the scientific management movement was strong and growing in Europe. "No one can challenge its key influence," he insisted.[17]

Both radicals and conservatives were affected. Even before the Russian Revolution, Lenin had become thoroughly familiar with scientific management concepts. The idea of time-motion studies

140

especially intrigued him. The technique seemed a way both to increase production and to simplify manufacturing procedures so that peasants without industrial experience could be used effectively in factories. "We must organize in Russia the study and teaching of the Taylor system and systematically try it out and adapt it to our purposes," he said in 1918. Lenin also brought American engineers familiar with Taylorism to Russia as consultants. After his death, Josef Stalin continued this practice, with the result that the Taylor system had a large influence on the shaping of the first Soviet Five-Year Plan.

In the 1920s, German socialists saw in scientific management a possible way to increase production and thus to raise the living standards of workers. German industrialists and other conservatives also found scientific management and what they called *Fordismus* attractive because these techniques promised both greater efficiency and profit and more effective control of labor. A small scientific management movement also sprang up in France in the 1920s. But the resistance of both workers and most business leaders prevented it from making much headway. In Great Britain, where piecework was common and where strong unions and government support for "industrial democracy" limited the ability of employers to control how workers did their jobs, a somewhat different "human relations school" of management developed. Especially after the general strike in 1926, its advocates sought labor peace by putting less pressure on labor rather than more. A British automobile executive said in 1934, "The daily task system at fixed wages may perhaps be workable in America, or even [in] Continental factories, but the necessary . . . driving works policy, would not be acceptable either to English Labour or Management."[18]

The economic collapse of the 1930s reduced the influence and prestige of all industrialists, but the idea that the depression could be ended and prosperity restored by careful planning and efficient management of available resources had increased appeal. To many contemporaries, planning called for socialism of some kind; what institution but government had the power and public backing needed to regulate anything as complex as a nation's economy? "Why do

141

we need a plan?" the English socialist G. D. H. Cole asked in 1935. "Because, as matters stand, our physical power to produce goods has outrun our ability to provide for their consumption, and the result is seen in widespread unemployment, suffering, and bodily and mental deterioration. . . . Because reliance on a system whose defenders pride themselves on doing without a plan has brought us into this impasse. . . ."[19]

Socialists like Cole had been advocating government planning since long before the depression, and he at least recognized that it was "unlikely" that any of the democracies were about to "institute a planned economy in any real or thoroughgoing sense."[20] But more and more people were coming to think that because economic relationships were growing more complicated, Adam Smith's invisible hand was no longer guiding the economy efficiently. Since the automatic correction of the current decline predicted by business cycle theorists had not materialized, would not deliberate "artificial" adjustments be worth trying?

Because planning implies complex intellectual activity, many academics and other professionals found it appealing. In 1930 the historian Charles A. Beard edited a collection of essays by scientists and engineers on the subject, in the conclusion of which he stated, "Throughout the whole world of economic operations runs the imperative necessity of planning, of rationality in the engineering sense." "Planning," Beard wrote on another occasion, "is a hazardous industry, but it must be faced."[21]

"We must have social planning," the veteran economist Richard T. Ely, a critic of laissez-faire ideas since the 1880s, when he had been one of the founders of the American Economic Association, wrote in 1931. "We must pull together with all our resources to find the way, or the various ways out." Ely suggested that the Army General Staff should draw up plans "so elaborate . . . that overnight the peace-time army could be expanded indefinitely and take into its ranks those who had lost their employment." The recruits could perform useful tasks such as reforestation and "roadside improvements." When good times returned, the expanded army could function as a kind of employment agency. Suppose U.S. Steel

142

needed an additional 2,000 workers. Under Ely's scheme, the army "would immediately dispatch to the proper place men with the requisite qualifications."[22]

The Soviet Union's Five-Year Plan attracted much favorable attention in the western industrial nations. The plan was in full swing when the depression began. Apparently as a result, Russia had escaped the massive unemployment that capitalist countries were enduring. At a time when factories in the West stood idle and the public mood was glum, Russia seemed a beehive of activity, its people vigorous and hopeful. The English scientist Julian Huxley wrote in 1932 after a visit to the Soviet Union, "[Russia] is progressing upward, and shows little of the unemployment and none of the so-called overproduction that elsewhere have descended like a blight upon all capitalist countries."

"For the first time, a great people has embarked upon a consciously organized effort to plan its entire economic life," the American political scientist Frederick Schuman, an unfailing admirer of the Russian system, wrote in 1930. The English clergyman Hewlett Johnson (called by critics the "Red Dean") compared "this tottering capitalist world of storm and stress, where ancient pillars of society collapse" with the Soviet Union, where "the economic and social life of the country is planned in the public interest."[23]

Of course the Russians made much of their plan and of the supposed advantages of their system. "In capitalist production there is a general anarchy," said V.I. Molotov in 1932. "In the Soviet Union, on the other hand, there is a general plan." The Russians employed thousands of technicians and workers from the United States and other industrial nations during the early thirties in connection with the Five-Year Plan, and more thousands of western businessmen and plain tourists visited the country. There were so many Americans there, Louis Fischer, a correspondent resident in Moscow in the 1930s, recalled in his autobiography, that "often it seemed as though everybody I ever saw or heard of in America turned up in Moscow."

Soviet officials spared no expense in their efforts to impress these people. Ordinary technicians were provided with first-class accommodations, free tickets to the opera, and treated in general like high-level diplomats. For one group of touring American businessmen, Intourist supplied a special deluxe train dating from the days of the Czar and stocked it with unlimited supplies of vodka and caviar.

Such treatment, and far more important, the all-out effort that the Russians were making to expand industrial output at a time when western economies were stagnant, had a powerful impact on large numbers of these visitors. A group of British politicians who visited Russia in 1931 and who recognized the limitations of the Soviet system, were nonetheless impressed by "huge factories being built, vast machines being installed, rivers being dammed" and other signs of economic growth. So was the American journalist William Allen White, who traveled there in 1933. "Russia," he wrote his friend Secretary of the Interior Harold L. Ickes, "is the most interesting place on the planet. Their experiment is colossal."[24]

Many westerners who commented favorably on the Five-Year plan were communists, or at least enthusiastic supporters of the Soviet regime. But even critics of that regime could be impressed by the planning effort. "The Russians have drafted a Five-Year Plan," a German legislator said in 1931. "It is doubtful whether it can be carried out. But I will say this for it—those people are working with fanatical enthusiasm. . . . They are leading a dog's life, but they keep hoping that some day things will be better. I wish the German people too could be inspired with . . . such faith." A British reporter made the same point after a visit to Berlin in 1932. "I saw there poverty more terrible than anything I saw during weeks spent with the workers and peasants of Soviet Russia. For the Russians at least have hope."

In *The Red Trade Menace* (1931), another journalist, H. R. Knickerbocker, dismissed the Soviet economic system as state capitalism rather than communism. He considered the system an effort by Russia "to starve itself great" by a combination of "zeal and terror." The objectives of the plan were, he wrote, pretentious. But he admitted that it might enable the country to double its economic output in five years. The French writer André Gide, though shocked by the repression of individual rights that he observed in Russia, was nonetheless impressed by the dynamism and spirit of the people.[25]

The publicity given to the Russian experiment increased the attention given to planning both by enthusiasts and those who opposed the idea. In 1931 the critic Edmund Wilson called upon his fellow Americans to "take Communism away from the communists," while the conservative *Saturday Evening Post* urged in an editorial that the United States develop "a real five-year plan." In 1931 President Hoover, who opposed government planning, told a midwestern audience that "the 'plan' idea is an infection from the slogan of 'five-year plan' through which Russia is struggling."

On the other hand, Charles A. Beard insisted that there was "nothing Russian" about planning. Indeed, he added, planning "was anathema to the Bolsheviks until, facing the task of feeding enraged multitudes, they laid aside Marx, took up Frederick Winslow Taylor, and borrowed foreign technology to save their political skins."[26]

In any case, no nation tried to imitate the Russian example. Even when socialist political parties controlled the governments of capitalist countries, as they did in the first stages of the depression in Great Britain under Ramsay MacDonald, in Germany under Hermann Müller, and in Australia under James H. Scullin, and in France under Léon Blum in the mid-thirties, they made no effort to nationalize the means of production or control all economic activity. Throughout the period, most socialist politicians favored compromising with capitalism; or better, they believed that compromise was the only practical way to achieve reform and break the back of the depression.

One of these socialists was Henri de Man, a Belgian long prominent in his country's labor movement. In 1934 de Man announced his *Plan du Travail*, for creating a "mixed economy" that would combine structural changes with measures to fight the depression— "the objectives of Lenin with those of Roosevelt."

De Man's plan was long on organization but short on explanations of how the organization would function. The financial system and certain key industries such as public utilities and others that were dominated by big combinations and cartels should be nationalized. But artisans, shopkeepers, and small manufacturers should continue to function under the free enterprise system. Each nationalized sector would be managed by a government commissariat or consortium in accordance with the general principles of the plan. But these enterprises would not actually be owned by the state. "The essence of nationalization," said de Man, "is less the transfer of ownership than the transfer of authority."

These principles, while unexceptionable, were terribly vague. The policy of the Commissariat of Credit, for example, should be to "favor especially the branches of the economy the development of which will lead to the success of the plan." A central object of the system was "the enlargement of the domestic market," but commercial policy, "far from tending towards autarchy," should foster "the development of foreign commerce."

The appeal of the *Plan du Travail* rested largely on de Man's impressive credentials as a socialist combined with his gradualist approach. He insisted that the working class and the middle class must work together. The plan would only succeed when put into effect in individual countries and by peaceful democratic procedures. Nationalization of industries involved control of policy, not the seizure of property. The object was to benefit everyone, not a single class.

De Man went on to become minister of public works and then finance minister in the Belgian government. His plan, however, was not put into effect. His ideas did receive a great deal of attention in the French labor federation, which set up a special bureau of economic studies to develop proposals of a similar type. But nothing came of these either.[27]

The idea of planning attracted conservative thinkers as well as those on the left. Large corporations, by their nature, could not operate efficiently without central planning of some kind. Trade associations, cartels, and other business organizations that sought to plan and control production and prices and allocate markets had existed long before the 1930s. Executives who had seen what could be done by rationalizing the way factories were run found the idea of general economic planning entirely logical, especially when separated from the idea of government ownership of the means of production. At a time of shrinking markets and falling prices, the need to prevent disastrous competition by this type of voluntary cooperation seemed particularly urgent. The depression put so much pressure on cartels and other organizations of this sort, however, that members began to violate their agreements in a desperate search for business. This led corporate executives to think that some kind of government supervision of cartels and trade associations was necessary to enforce discipline.

At the same time, the failure of the capitalist system to break out of the depression caused some of these businessmen to worry lest their workers be radicalized. This concern encouraged them to consider bringing labor into a kind of loose coalition too. A combination of existing institutions—employers' trade associations, labor unions, and the government—might stifle radical tendencies by demonstrating the harmonious nature of the existing social and economic system. Such an arrangement would also stimulate recovery by insuring that production and pricing would be controlled in an orderly and fair-minded manner. "It is necessary to establish a compulsory organization uniting owners, managers, and workers and controlled by the state," the president of the French wool manufacturers association wrote in 1932.[28]

This concept, called corporatism, had emerged in the nineteenth century—indeed, it can be traced back to the guilds of the Middle Ages. The root of the word, *corpus*, or body, encapsulates the idea. As with the human body, the production of goods could be visualized as a harmonious relationship of many parts functioning together in a single organism.

In the 1930s, some saw in corporatism an antidote both to Marxist class conflict and rampant, competitive, capitalist individualism. The historian Richard Kuisel provides an excellent summary of the relationship of corporatist thinking to the idea of planning during the Great Depression.

Corporate theorists . . . looked to reconstituting the natural cells of the social organism as a way of overcoming

147

the anarchy of individualism whereas planners sought to manage the economy. To the extent that rebuilding a hierarchy of intermediate associations, such as professional or regional bodies, to stand between the individual and the state brought collective discipline, corporatism abetted economic management. Some planners accordingly introduced corporatist bodies to their designs. Yet at heart corporatists regarded balancing production and consumption and similar economic problems as secondary. . . . Their agent was the mixed professional association that grouped together those engaged in a common economic activity.[29]

Mussolini's success in establishing a corporate state in Italy in the 1920s added to the popularity of the approach. For a time in the early 1930s, Il Duce, projecting an image of purposefulness and determination, seemed the only important western leader who was attacking the problems of the depression forcefully. The socialist G. D. H. Cole, while dismissing corporatism as impractical and fascism as "nationalistic megalomania," described Mussolini as "much cleverer" than Hitler and "far more determined than the Nazis to make capitalists and other property-owners into feudatories of the State."* An American observer defined Italian corporatism as "industrial self-government under Federal supervision."[30]

However, the corporatist movement was not necessarily fascist. Most of the business leaders who found the idea attractive envisioned it as a way of using government authority without creating a totalitarian state in the Italian mold. They saw state participation as good public relations. In addition, the government could serve as a mediator of labor disputes and as a kind of benevolent uncle entrepreneurs could turn to for guidance and material assistance in hard times. They had no taste for totalitarian powers that could dictate to industry in the name of the entire nation. Each industry should be managed by a council representing "all persons

* Cole added that Mussolini had "graduated in the school of Socialism" and suggested that he "might well pursue in the end a sort of bastard 'Socialism' without class equality."

practicing the same métier," a French corporatist writer argued. The government should have the last word, but capital and labor should cooperate in day-to-day management. "Authority at the head of the state . . . but *liberty below*."[31]

The best-known American proposal of this type was the one advanced by Gerard Swope, the president of General Electric. "Production and consumption should be coordinated . . . preferably by the joint participation and joint administration of management and employees," Swope explained in a speech before the National Electrical Manufacturers Association in September 1931. In each industry, all companies that employed 50 or more workers should be grouped in a trade association supervised by the Federal Trade Commission. The associations should regulate output, fix prices, and otherwise organize the activities of the member companies.

The Swope Plan included life insurance, pensions, and unemployment insurance for workers, paid for in part by employers. It appeared somewhat radical coming from the head of a major corporation, yet it attracted the enthusiastic support of the Chamber of Commerce and other conservative Americans.

Charles A. Beard advanced a planning scheme that closely resembled Swope's. He wanted Congress to repeal the antitrust laws and create a National Economic Council representing "all the great industries" along with "organizations in agriculture, wholesaling, and retailing" and spokesmen for labor, "organized and unorganized." A Board of Strategy and Planning modeled after the War Industries Board of 1918 and headed by "a production engineer" would administer the plan. Each industry would be formed into a kind of holding company to plan and carry out production and distribution. "Everything hangs on management," Beard insisted. "Cave-man methods on the part of capital and labor in a technological civilization indicate a lack of common-sense."

Corporatism appealed to many businessmen because it seemed a middle way between socialism and monopoly capitalism, a system that would resolve or at least paper over conflicts and provide rational, orderly leadership without undermining freedom of choice and the incentives supplied by the profit motive. In Swope's scheme,

149

"the federal supervisory body" would not regulate or manage the trade associations. Rather it would "act as a referee or umpire" in order to "protect the public interest."[32]

But nearly all advocates of planning in the 1930s were displaying in some sense their disillusionment with capitalism. Competition no longer seemed to work; the system was breaking down. Planners differed only as to whether the system should be repaired, or simply scrapped.

Another possible way of dealing with the depression was to try to encourage consumption by some kind of inflation. Since people did not have enough money to buy all the goods that were glutting markets everywhere, why not find some way to put more money in their pockets? Then they would buy the unsold goods. That would mean profits for producers and middlemen, which, in turn, would lead to the resumption of stalled production and the hiring of laid-off workers.

The difficulty was that most people thought inflation dangerous, psychologically corrupting, and immoral. Just about every country had historical memories of runaway inflation, times when for one reason or another, the printing press had been substituted for more conservative means of raising money. The American expression, "not worth a continental," was a reference to the deterioration of the value of the continental dollar during and after the Revolution, a decline that was not corrected until the drafting and ratification of the Constitution gave the central government the means of raising money in more conventional ways. The sad tales of what happened to Confederate money and (to a lesser degree) to northern greenbacks during the Civil War were more recent American examples of the danger of inflationary excess. The French had the case of the *assignats* during their revolution.

More graphic because so recent and so widespread was the inflation that had followed the Great War. As everyone knows, the most extreme inflation occurred in Germany, where by 1923 a newspaper cost 200 billion marks. But except for Great Britain, Switzerland, Holland, and the Scandinavian countries, every European nation suffered drastic inflation in the early 1920s. The Austrian crown fell from a prewar five to the dollar to 83,600 in 1922. The Polish zloty plunged to one 2.5 millionth of its prewar value, the Russian ruble to one 4 millionth. Portuguese money fell to about 5 percent of its prewar value, Belgian to a little more than a quarter. The French franc was stabilized in 1926 at a bit less than one-fifth of its gold value in 1914.

Even in the countries that did not experience inflation of these dimensions, including the United States, prices rose steeply before settling at a level that was between 40 and 60 percent higher than what it had been before the war. The result was to make governments extremely wary about future inflation. After the stabilizing of the franc in 1926, Richard Kuisel reports in his study of French economic planning, "the French were to be extremely protective about any further loss in the value of their currency. Maintaining the *franc Poincaré* assumed immense political and psychological importance."[33]

Inflation seemed to the financially unsophisticated masses morally wrong. If paper money was supposed to "represent" something specific, such as gold, or to be "worth" something or other, such as a person's labor, creating it arbitrarily in order to stimulate economic activity appeared to be some kind of fraud against those who already had money, because the purchasing power of that "old" or "real" money was likely to go down as a result. Furthermore, such people reasoned, giving money directly or indirectly to anyone would undermine the recipient's character. The almost universal fixation on the necessity of balancing national budgets in hard times was a further reflection of this deeply felt attitude.

None of these reasons prevented advocates of various schemes for getting money into the hands of those who needed it from advancing inflationary proposals. As Joseph Dorfman put it in his survey of American economic thought, during the depression "monetary heresies of earlier days—long considered dead—were revived in old and new forms."

One of the most strident inflationists was the American "radio priest," Charles E. Coughlin. The Great Depression enabled Father

Coughlin to turn what had been a religious program on one Detroit station into a nationwide political crusade. Coughlin was vehemently anticommunist, which was hardly controversial, but in 1932 he began to attack President Hoover, calling him "the bankers' friend, the Holy Ghost of the rich, the protective angel of Wall Street." He urged listeners to vote for Franklin D. Roosevelt in the 1932 presidential election.

Coughlin approved of most of the early New Deal, which he called "Christ's Deal." He especially liked Roosevelt's money policies, such as raising the price of gold. As the depression dragged on, he gradually focused his attention on inflation as the way to end it. He suggested remonetizing silver and creating a government bank with the power to issue unbacked paper money. Along with these proposals went a constant barrage of invective aimed at New York City congressmen, Wall Street lawyers, bankers with "grouse hunting estates in Scotland," and "the erudition of Harvard, of Yale, of Princeton, of Columbia."

In 1934 Coughlin founded the National Union for Social Justice. Within two weeks, 200,000 people joined, and eventually the organization had over a million members. Soon Coughlin began to criticize Roosevelt because New Deal monetary policy was not as inflationary as he desired. When Roosevelt refused to back an inflationary farm refinancing bill, the priest was furious. Early in 1936, he called the New Deal "a government of the bankers, by the bankers, and for the bankers."

Coughlin was a blatant demagogue as well as an inflationist. He was incapable of developing a plausible program for combating the depression. Although his followers found his denunciations of bankers emotionally satisfying, his popularity depended mostly on his ability to convince listeners that they were being mistreated by forces too powerful and too distant to be effectively controlled. Practical measures were not his forte. His villains were personifications of historical forces—urbanization, industrialization, modern science—and he had not the slightest idea what to do about them.[34]

Inflation was a constant temptation to more thoughtful and disinterested persons who were struggling to find ways to stimulate the economy. Coughlin and others like him were in the tradition of American Populism, and ideas that the Populists had found attractive in the 1890s again came to life. Coining silver, which was plentiful and relatively cheap, as a way of increasing the amount of money in circulation in gold standard countries received considerable attention. Surely, many respected economists argued, it was possible to increase the amount of money in circulation without flooding the economy with an ocean of paper. "The one question that ought to occupy us today is, how can we get out of this deflation," wrote Professor Wilhelm Röpke of the University of Marburg in 1932. "Does anyone really believe that there is no middle way between the icy hell [Eishölle] of deflation and the burning heat [Gluthitze] of inflation?"

The answer to Röpke's rhetorical question was, "Not many, and especially not in Germany." In March 1932, the banker Hans Luther was making a speech in Berlin. He attacked a proposal to put 600,000 jobless men to work on public projects. "I do not even know how long they are to be kept busy," he said. "A year," someone in the audience cried out. "All right, let's say a year," said Luther, "and when the year is up what next?" "Again from the beginning," came the response. "And after that from the beginning again!" Luther retorted. "Then we are right in the middle of rampant inflation."[35]

One way to stimulate consumption without creating additional paper money would be to increase the velocity of money by compelling people to spend it. The Revolving Old Age Pension Plan concocted by Dr. Francis E. Townsend was such a scheme. Townsend proposed giving every American citizen over the age of sixty $200 a month, with the proviso that the recipients must spend the money within the month. The scheme was not inflationary in that it was to be financed by a transactions tax. Compelling pensioners to spend the money within a month, however, was designed to increase the turnover of money enormously and thus to stimulate production. The plan was totally impractical; Townsend knew nothing of economics and apparently not much more about arithmetic—the cost of the pensions, perhaps $24 billion a year, would have absorbed about half the entire national income. He decided upon the sum of $200 a month, he said, because "with our figure so high we could feel reasonably sure that no one would bring out a plan with a higher amount." The impracticality of the idea did not, of course, prevent tens of thousands of people from joining Townsend clubs.[36]

A few techniques for forcing people to spend money found advocates among competent economists. One such idea was stamped money. A government would give everyone a specified amount of special money, but to spend the money the owner must attach a dated stamp that would cost, say, 1 percent of the value of the bill. If at any time such a bill was not spent within a month of the latest stamp, it would become worthless. In 100 months, advocates of the idea claimed, the government would get back all of the original gift, which would have been no more than an interest-free loan. John Maynard Keynes thought stamped money "sound" in principle, though presenting "many difficulties" in practice, and no less an establishment economist than Irving Fisher of Yale proposed a modified form of a stamp plan. Fisher suggested giving the money only to unemployed people. This would combine relief for the jobless with a shot in the arm for the economy.[37]

In practice unemployed people rarely needed the incentive of stamps to spend whatever money they could lay their hands on. Their needs were too urgent and their resources too slim to afford them the luxury of squirreling away anything. But getting people to spend money when times were hard and prices falling was one of the main problems of the day. Businessmen were engaged in "a spenders' strike," J. R. Bellerby, an English economist, said in 1932. They were lowering wages, not paying dividends to stockholders in order to build up reserves, and reducing inventories to the bone. Bellerby suggested that the only thing that would induce them to expand their activities would be a negative interest rate produced by "State-guaranteed inflation." If a merchant borrowed money at 5 percent interest to buy goods that increased 15 percent in price over the life of the loan, the actual cost of the loan would not be 5 percent but −10 percent.

To produce the inflation, the government ought to give money

154

outright to people who could be counted upon to spend it, Bellerby said. Poor people would be logical recipients because they had so many needs. So, he added, only half humorously, would spendthrifts. "This is the awful paradox that confronts the world: that in order to save the strong and virtuous it must subsidize the thriftless and the half-starved."[38]

More persuasive advocates of fighting the depression by "inflationary" means did not suggest directly printing and distributing money, stamped or otherwise. They proposed stimulating economic activity by making it easy to borrow—that is, by lowering interest rates. As Bellerby's extreme example made clear, if producers could borrow money cheaply, they could afford to expand. This idea had been advanced before the Great War by the British economist Ralph G. Hawtrey and in the immediate postwar years by (among others) the American business cycle theorist Wesley Clair Mitchell, Knut Wicksell and other Swedish economists, L. Albert Hahn of the University of Frankfurt, and a number of British economists, including, besides Hawtrey, Keynes. The postwar inflations, however, frightened most people away from this approach. Yet as early as 1925, a connection between rising prices and falling unemployment was being noticed by statisticians, and the high unemployment of the 1930s made the idea of pushing up prices increasingly tempting.[39]

By far the most original of the "inflationists" was Keynes. Keynes did not believe that inflation was a good thing in itself. In *The Economic Consequences of the Peace* he wrote that inflation undermined "confidence in the existing distribution of wealth," and he quoted Lenin as saying that the best way to overturn capitalism would be to "debauch" the currency. In 1920, when prices were soaring, he had tried to persuade the British Chancellor of the Exchequer, Austen Chamberlain, to raise interest rates steeply—the way he put it was "to go to whatever rate is necessary" to make borrowing prohibitively expensive and thus change businessmen's expectations and cool off the economy. "We must make it a prime object," Keynes wrote in 1923, "that the standard of value . . . should be kept stable." But he felt strongly that in times of severe deflation, measures should be taken to turn prices in the other direction. In May 1932, the Melbourne *Herald* asked him to comment on a proposal to reduce the real wages of Australian workers by 10 percent in order to enable manufacturers to lower the price of goods. He took a dim view of the scheme. Adjusting to already much-deflated prices, he said, "is one of the things, like the end of the world, against which, although possible, it is not sensible to insure."[40]

Keynes argued that over time, prices tend to rise, thus reducing the value of money. "In every country which has a history, back to the earliest dawn of economic record," he wrote, there has been "a progressive deterioration in the real value of the successive legal tenders which have represented money." He did not deny that inflation injured creditors and people with fixed incomes, such as bondholders and pensioners. He insisted, however, that inflation benefited "the active and constructive elements" in society. "The tendency of money to depreciate has been in past times a weighty counterpoise against the cumulative results of compound interest and the inheritance of fortunes. . . . By this means, each generation can disinherit in part its predecessors' heirs." By way of contrast, deflation caused economic stagnation and unemployment. Deflation was therefore worse than all but the most uncontrolled inflation, "because it is worse, in an impoverished world, to provoke unemployment than to disappoint the rentier."

In the 1920s, Keynes disapproved of Great Britain's returning to the gold standard at the prewar rate because, by overvaluing the pound, it caused prices to fall and unemployment to rise. During the early 1930s, as the British economy slumped deeper into depression, he shocked conservatives by the casual way he urged people to spend money rather than to save it. "Whenever you save five shillings, you put a man out of work for a day," he said in 1931. "On the other hand, whenever you buy goods you increase employment."

Therefore, oh patriotic housewives, sally out to-morrow early into the streets and go to the wonderful sales which are everywhere advertised. You will do yourselves good— for never were things so cheap, cheap beyond your dreams.

Lay in a stock of household linen, of sheets and blankets
to satisfy your needs. And have the added joy that you
are increasing employment. . . .[41]

That Keynes expected this reasoning to change the behavior
of "patriotic housewives" or other potential consumers is doubtful
at best. In any case, they did not follow his advice, and by the end
of 1932, as the depression sounded the depths, he was taking a
different, more subtle approach. Cheap money would not cause
producers to borrow in order to expand output if they were so
demoralized by the long depression that they did not think they
could sell the goods at any reasonable price. Governments, therefore, should undertake extensive public works financed by borrowing. After government-created demand had caused the economy to
begin to recover, a policy of low interest rates could be counted
upon to sustain the trend.

By 1932 Keynes was hard at work on his *General Theory of
Employment, Interest, and Money*, a book that changed the way
economists thought about depressions and booms and led government officials to abandon their conviction that budgets must always
balance and adopt inflationary techniques enthusiastically. But that
book was not published until 1936. It had almost no impact on
policymakers until very late in the Great Depression; therefore its
role in ending the depression was minuscule. In any case, Keynes's
originality lay in his explanation of how a depression could last so
long, not in his ideas about what should be done to end the particular
depression of the thirties.

Keynes's practical proposals, including countercyclical deficit
spending, were by no means original. They had been used in the
past and were being employed independently in a number of countries in the early 1930s, sometimes because government leaders
had been persuaded by the arguments of economists, sometimes
for purely political reasons, sometimes almost inadvertently. The
Swedish finance minister Ernst Wigforss, who had a solid knowledge of contemporary economics, had read and appreciated many
of Keynes's essays and articles. In 1933, with the backing of Swed-

ish economists of the Wicksell school, he persuaded the legislature to pass a bill putting into effect a countercyclical policy based on the idea that budgets should be balanced over entire business cycles, not each year. But while Wigforss may properly be considered a Keynesian, the leading Swedish economists—an unusually talented group—did not really understand the General Theory in 1936. According to one of them, Gunnar Myrdal, the Swedish economists considered Keynes's works "brilliant and important" but based on already familiar ideas and certainly not "a revolutionary break-through."[42]

In the United States on the other hand, while the Roosevelt administration spent heavily on public works and unbalanced the budget in order to do so, Keynes had little impact, although he was something of a celebrity, and his work was well known to economists. His lack of influence was certainly not due to any lack of trying. During the early 1930s, his frequent comments on economic conditions were reported in American newspapers, and he wrote a number of articles for American magazines. While on a trip to the United States in 1931, he made several speeches before important audiences, including a widely noticed lecture on unemployment at the University of Chicago, and he discussed the world situation with a number of business and political leaders, including President Hoover. In June 1933, he engaged in a radio discussion of the then-upcoming London Economic Conference with the American political commentator Walter Lippmann on a telephone hookup that was said to be the first broadcast of a transatlantic conversation in history.

That December Keynes published an open letter to President Roosevelt in the *New York Times*. In it he criticized New Deal efforts to raise prices by limiting production, including the New Deal centerpieces, the Agricultural Adjustment Act and the National Industrial Recovery Act. He urged the president to fight the depression by increasing government spending rather than by expanding the money supply. The latter approach, he remarked wryly, was like trying to get fat by buying a larger belt. The following year, while in the United States to accept an honorary degree from Columbia University, Keynes had an interview with Roosevelt.

(Afterward the president reported that he liked Keynes "immensely," but apparently he was not much impressed by Keynes's ideas about fighting the depression.)[43]

All these activities enhanced Keynes's prestige in the United States but not his influence. Although from early in the depression, many important American economists had been advocating expansionary programs, they did not base their recommendations on Keynesian logic. Jacob Viner and other economists at the University of Chicago "had reached Keynes's policy conclusions through common-sense observation while continuing to hold to traditional theory." One modern partisan of this group goes so far as to surmise that economists like Viner and his colleague Frank Knight, considered Keynes's policy recommendations "old hat."[44]*

Other nations adopted at least moderately stimulatory policies as the depression dragged on. The Japanese, already at war, broke away from budget balancing in 1931, when Korekiyo Takahashi became minister of finance. The yen was devalued, and interest rates were reduced. Government spending rose, financed by heavy borrowing. By 1936, writes the historian G. C. Allen, "Takahashi had successfully practiced, without benefit of Keynes, a policy in full accord with what was soon to become the new economic orthodoxy." This policy worked so well that industrial output in Japan in 1936 was more than 50 percent larger than it had been in 1929.

Even in Germany, where inflation was such a bugaboo, ideas similar to those of Keynes were "in the air" by 1931. Because so many workers were unemployed, job creation (*Arbeitsbeschaffung*) was the slogan of the day. Some Germans were also pushing the idea of reducing interest rates and getting more money into the hands of consumers. In 1929 Fritz Tarnow of the Trade Union Federation argued in *Why Be Poor?* that if consumers had more money to spend, their purchases would lead to an increase in employment.[46]

***

* There were sharp limits, however, to Viner's tolerance of deficit spending. When Roosevelt came out strongly for such spending in 1938 because of the recession, Viner resigned his post in the Treasury Department in protest. "I believe that heavy deficit spending . . . will involve serious dangers," he explained.[45]

In 1931 Wladimir Woytinsky published *Internationale Hebung der Preise als Ausweg aus der Krise* (International Raising of Prices as a Way Out of the Depression). Woytinsky sent Keynes a copy of this work along with a letter saying, "I have reached essentially the same conclusions with regard to economic policy as those which you have been advocating," and noting ruefully that "the deflationary psychosis is still very strong in Germany." (Keynes responded with what may be described as polite indifference, sending Woytinsky a copy of his collection of popular writings, *Essays in Persuasion*). The next year Woytinsky, Tarnow, and Fritz Baade, an agricultural economist, persuaded the Trade Union Federation to support their W-T-B Plan for stimulating consumption by inflating the currency.[47]

In 1932 Heinrich Dräger, a Lübeck manufacturer, published *Arbeitsbeschaffung durch produktive Kreditschöpfung* (Creating Work by Productive Credit Creation), which recommended spending 5 billion marks a year on housing, dams, roads, sports facilities, and other public works, the money to come from long-term, low-interest loans made by the Reichbank. At about the same time, Gottfried Feder, a radical National Socialist, put forth a plan for creating 5 billion marks in new money to build electric power plants and relocate idle workers in the eastern part of Germany. Another radical Nazi, Gregor Strasser, speaking in favor of such a proposal before the Reichstag in May 1932, said, "Never ask 'Have I the money for it?' but 'How shall I use the money?' " Shortly before Hitler came to power, the German trade union economists even tried to persuade the Strasser element in the National Socialist Party to join them in support of a modified version of the W-T-B Plan.[48]

By early 1933, with the depression at its most severe, pressures were mounting nearly everywhere in behalf of policies such as these. Conservatives continued to warn that spending large sums on public works was robbing Peter to pay Paul and that deficit spending was both immoral and in the long run dangerous. But they offered few alternatives other than patience, and increasingly, people were demanding that some positive actions be taken.

CHAPTER VII

RADICALISM

In 1931 Paul Einzig, an economist, published *The World Economic Crisis: 1929–1931*. At the time, Einzig still believed that the depression was just another cyclical downturn that would soon end. By the end of the year, however, he had changed his mind. "In May 1931 there was reason to hope that the crisis would take its course without culminating in a disaster," he explained. "The events of the last eight months . . . have frustrated these hopes." Incidents "of unprecedented gravity" had "shaken the very foundations of our economic system" and made the depression "the worst . . . of modern history." Actually, even in 1930 Keynes, a more brilliant and influential economist, was calling the depression "one of the greatest economic catastrophes of modern history" and "a colossal muddle . . . the working of which we do not understand." A year later, Keynes predicted that the depression might well last another five years.[1]

During the depression, the League of Nations published an annual *World Economic Survey*. The 1933 volume contains the sentence: "Economic activity in the world as a whole had touched depths unprecedented during the present depression, and international economic organisation was in a state of extreme confusion." League economists compared the collapse to "a landslide which carried with it buildings, fields, walls, and living objects. As the landslide continued, the more vulnerable of the buildings collapsed and, in collapsing, started a fresh downward movement."

In *The Great Depression*, Lionel Robbins insisted that a cure could be achieved by ceasing to meddle with economic forces. Nevertheless, even he admitted that "there have been many depressions in modern economic history but it is safe to say that there has never been anything to compare with this."[2]

To move from what would today be called the macro- to the microeconomic level, here are some examples of the human suffering that the Great Depression caused. *Fortune*, bulwark of the defenders of American capitalism, published this generalization about unemployment in September 1932:

You are a carpenter. Your last cent is gone. They have cut off the gas. The kid is white and stupid looking. . . . You can't get a job now for love or money. What do you do? In some, but by no means all, cities you can get a meal at the Salvation Army. . . . But that's no use now. So you go to the cop. He pulls out his directory and sends you to one of the listed charitable societies. . . . You draw the Episcopal Family Relief Society. The Relief Society clears your name through the central agency to see that you are not receiving help elsewhere. . . . Eventually it will allot you $2 to $8 a week, depending on the locality and the funds available. If its funds are exhausted it asks you to wait.[3]

On October 7, 1932, the *New York Times* printed this news item:

Fifty-four men were arrested yesterday morning for sleeping or idling in the arcade connecting with the subway through 45 W. Forty–second Street, but most of them

163

considered their unexpected meeting with a raiding party of ten policemen as a stroke of luck because it brought them free meals yesterday and shelter last night from the sudden change in the weather.

Here is Malcolm X's recollection of what it was like for a poor black family living on the edge of a small city in Michigan during the depression:

> . . . by 1934, we really began to suffer. This was about the worst depression year, and no one we knew had enough to eat or live on. Some old family friends visited us now and then. At first they brought food. Though it was charity, my mother took it. . . . In Lansing, there was a bakery where, for a nickel, a couple of us children would buy a tall flour sack of day-old bread and cookies, and then walk the two miles back out into the country to our house. . . . But there were times when there wasn't even a nickel and we would be so hungry we were dizzy. My mother would boil a big pot of dandelion greens and we would eat that.[4]

In England, the writer J. B. Priestley penned a description of a reunion of his World War battalion that he attended in 1933. Learning that some of the members of his old unit could not afford tickets to the affair, he and some of the others bought tickets for them. Still, they did not attend. "They were so poor, these fellows, that they said they could not attend the dinner even if provided with free tickets because they felt that their clothes were not good enough," Priestley explained. "We could drink to the tragedy of the dead," he added, "but we could only stare at one another, in pitiful embarrassment, over this tragi-comedy of the living, who had fought for a world that did not want them, who had come back to exchange their uniforms for rags."[5]

One family of four in Marienthal, Austria, according to one of Paul Lazarsfeld's associates, was so poor that the seven-year-old "had to stay away from school for eight days because he had no shoes to wear." German accounts speak of children fainting in their classrooms from lack of food, of bars where most of the "customers" sat empty-handed and watched the few lucky ones who could afford to buy a glass of beer. In his autobiography, a German archaeologist recalled picking up young hitchhikers on his travels. Not wanderlust but necessity had put these youths on the road. Their stories were all substantially the same—parents and older brothers unemployed, savings exhausted. "What could I say to them?" the archeologist asked.[6]

One might well expect that conditions such as these, extended over a long period without visible sign of improvement, would cause violent reactions or at least demands for fundamental changes in the economic system and in the political structures that supposedly administered the system. Many contemporaries, radicals and conservatives alike, predicted that outbreaks of violence would soon occur. In 1931 a German commission studying unemployment reported, "The present crisis is so widespread in its effects and is so dire in its consequences to those who suffer from them that social disturbances of the most serious nature . . . are to be feared on a larger scale, unless some way is found of relieving and overcoming the crisis." At approximately the same time in the United States, the Hoover administration decided not to risk reducing the armed forces as part of its economy-in-government campaign because doing so would "lessen our means of maintaining domestic peace and order." In 1934 the communist Eugen Varga, director of the Institute for World Economy and World Politics in Moscow, wrote:

> There is only one way out for the proletariat: the revolutionary overthrow of the rule of the bourgeoise. . . . Never before has there been such a glut of commodities alongside the misery and starvation of the working-class masses. Never before has it been so clear that the capitalist system of society must be overthrown, if mankind is to live as men![7]

The radical upheavals that these and countless other people claimed the Great Depression would cause failed to materialize. The Great Depression was finally ended by World War II, and it can be argued that the depression was an important cause of that war. But no one has ever suggested that the war was started by the people who were suffering from the depression most acutely. Put differently, when war broke out in 1939, none of the industrial nations was controlled by anticapitalists. In America the reform period of the New Deal was over, even in President Roosevelt's eyes, and this despite the fact that double-digit unemployment was still plaguing the nation. Neville Chamberlain was prime minister of Great Britain. The historian A. J. P. Taylor has described Chamberlain as "a meticulous housemaid," presiding over a "humdrum government" consisting of the " 'old gang' slightly reshuffled."

The premier of France was Edouard Daladier, the same kind of middle-of-the-road conservative that had been running the country ten years earlier. The only industrial nation where drastic change had occurred was Germany, and the German revolution had been a rightist coup, engineered by the Nazis and supported not by the unemployed or the urban masses but by shopkeepers, farmers and other small landowners, and by some big business interests.

There was certainly a good deal of protesting during the depression, some of it lawless in character. The historian Bernard Sternsher has counted 17 cases of violence in the United States associated with the depression during a 2½-year period, and there may have been many more. On International Unemployment Day (March 6, 1930), large gatherings took place in many American cities, and at some of these meetings, serious clashes with the police erupted. Rural protests against low prices for farm products and against farm foreclosures were frequent. Strikes by agricultural workers for higher wages occurred all over the United States— among cranberry pickers in Massachusetts and apple pickers in Washington.

In 1934 a waterfront strike in San Francisco resulted in clashes between longshoremen and policemen in which several strikers lost their lives. Here is how an eyewitness described the scene: "The air was filled with blinding [tear] gas. The howl of the sirens. The low boom of the gas guns. The crack of pistol-fire. The whine of the bullets. . . . Men lay bloody, unconscious, or in convulsions—

in the gutters, on the sidewalks, in the streets." The fighting only ended after state troops were called in. A strike in Minnesota caused so much damage that the governor had to summon the National Guard.[8]

In Great Britain a National Unemployed Workers' Movement staged many demonstrations, some of which ended in rioting. Hunger marches were frequent in Germany, and mobs of poor people caused much damage in many cities. In the winter of 1932, in Halle, Germany, a mob broke into a coal yard and carted away coal by the wagon load while the frightened owner stood by helplessly.

The major popular explosion in France did not occur until 1936, perhaps because the full impact of the depression occurred later there than elsewhere. It assumed the form of a wave of sit-down strikes that swept over the land that spring. Historians have counted 8,941 establishments that were occupied by striking workers, and there were probably many other small ones that were seized. At least a million workers were involved. All this developed within a matter of days and with major results that will be discussed later. The next year saw the occupation by automobile workers of the General Motors plant in Flint, Michigan, which inaugurated an outbreak of no less than 477 sit-down strikes in America.

Countless smaller outbursts of violence occurred that were ignored by the authorities and the press. John Dos Passos, writing for the *New Republic* in 1932, reported one such incident. A group of men entered a large food store in Detroit and asked for credit. When they were told that the store only sold for cash, they pushed the clerks aside and took what they wanted from the shelves. The manager did not summon the police. "If more people heard about affairs like this, there would be more trouble," he explained to Dos Passos.[9]

Beyond signs of discontent among ordinary people was the reaction of intellectuals to the depression. Most liberal intellectuals were as unprepared for the depression as the rest of society.* But

* In the United States, for example, the *New Republic* predicted after the stock market crash that "the ultimate result will, of course, be extremely good for business and the country."

by 1932 large numbers of them had been radicalized. The persistence of high unemployment and stagnating production convinced them that capitalism would have to go if social justice was to be achieved and prosperity restored.

The thinking of such people was well reflected in *The Coming Struggle for Power* by John Strachey, an English radical. Strachey, a nephew of the biographer Lytton Strachey, was a recent convert to Marxism. (While writing the book, he was still working his way through *Das Kapital*.) But he made a persuasive if superficial argument.

Capitalism, according to Strachey, meant monopoly, "ferocious" nationalism, and recurring depressions. The system had "reached an economic impasse" and was "visibly, obviously, and now rapidly, declining." Soon it would be dead and gone, to be replaced by communism. "There is no force on earth which can long prevent the workers of the world from building a new and stable civilization for themselves upon the basis of the common ownership of the means of production." Strachey insisted that although the Soviet Union was not yet a true communist society, it was moving rapidly in that direction. If all went as anticipated, he predicted, it would achieve that happy state by the end of the Second Five-Year Plan in 1937. *The Coming Struggle for Power* was not a best seller in Great Britain, although in the United States, it went through five printings in a year. It was, however, widely and favorably reviewed, and unquestionably influential.[10]

The success of the Five-Year Plan in stimulating economic growth in the Soviet Union had a profound effect on thinking in the industrialized nations. Richard H. Pells has summarized the common reaction in *Radical Visions and American Dreams*: "While the West struggled helplessly with the depression, its people at the mercy of economic forces over which they had no control, the U.S.S.R. strode purposefully into the future." Intellectuals were particularly attracted to the idea that planning (by its nature an organized, logical mental activity) could provide solutions to problems that the mindless automatic operation of the so-called free market could not supply. Many who were not Communist Party members or even Marxists found the Russian experiment appealing because, in Pells's words, the Bolsheviks "were using human intelligence in the interests of social control."[11]

Communists or not, considering that intellectuals were not as a class among the leading sufferers, a remarkable number of them were radicalized by the experience of living through the depression. And, being intellectuals, they did not hesitate to make their feelings known to anyone who would read or listen. Novelists were among the most effective in reaching a wide audience. In addition to John Steinbeck's *Grapes of Wrath*, which was not published until 1939, when the depression was finally ending, there were a number of international best sellers that dealt with the impact of the depression on ordinary people. Almost invariably the authors of these works took a radical position. In *Little Man, What Now?* the German Hans Fallada wrote:

> How could one laugh, really laugh in such a world as this,
> a world of respectable and blundering captains of industry
> and little degraded down-trodden people always trying to
> do their best? . . . Order and cleanliness; they were of the
> past. So too were work and safe subsistence. And past too
> were progress and hope. Poverty was not merely misery,
> poverty was an offense, poverty was evil, poverty meant
> that a man was suspect.

And the Belgian Maxence van der Meersch remarked in his 1933 novel *Quand les Sirènes Se Taisent (When the Factory Whistles Fall Silent)*, "Those who are well off during these depressions benefit from the poverty. They buy at very low prices and make good deals. . . . A happy minority enrich themselves by speculating on the starvation [famine] of the district."[12]

Perhaps more significant, though less widely circulated, were the comments of novelists in works of nonfiction. After recounting a discussion he had with a bankrupt businessman, J. B. Priestley wrote in *English Journey*, "I do not blame him in particular, I blame us all for allowing such a daft chaos to go blundering on." On another occasion, Priestley watched some unemployed young men playing Ping-Pong at a hostel. "Many of these unemployed lads . . . are very good at table tennis," he wrote. "Probably by the time the North of England is an industrial ruin, we shall be able to beat the world at table tennis."

In 1931 Theodore Dreiser published *Tragic America*, a book describing what he called "the haphazard anarchy of the whole régime of Capitalism."

I insist [he wrote] that without a fundamental change in our Government, the rights and needs and just desires of the laborer can never be met. . . . How can any good come of the present situation: the employer or corporation absorbing nearly all of the profits and deliberately degrading labor in order to do it?[13]

The number of statements like these, many far more sophisticated than Dreiser's, is almost infinite. In particular the great gap between rich and poor, accentuated by the shrinking of the economy as a whole angered the critics. The stagnationist Ferdinand Fried, no Marxist, denounced what he called the "Upper Hundred" German capitalists in *Das Ende des Kapitalismus*. "In Germany, 80,000 persons possess twice as much wealth as 62.5 million!" Fried wrote. He compared the condition of a poor family where "five persons live in a tiny whitewashed room, no one having a bed to himself, eating grits and potato soup," with the lifestyle of the "plutocracy who ape the formality of the old nobility, build themselves costly country seats, travel for the season to Baden-Baden, and would gladly let themselves be called Kaisers, Kings, or Princes of their businesses." One hundred and ten families, Fried stated, "own altogether property worth about 3.4 billion marks."

Here is another example. In the conclusion of his best-selling history of late-nineteenth-century American industrial development, *The Robber Barons* (1934), Matthew Josephson wrote:

Soon there would be few who hoped that the old economic rulership . . . could minister to the just interests of the masses. . . . And during long years of industrial lethargy, while grass literally grew upon the floors of magnificent factories, the lesson would finally be driven home of the fearful sabotage practiced by capital upon the energy and intelligence of human society. . . . When the busy workers of our cities were turned into idle and hungry louts, and our once patriotic farmers into rebels and law breakers, there would arise hosts of men and women, numerous enough, who knew that "they could no longer live in a world where such things can be. . . ."

And in France, where the notorious "200 Families" had long dominated the economy and exercised a disproportionate influence on the government, Augustin Hamon wrote a vivid three-volume denunciation of *The Masters of France.* Among the bankers, insurance executives, newspaper publishers, government administrators, and legislators who dominated French life, Hamon charged, "the intermixture of families one with the other is the same. The intermixture is so deep and so extensive that almost everyone is related to everyone else. It is the same as in a village isolated from the world, where the inhabitants marry among themsleves."[14]

One of the most formidable of the critics who focused on maldistribution of wealth as the chief cause of the depression was an American, Senator Huey P. Long of Louisiana. Long proposed enacting a steeply graduated income tax that would reach 100 percent at $1 million. Still more drastic, he called for an annual capital levy that would confiscate fortunes of more than $8 million. The money so collected, Long promised, would provide every American family with a stake or "homestead" of $5,000 and an income of at least $2,000 a year. Old people would receive pensions. (To deal with unemployment, Long proposed reducing the work week to 30 hours.)

It is hard to know how sincere the raffish "Kingfish" was about his "Share Our Wealth" plan. Critics then and later charged that he was using it to advance his presidential ambitions, but his biographer, T. Harry Williams, thought that Long believed the plan workable, though not in the simple form he advanced early in 1934.

Long's rhetoric was extremist. The rich, he said, are "pigs swilling in the trough of luxury." Actually, he was not really very radical. Even if he meant precisely what he said, he was denouncing the excesses of capitalism, not capitalism itself. He was bitterly critical of socialism and did not favor any substantial increase in the power of the federal government. The government he seemed to favor would be strong but unobtrusive.[15]

Most historians place Long in the tradition of American populism—his was the protest of rural and small town people who believed that they were being oppressed and dominated by powerful faraway forces. Wily big-city bankers, Wall Street speculators, anonymous Washington bureaucrats, effete eastern aristocrats—these were Long's targets, along with Franklin Roosevelt, whom he saw as the master manipulator of the phalanx of special interests who were exploiting the citizenry.

Long appealed to a wide audience. Had he not been assassinated, he might well have posed a formidable threat to Roosevelt in the 1936 presidential election, though more likely he was aiming for 1940. Similarly, the works of writers like Fallada, Fried, and Josephson were read and praised by large numbers of people. Even van der Meersch's novel, less well known than most of the books cited above, sold more than 100,000 copies. Yet most of those who suffered from the depression accepted its burdens and endured its indignities without reacting violently or pressing for basic changes in the economy or in society. No significant alterations of the capitalistic system were made, even in Germany and the United States, where the most important changes in the status quo were attempted.

That radical changes did not occur is easier to explain than why there were so few organized efforts to make them. That question has many possible answers, some of which are the following.

Probably the most important, though rarely verbalized at the time, was the fact that it was a world depression, so widespread that people saw it as an act of God or of Nature, depending on their philosophy. Like an earthquake or a drought or like one of the great plagues of the Middle Ages, the depression seemed a cataclysm beyond human control. What good to protest, let alone organize a revolution, against an earthquake? Moreover, the fact that the depression extended beyond national boundaries inhibited political protests, which by the nature of the situation had to be national. (The fact that the world was divided into autonomous political structures called nations, but integrated economically, was one reason why the depression lasted so long.)

The lack of agreement as to what to do about the depression was another inhibiting force. The din of so many insistent yet conflicting voices urging this reform, that change, some other panacea, was likely to paralyze rather than galvanize the public. Those who were convinced by one or another of the self-proclaimed saviors often neutralized each other as they went off in different directions, and their activities only further confused the passive remainder.

In this connection, the arguments of the conservative economists had a sobering impact. Their own prescriptions were not curing the disease, but they spoke from the vantage point of long experience, and the best of them were powerful intellects, not mere mossback defenders of the status quo. (John Strachey described Lionel Robbins in *The Coming Struggle for Power* as "the vigorous young economist of the London School of Economics.") They excelled at pointing out the indirect effects of policies designed to solve this or that problem—that tariffs and subsidies fostered inefficiency and increased the cost of living, that government borrowing discouraged private investment by raising interest rates, and so on. "Governments could hardly have been expected," the British historian W. R. Garside writes, "to have adopted alternative policies which . . . lacked sufficient intellectual rigour to challenge the ruling canons of classical economic theory."[16]

More important, the Marxists, the most militant and persuasive advocates of root-and-branch change, were split into socialist and communist camps during the worst stages of the Great Depres-

173

sion. The communist parties in the western nations opposed any effort to *reform* the capitalist system. They would join no government coalition, preferring to stir up trouble and stand by smugly while capitalism went through what they assumed were its death throes. Before 1933 the German Communist Party often sided with the National Socialists, employing the fatuous logic that the destruction of democratic government would clear the way for a communist revolution.

While the European socialist parties sometimes accepted political responsibilities in capitalist governments, they had few constructive suggestions for ending the depression. The socialist legislative program, John Strachey wrote scornfully, "turns out to be the most weary, stale, flat and unprofitable liberalism." Strachey was not a very objective critic, but the British Labour Party was indeed intellectually bankrupt. Robert Skidelsky, the leading student of the party's history during the depression, put it this way: "Alone of those in a position to contribute to the 'pool of ideas,' the Labour Government offered nothing." When a high-level British civil servant wrote Prime Minister Ramsay MacDonald in 1930 that the economy was like "a great ship which has run aground on a falling tide; no human endeavour will get the ship afloat until in the course of nature the tide again begins to flow," MacDonald responded, "Your letter expresses exactly my own frame of mind."[17]

MacDonald and most other British socialist politicians believed that capitalism was doomed. But they did not think the British public was "ready" for socialism. They acted, one witty historian suggests, as though "capitalism must be put back on its feet before it was got rid of." Such an attitude was uninspiring, irresolute—and unlikely to produce much public pressure for radical change. The German Socialist Party, like the British Labour Party, put an inordinate emphasis on maximizing wages and unemployment benefits. It surrendered power in 1930 rather than accept responsiblity for a small increase in the unemployment insurance tax paid by workers. Out of power in the depths of the depression, it chose to "escape into noisy opposition without tangible aims." When the Nazis swept to power in 1933, the Socialists followed what the historian Karl Bracher describes as a "course of acquiescence devoid of all possibility of exerting political leverage."[18]

The French socialists were deeply affected by the fate of the German party in 1933. Until then they had adopted a policy similar to the communists; they refused to participate with "capitalist" parties in coalition governments. Even in 1934, when some left-leaning intellectuals and union leaders proposed a scheme for fighting the depression, doctrinaire French socialists refused to cooperate. "Before any plan," they insisted, "first . . . the total conquest of power by socialism." Small wonder that the Marxist critique of capitalism had little appeal to most of the victims of the depression.

Many observers, including some of the most radical, commented on how difficult it was to interest the unemployed in revolutionary movements. Down-and-outers in New York City told Matthew Josephson that they were " 'good Americans' and didn't go for the 'communist stuff.' " Two sociologists in Chicago who worked with the residents of local shelters reported, "While the men applaud anyone who makes a radical statement, they are generally indifferent to such radical programs as communism and fascism."[19]

Fear was still another reason why radical outbursts were relatively rare. It is often said that force is useless when "the people" are roused by some injustice. That has seldom been the case. For the majority of the unemployed in every country, the mere threat of further deprivation inhibited protest. When Josephson asked the same down-and-outers why they did not complain about conditions in the municipal lodging house where they were staying, they answered, "We don't dare complain about anything. We're afraid of being kicked out." In all the industrial nations, governments cracked down hard on mass expressions of discontent, in large measure because they were aware of their inability to satisfy the protesters' demands that they do something to improve conditions.

With unemployment so high, those who had jobs did not feel free to criticize the system too vigorously, lest they find themselves replaced. The fact that the jobless were possible competitors could never have been far from any worker's consciousness. Two Australian historians make this point: "A depression is no time to take industrial action against attacks on living standards—there are too many men waiting at the factory gate. Throughout the depression years, there was an undercurrent of fear, resentment and jealousy splitting the employed from the unemployed."[20]

The debilitating physical and psychological effects of poverty and prolonged unemployment on their victims provides a further explanation of the dearth of radical reactions during the depression. Contemporary observers were struck by the political passivity of the unemployed. Jobless people often expressed anger and then disillusionment with the authorities. Here are a few examples: "Just nationalise everything," said an Englishman. "Unemployment is due to an agreement between capitalists and the Government to crush the worker and make a slave of him," wrote a Pole. "I don't think things will improve until we have a revolution." An American investigator quoted idle people "giving the capitalist system hell in a big way." But words like these were mostly mere talk.[21]

In deeply depressed Marienthal, people seemed to lose interest in political parties of any persuasion. After his research in Great Britain, E. Wight Bakke reported no difference in the political attitudes of English workers and their unemployed neighbors. Later, in New Haven, Bakke once attended a communist May Day rally on the town common. The speaker ended by urging his audience to march to City Hall to protest conditions. Few followed him. According to the sociologists who studied unemployed men in Chicago, most of the jobless insisted (perhaps correctly, considering the nature of politics in that city) that all politicians were crooked. They claimed that they sold their votes on election day to whichever party boss made them the best offer. After discussing the efforts of radicals to rouse the unemployed of Boston, Charles H. Trout writes, "The Boston [jobless] worker . . . did not take to the streets to plead for a revision of the system, but instead throngs milled outside the Municipal Employment Bureau in the Micawber-like hope that something would turn up."[22]

Walter Greenwood, author of the novel *Love on the Dole*, described the following incident in his autobiography. He was talking with a radical acquaintance at a British Labour Party headquarters. An unemployed man came in complaining about a faithless friend who had refused to help him out so that he could get back on unemployment relief. "What the Government ought to do," said the radical, "is freeze us solid, shove us in cold storage and bring us out when they need us." But the other man merely continued to grumble about his faithless friend. "It was as though he had not been listening," Greenwood wrote.

An Italian historian has summed up many of these reasons in an essay on the condition of Italian workers during the depression. For a decade, he writes, people lived through a time of economic stagnation difficult for anyone accustomed to economic growth to envisage. The era was characterized by "the desire to conserve and not necessarily to make progress. . . . The obsession of unemployment, the general economic stagnation, and the pressure exercised by the [fascist] party on the consciences and actions of men, stifled the spirit of initiative, reduced ambition, quite often annihilated the will to act."[23]

There was also a positive side to the lack of much radical response to the depression. Forces were at work in all the western nations that blunted the impact of hard times and soothed the indignation of the dissatisfied. It is obvious, but worth emphasizing, that patriotism remained a powerful social cement. In Great Britain, the remarkable popularity of Noel Coward's play *Cavalcade* (1932), with its nostalgic reminders of the English past, and of the film based on that play, illustrate this point. When the British government proposed spending an enormous amount of money celebrating the twenty-fifth anniversary of the coronation of George V, the king expressed concern about spending so much in the midst of a depression. But huge crowds turned out for the ceremonies, and their mood was cheerful rather than resentful. In the dreariest London slums, people marched carrying banners that read "Lousy but Loyal."[24] The lack of such a commitment had much to do with the collapse of the Weimar Republic in Germany, and however awful its consequences, the Nazis' frenzied superpatriotic nonsense about the superiority of the so-called Aryan race had something to do with the economic revival that occurred under Hitler.

Related to this patriotic element was the sense that however bad the situation, everyone was more or less in the same boat. The popularity of the American song "Brother, Can You Spare a Dime?" reflects this. The words are bleak, but somehow, for the people of the thirties, the song was inspiring.

In every community, individuals and private organizations tried to help those in need. In 1931, deep into the depression, the American Community Chest drive collected 25 percent more money than in the boom year 1928. In 1930 a group of New York City businessmen raised $8 million for relief; in 1932 nongovernmental relief in the city rose to $21 million. The Community Fund of Muncie, Indiana, raised its collections from $80,000 in 1929 to $115,000 two years later.

When the depression began, James Michael Curley, the mayor of Boston, opposed direct relief to the jobless. Such aid, he said, "saps initiative, and makes of a man a chronic loafer." Experience soon caused Curley to change his mind. In December 1931, having already given 20 percent of his salary to charity, he authorized a major municipal fund-raising effort. To publicize the effort, a dummy named General D. Pression was stuffed into a coffin, hauled to the harbor on a garbage truck, and pushed into the water by Mayor Curley while a band played "Happy Days Are Here Again" and harbor craft sounded their horns.

Boston's schoolchildren wrote appeals to take home to their parents. A thousand boy scouts and five thousand adult volunteers rang doorbells and distributed fliers. At the formal opening of the drive at the Boston Opera House, the audience sang the "Star Spangled Banner" before a flag made of red, white, and blue lights. In less than three weeks the people of the city contributed more than $3 million to the effort.[25]

Similar efforts were made in the European nations. By 1931 two-thirds of the unemployed of the town of Thalburg, Germany, had exhausted their government unemployment benefits. In this difficult situation, the townspeople made a massive effort to care for the unfortunate. Most of the charitable organizations of the community combined their resources. They made street collections and distributed food, clothing, and fuel. Merchants contributed some of their wares. Coal dealers sold lignite blocks to the unemployed at a special low price. Bakers reduced the price of bread. Free "cultural" movies were shown at the school. The labor unions put on a gymnastic exhibition, charging 75 pfennigs for admission and donating the proceeds to the jobless.[26]

Far more significant were government relief and insurance programs. In the depths of the depression, American state and local governments could not meet the demand for relief funds, but most of them exhausted their resources trying to do so. By late 1932, they were spending a combined total of more than $50 million a month. After Franklin Roosevelt took office, the federal government began spending billions on direct relief and on job-creating public works projects. Despite their inadequacies, these programs were enormously popular—a major reason for the failure of radicals to have much influence in the country. The Europeans had their systems of social insurance from the start of the depression. The hard times weakened the effectiveness of these programs, and that caused much suffering and resentment. But the help they did bring to millions was a force for social peace. The tendency worldwide was toward a broader acceptance of the responsibility of government to help the victims of the depression. This served to moderate discontent.

Any sign of official support, no matter how routine or trivial, was likely to win the gratitude of suffering people. In 1931 the governor of New South Wales, Sir Philip Game, visited a shantytown on the edge of Sydney. He and his wife toured the settlement and talked with some of the 350 people living there. (Lady Game was quoted in the press as saying "she had seen one little home in which she would not mind living herself.") When they were ready to leave, the inhabitants gave them a vote of thanks, to which Sir Philip responded modestly, "I have only come here as part of my job, and I don't want any thanks at all."[27]

In sum, the Great Depression was a radical event, one that

179

exposed glaring weaknesses in the capitalist system. It radicalized many persons all over the world. The depression also caused enormous changes. But the changes that were in any sense fundamental came so slowly that they can better be described as having evolved than as having arrived in a radical or revolutionary manner. On the one hand, they had roots in developments that long antedated the depression—the decline of laissez-faire is a good example. On the other hand, they were produced as much and probably more by World War II as by the "Great Crisis" that Eugen Varga and so many other radicals of the 1930s believed was the death knell of the capitalist system. These radicals failed to achieve nearly all their objectives; the system they denounced still exists, patched up, modernized, reformed, but essentially the same as before 1929.

The Bettmann Archive

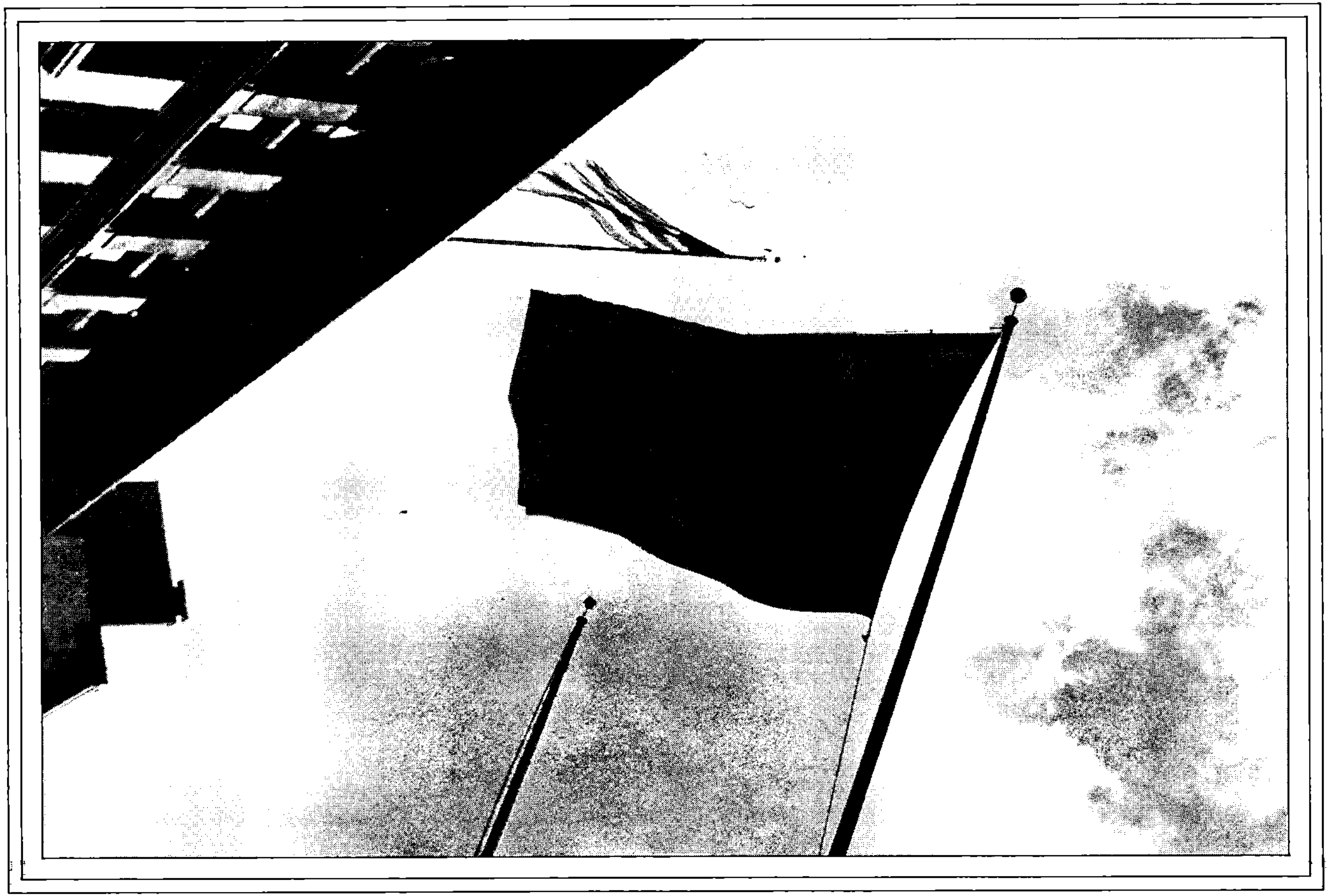

CHAPTER VIII

NEW DEAL AND NAZI REACTIONS

In early 1933, the Great Depression was at its low point, and the worst-hit countries were Germany and the United States. In both nations, industrial production had plumbed the depths. Unemployment was in the area of 25 percent of the work force, somewhere between 13 and 16 million in America, 6 million or more in Germany. Both countries had experienced periods of poor or at best, uninspired, leadership. Herbert Hoover lacked both political skill and popular appeal. One biographer mentions his "inability to master the political techniques of leadership," and the *New York Times* columnist Arthur Krock, who admired Hoover and shared his political philosophy, spoke of his "awkwardness of manner and speech and lack of mass magnetism."[1]

Like Hoover, the German chancellors in 1932 proved incapable of dealing with the deepening depression. Heinrich Brüning was too rigid to be a good politician and too reserved to win the affection of the public. In his 1931 New Year's Day message to the people, for example, Brüning said, "I am anxious to stress the limitations of any policy so that you will not indulge in any illusions." Statements like this were certainly candid but, as the historian Andreas Dorpalen once wrote, most Germans "mistook the chancellor's sober factualness for cynical coldness."[2]

Brüning's successor, Franz von Papen, was a political light-weight. When a friend said to General Kurt von Schleicher, who had recommended Papen to President Hindenburg, that "Papen did not have much of a head," Schleicher replied with a smile, "He need not have, but he'll make a fine hat!" A German historian once compared Papen's approach to the problems of the day to that of "a buoyant officer riding in a cavalry attack or a steeplechase."[3] As for Schleicher, who replaced Papen in December 1932, he was primarily a behind-the-scenes manipulator. He soon resigned.

On January 30, 1933, Adolf Hitler became chancellor, and on March 4, 1933, in the midst of a financial panic that had caused thousands of banks to close their doors, Franklin D. Roosevelt took the oath as president of the United States. Thus, barely a month apart, the two most powerful and effective depression leaders of the western world took office. Although it is possible to argue that the long-sought economic upturn had already begun, their rise marked, if it did not cause, the beginning of the end of the Great Depression. Their methods and their personalities had enormous effects, both on their own nations and on the rest of the world.

Although two more different people than Roosevelt and Hitler would be hard to imagine, at the time neither seemed particularly well suited for his position. Roosevelt had been born to wealth and social prominence. He had attended elite private schools (Groton, Harvard, Columbia Law). His political career, culminating in two terms as governor of New York, had been successful but not particularly brilliant. He was widely regarded as an intellectual lightweight; the political commentator Walter Lippmann, in a now-famous phrase, described Roosevelt in 1932 as "a pleasant man who, without any important qualifications for the office, would very much like to be President."[4]

Roosevelt had only the sketchiest understanding of economics, and that outdated, as witness his referring to John Maynard Keynes as "a political economist," a term rarely used since the nineteenth century. That such a person could be elected president at a time when entrenched wealth was in disrepute and when everyone believed that solving complex economic problems was the nation's top priority is best explained by Hoover's inadequacies and the widespread public feeling that no matter what, it was time for a change in the White House and in Congress.

Hitler was the son of an Austrian customs official of modest means. He had been a poor student and lazy. He dropped out of school at the age of 14. Later he lounged around Vienna for five years, pretending to be studying art but mostly absorbing his ultranationalist, anti-Semitic ideas. He spoke a most uncultivated form of German, and of course with an Austrian accent—not the kind of speech that one would expect to appeal to German voters. After serving in the army in the Great War, Hitler became involved in reactionary political movements. His National Socialist Party was scorned by most decent Germans in the 1920s, both for its ideology and because of the rowdy, violent behavior of its members.

Yet despite all these apparent disadvantages, Hitler became the leader of a country whose citizens were supposed to have an exaggerated respect for hard work, education, high culture, and family lineage, and who had a reputation for orderliness and rigid obedience to the law.

For some reason, Roosevelt and Hitler were especially appealing to their social and economic opposites: Roosevelt to industrial workers, farmers, the unemployed, Hitler to hard-working shopkeepers and peasants and then (after he achieved power) to industrialists, large landowners, and the military.

These strange contradictions may not be significant. Probably any Democrat would have defeated Hoover in 1932, and what Hitler did after he became chancellor was accomplished without the formal consent (though not necessarily without the approval) of a majority of the German people. Yet the personal impact of Roosevelt and Hitler on the two societies in the depths of the depression was very large. Their policies aside, both exerted enormous psychological influence on the people.

Roosevelt's patrician concern for mass suffering, his charm, his calm confidence, his gaiety, even his rather cavalier approach to the problems of the day had an immediate effect on most Americans. Hitler's resentment of the rich and well born, while probably psychotic in origin, appealed powerfully to millions of Germans. His ruthless, terrifying determination, always teetering on the brink of hysteria, combined with the aura of encapsulated remoteness that he projected to paralyze his opponents and turn his supporters into toadies. He inspired awe among millions of ordinary Germans. Both the euphoria of the early days of Roosevelt's New Deal and the nationalistic fervor that swept over Germany in early 1933 made millions almost incapable of organized thought, let alone of judgment.

Both Roosevelt and Hitler made clever use of the crisis psychology of 1933, emphasizing the suffering of the times rather than attempting to disguise or minimize it. "The misery of our people is horrible," Hitler said in his first radio speech after becoming chancellor. "To the hungry, unemployed millions of industrial workers is added the impoverishment of the whole middle class and the artisans. If this decay also finally finishes off the German farmers, we will face a catastrophe of incalculable size."[5] Roosevelt's style was more reassuring than alarmist, but he too stressed the seriousness of the situation and the urgent need for decisive action: "Action, and action now," as he put it in his inaugural.

Basic rights were abolished in Germany without causing even an attempt at resistance. "Judgment must be waived . . . argument must be silenced," a *Republican* congressman said during what passed for the debate on the bill drastically reforming the American banking system in March 1933. (The debate lasted exactly 38 minutes.) The personalities of the two leaders had a great deal to do with this submission of legislators and mass opinion to executive domination.[6]

The sweeping approval that Roosevelt and Hitler won on first taking office was due to a spontaneous public reaction based mostly on the hope that things would get better. But not entirely. Both Roosevelt and Hitler employed the latest technologies to dramatize themselves and to influence public opinion. When the Democratic convention nominated him in 1932, Roosevelt flew to Chicago in order to make his acceptance speech on the floor of the convention. Both the flying and the personal appearance before the delegates were unprecedented acts for a presidential nominee. Hitler pioneered in making whirlwind speaking tours. By using airplanes, he spoke at 21 different cities in a seven day period, 50 in two weeks on another occasion. Here is how the German historian Joachim Fest has described the effect: "Hitler descended like a saviour to the seething crowds of despairing people; on one day alone he would address several hundred thousands, sweeping them into a 'forward-thrusting hysteria', as he called it himself. The collective feelings, the fascination of the vast mass, of which each individual could feel himself a part, gave people a sense of power which they had long lacked and which found fulfillment in Hitler's rhetoric in this atmosphere of rapturous emotion: extreme self-elevation was brought about by extreme self-surrender."

Roosevelt and Hitler were masters at speaking on radio, a skill that was still quite undeveloped by politicians in the early 1930s. Roosevelt specialized in low-key "fireside chats," Hitler in shrill harangues delivered before huge audiences. Hitler put so much energy into his speeches that (at least he claimed this was true) during any major speech he lost from 4 to 6 pounds. In his memoirs, Albert Speer recalls listening to a speech Hitler made before he became chancellor:

> I was carried on the wave of the enthusiasm which, one could almost feel this physically, bore the speaker along from sentence to sentence. It swept away any skepticism, any reservations. . . . The peril of communism which seemed inexorably on its way could be checked, Hitler persuaded us, and instead of hopeless unemployment, Germany could move toward economic recovery.[7]

Judgments of Roosevelt's and Hitler's abilities as administrators are of course subjective. In addition, the internal workings of any government are likely to seem confused when examined in detail. It is nevertheless clear that both Roosevelt and Hitler were exceptionally prone to set up confused lines of responsibility among their subordinates and to tolerate and at times encourage inter-departmental and intradepartmental rivalries. Waste and ineffectiveness frequently resulted.

Roosevelt's biographer James MacGregor Burns, a political scientist who should know about such things, writes, "Again and again Roosevelt flouted the central rule of administration that the boss must co-ordinate the men and agencies under him. . . . [He] put into the same office or job men who differed from each other in temperament and viewpoint." Karl Bracher, a leading authority on the Nazi period, concludes that "friction, waste, duplication" were deliberate Hitlerian techniques, whereas another important German historian, Wolfram Fischer, argues that when Hitler "made at least two and most often many more boards, agencies, and men responsible for each assignment," he was merely revealing the senselessness and lack of guiding principles in the Nazi system. But Bracher and Fischer and other scholars agree as to the facts. Burns considers Roosevelt "an artist in government," a master of the technique of divide and rule, whose "first concern was power," the subjection of the bureaucracy to executive control. Bracher writes that Hitler displayed "matchless virtuosity" in making others dependent on him, "the sole figure standing above the confusion."[8]

It seems clear that Roosevelt and Hitler were terrible administrators in the formal sense but virtuosos at handling subordinates. Their governments were marked by confusion, overlapping jurisdictions, and factional conflicts. Yet somehow they transformed these inadequacies into political assets. They seemed symbols of energy and commitment, not of weakness or inefficiency or indecisiveness.

The depression-oriented policies of New Deal America and Nazi Germany also displayed many remarkable similarities. Both gave providing aid to the unemployed a top priority. Building on a program begun by Papen, the Nazis offered subsidies and tax rebates to private companies that hired new workers. They granted marriage loans to persuade women to leave the work force and to encourage consumer spending, and they launched a huge public works program that included numerous railroad and navigation projects, the building and repair of private homes, the construction of public buildings, and the *Motorisierung* program that involved the design and construction of the autobahn network.* Soon wits in Germany were saying that Hitler was going to put the unemployed to work painting the Black Forest white and laying linoleum on the Polish Corridor.[9]

American work creation programs were relatively smaller—at no time were more than one-third of the unemployed enrolled. The programs were nonetheless impressive. Besides swiftly appropriating federal funds for direct relief for the jobless, in 1933 Congress set up a $3.3 billion program under which more than 4 million people were put to work. Somewhat later came the Works Progress Administration (WPA) and the Public Works Administration (PWA), which employed more millions building roads, schools, bridges, and similar public structures.

Some New Deal projects seemed to critics wasteful and unnecessary. So did the Nazi penchant for gigantic stadiums and other public structures, described so graphically by the architect Albert Speer in his memoirs. The American term *boondoggle*, meaning a useless make-work project, had its parallel in what the Germans called *Pyramidenbau*, pyramid building. It is fashionable, and also accurate, to note the military aspect of Nazi public works policies, although in fact, the Nazis spent relatively little on arms before 1935. It is less fashionable, but equally correct, to point out that in the United States, PWA money—more than $824 million of it— went into armaments. The aircraft carriers *Yorktown* and *Enterprise*, four cruisers, many lesser warships, as well as more than a hundred army airplanes and about 50 military airports were built with these funds.

---

* Road building also stimulated the demand for automobiles. The stiff tax on the purchase of cars was repealed in 1933, and by 1934 German auto production was four times larger than in 1932. Hitler, being an admirer of Henry Ford, saw the development of good roads and of small, moderately priced automobiles as a way of creating social harmony as well as of reducing unemployment.

Another way that both regimes dealt with the jobless was by opening work camps; one of Roosevelt's first actions in March 1933 was to propose the creation of the Civilian Conservation Corps. Unlike the German and American public works projects, these camps did not employ many idle industrial workers. They were not expected to have much stimulating effect on private business. Both used enrollees for forestry and similar projects to improve the countryside, and both were intended primarily to keep young men out of the overcrowded labor market. Roosevelt described work camps as a means of getting youth "off the city street corners." Hitler said they would keep young men from "rotting helplessly in the streets."[10] In both countries, much was made of the beneficial social results of mixing thousands of young people from different walks of life in the camps, and of the generally enthusiastic response of youth to the camp experience.

Furthermore, both were organized on semimilitary lines, with the subsidiary purposes of improving the physical fitness of potential soldiers and stimulating public commitment to national service in the emergency. Putting the army in control of hundreds of thousands of young civilians roused considerable concern in the United States. This concern proved to be unfounded; indeed, the army undertook the task with great reluctance and performed it with admirable restraint. It is also difficult to imagine how so large a program could have been set up in so short a time in any other way.

Nevertheless, the CCC served paramilitary and patriotic functions not essential to its announced purpose. Corpsmen were required to stand "in a position of alertness" while speaking with superiors and to address them as "Sir." Camp commanders possessed mild but distinctly military powers to discipline the men, including the right to issue dishonorable discharges. Morning and evening flag-raising ceremonies were held. The civilian head of the CCC, Robert Fechner, described the ceremony as a mark "of patriotism, of good citizenship and of appreciation by these young men of the thoughtful care being given them by their government."

Army authorities soon concluded that six months in the CCC

was worth a year's conventional military training, and the secretary of war, George Dern, said that running the camps had given the army the best practical experience in handling men that it had ever had. John A. Salmond, who has written a detailed history of the organization, says of the CCC in this regard:

> To a country engaged in bloody war, it had provided the sinews of a military force. It had given young officers valuable training in command techniques, and the nearly three million young men who had passed through the camps had received experience of military life upon which the Army was well able to build.[11]

New Deal and Nazi attempts to stimulate industrial recovery also resembled each other. Despite the "Socialist" in National Socialist and the charge of American mossbacks that Roosevelt was a "traitor to his class," neither administration sought to destroy the capitalist system. In both cases, there was at the start much jockeying for positions of influence between small producers and large, between manufacturers and merchants, between inflationists and deflationists, between planners, free enterprisers, and advocates of regulated competition.

In Germany the great financiers and the heads of cartels, most of them determinedly antidemocratic, demanded an authoritarian solution that would eliminate the influence of organized labor and increase their own control over the economy. Small operators, shopkeepers, and craftsmen wanted to reduce the power of bankers and to destroy not only the unions but the industrial monopolies and the chain stores. The tycoons sought to manipulate the Nazis, the others comprised the Nazis' most enthusiastic supporters, but Hitler and the party responded to pressure from both camps.

In the United States, most big-business interests had no open quarrel with the existing order. But because of the depression, by 1933 many were calling for suspension of the antitrust laws in order to end competitive price cutting. Other interests wanted to strengthen the antitrust laws. Still others favored some attempt at national economic planning. All clamored for the attention of the new administration.

The goals of these groups were contradictory, and neither Roosevelt nor Hitler tried very hard to resolve the differences. Roosevelt's method was to suggest that the contestants lock themselves in a room until they could work out a compromise. But Hitler, who freely admitted to being an economic naïf, was no more forceful. "I had to let the Party experiment," he later recalled in discussing the evolution of his industrial recovery program. "I had to give the people something to do. They all wanted to help. . . . Well, let them have a crack at it."[12]

Out of the resulting confusion came two kinds of that conservative, essentially archaic concept of social and economic organization called corporatism. In America, when the depression undermined the capacity of the "voluntary" trade associations to force individual companies to honor the associations' decisions, some were ready to accept government policing as a necessary evil. Gerard Swope's 1931 plan is the best known of these proposals.

President Hoover, who had been among the most ardent supporters of trade associations, denounced the Swope Plan as both a threat to industrial efficiency and "the most gigantic proposal of monopoly ever made." He considered all such compulsory schemes fascistic. But a number of early New Dealers found corporatism appealing.

In Germany the concept of government-sponsored cartels that regulated output and prices had a long tradition. Before 1933, however, the existence of powerful trade unions precluded the possibility of an effective corporatist organization. Hitler's success changed that swiftly. The Nazis created a complex system of 13 "estates" governing all branches of industry. These estates were, in effect, compulsory cartels. Each was subdivided into regional organizations, and at least in theory, the whole system was controlled by the Nazi minister of economics.

In America the process did not go nearly so far. But the system of self-governing industrial codes established under the National Recovery Administration (NRA) was in the same pattern. No less an authority on corporatism than Benito Mussolini saw the relationship. "Your new plan for coordination of industry follows precisely the lines of our cooperation," he told an American reporter in June 1933, though elsewhere he pointed out that Roosevelt had refused to go to the root of the problem by setting up labor-management associations and labor courts and by outlawing strikes. When a reporter asked Roosevelt in November 1933 for his opinion of an updated version of the Swope Plan, he replied, "Mr. Swope's plan is a very interesting theoretical suggestion in regard to some ultimate development of N.R.A."[13]

Under the law, the code system was voluntary. Each industry was supposed to draft its own code, tailored to its particular needs. But when the codification progress bogged down, a generalized "blanket" code called "the President's Re-employment Agreement" was drafted. The blanket code exempted arrangements made by previously competing companies from the antitrust laws so that they could fix prices and limit output. It also provided for minimum wages and maximum hours of labor, and it supposedly guaranteed workers the right to form unions and bargain collectively.

Production controls to prevent gluts, limitation of entry of new companies to lessen competition, and price and wage manipulation were characteristics of industrial policy in both countries. So were the two governments' justifications of drastic and possibly illegal or unconstitutional changes in the way the economy functioned on the ground that a "national emergency" existed, and so were the enormous propaganda campaigns they mounted to win public support.

During the early stages, big-business interests dominated the new organizations and succeeded in imposing their views on government. In Germany the radical Nazi artisan socialists who wanted to smash the cartels and nationalize the banks, led by Gregor Strasser and Gottfried Feder, lost out to the bankers and industrialists, represented by the financier Hjalmar Schacht. In the United States, victory went to the large corporations in each industry, which dominated the NRA code authorities.

This happened not because the governments favored big business, but because of basic relationships within industries. The large companies had the prestige and also more information, bigger and better legal staffs, and so on. Small producers dutifully deferred to "their betters."

But bewildering crosscurrents of interest and persistent factional rivalries hampered the functioning of corporatist organizations. In theory the system promised harmony and efficiency within industries. In practice it seldom provided either. It did not even pretend to solve interindustry problems, yet these were often more disturbing to government authorities. Under corporatism workers were supposed to share fairly in decision making and in profits resulting from the elimination of competition. In both countries, industrialists resisted allowing them to do so, with the consequence that the governments found themselves under pressure to enforce compliance. In America workers were a potent political force and vital to the New Deal coalition. German workers did not count as voters after 1933, but their cooperation and support remained essential to Nazi ambitions. Small businessmen also maintained a drumfire of complaint, and New Dealers and Nazis were sensitive to their pressure too.

Even the great industrialists were sometimes at odds with the system. Many German tycoons objected to sharing authority with labor and small producers. Others disliked particular decisions imposed on them by the government. After 1935 German steel and chemical manufacturers, such as the Krupps and the I. G. Farben interests, benefited from Hitler's emphasis on building up war-oriented industry. They backed him enthusiastically. But producers who were dependent on foreign raw materials or primarily concerned with the manufacture of consumer goods suffered from Nazi trade and monetary policies and held back. As for American industrialists, however much they profited under NRA codes, most of them came increasingly to resent both the regimentation the codes entailed and the growing interference in their affairs by the government.

To the Nazis, corporatism seemed at first compatible with the political process called *Gleichschaltung*, or coordination.* This was

---

* In German a *Gleichschalter* is a gear shift lever.

193

a process by which nearly every aspect of life was brought under the control of Hitler and the party. It quickly became apparent, however, that the autonomous character of any corporatist organization made precise control from above difficult. America, fortunately, was never *gleichgeschaltet*. But in any case, by 1935 and 1936, the Roosevelt and Hitler governments were abandoning corporatism and taking a more anti-big-business stance.

In America, after the Supreme Court declared NRA unconstitutional, this meant the passage of the Wagner Labor Relations Act, a far more effective guarantee of the right of workers to unionize and bargain with their employees in good faith. A government board was created to supervise elections and empowered to issue cease-and-desist orders when employers engaged in unfair labor practices. The Public Utility Holding Company Act made the pyramiding of control of gas and electric corporations illegal and gave the government power to regulate utility rates. In addition, the Social Security Act of 1935, which provided for both old age and unemployment insurance, was financed in part by a tax paid by employers, and other taxes paid by corporations were raised.

In Germany, although the cartel structure was retained, the Nazis limited the size of corporate dividends. The government constructed and operated steel, automobile, and certain other facilities in competition with private enterprise and imposed higher taxes on private incomes and corporate profits. As in the United States, but to a much greater degree, freedom of managerial decision making was curtailed.

After 1935 the increasing emphasis of the Nazis on preparing for war had much to do with the new restrictions on private business interests. They placed strict controls on imports in order to conserve the foreign exchange needed to buy raw materials used in the manufacture of munitions and other military necessities. These controls put nearly all industries at the mercy of the regime, whether they were making military or civilian goods. Under the Four-Year Plan of 1936, Hitler made Air Marshall Hermann Göring a kind of economic czar. The government undertook the manufacture of synthetic oil and rubber as well as steel and motor vehicles. Some businessmen earned profits from this activity, but their influence shrank, and their freedom of action disappeared.

In the last analysis, governments usually put their political objectives above their economic objectives. With Hitler, political ambition was all-consuming. The euphemism justifying Nazi policy toward business after 1936 was "the primacy of politics." In 1936 shortages of raw materials and the foreign exchange problem compelled Hitler to chooose between guns and butter. He chose, of course, guns. In his own crazy way, he insisted that production problems could be solved by an act of will. It was the job of the economy to supply the military needs of the state—so be it!

This kind of ruthless subordination of economic interests did not occur in the United States. Nevertheless, when military considerations began to dominate American policy after 1939, Roosevelt was also prepared to substitute guns for butter. One need only mention his famous announcement that he was replacing "Dr. New Deal" with "Dr. Win the War" as his prime consultant.

Conventional politics also affected economic policy in both nations. Consider Roosevelt's situation: Beset by depression-ravaged business interests seeking aid, by trustbusters eager to break up the corporate giants, by planners brimming with schemes to rationalize the economy, his administration survived in a state of constant flux, making concessions first to one view, then to another, acting in contradictory and therefore frequently self-defeating ways. The leading student of this subject is Ellis W. Hawley. "The New Dealers," he writes, "failed to arrive at any real consensus about the origins and nature of economic concentration." Nor did they follow any consistent policy in the fight against the industrial depression. And Roosevelt's inconsistency, Hawley adds, "was the safest method of retaining political power, . . . a political asset rather than a liability."[14]

Despite Hitler's stress on being the sole leader, the Nazis also permitted pressures from various interests to influence policy. They did so partly because even a totalitarian dictatorship could profit from the active cooperation of important economic groups, but also because the Nazi party had no fixed economic beliefs. Roosevelt responded to pressure groups; Hitler for a time permitted them to exist—a very important distinction. But the practical result was about the same.

Put differently, Hitler had a clear political objective—it was actually an obsession—but he was almost as flexible about specific economic policies as Roosevelt. "As regards economic questions," he boasted in 1936, "our theory is very simple. We have no theory at all."[15] This does not mean that the ideas of German and American economists were not taken up by the politicians. But the politicians did not adopt a consistent line of economic reasoning.

New Deal and Nazi labor policies were also shaped by the Great Depression in related ways. On the surface, this statement may seem not merely wrong but perverse, but only if one identifies labor with unions. Hitler destroyed the German unions and forced all workers into the *Deutsche Arbeitsfront* (German Labor Front) controlled by the Reich Trustee (another euphemism) for Labor. It is also true that Roosevelt, in part unwittingly, and with some reluctance,* enabled American unions to increase their membership and influence enormously.

However, New Deal and Nazi policies toward unions had little to do directly with the depression, and they do not throw much light on national policies toward workers. Hitler would no doubt have destroyed the German unions as autonomous organizations in any case—he destroyed all autonomous institutions in Germany. But it was because they were anti-Nazi that he smashed the unions so quickly. Roosevelt was at first indifferent to the fate of organized labor. He encouraged the American unions in order to gain labor's support, not because he thought doing so would speed economic recovery. In each instance the decision was essentially political.

The important New Deal labor legislation, especially the Social Security Act of 1935 and the Fair Labor Standards Act of 1940, benefited *workers*, not merely those who happened to belong to

* David Brody, an authority on New Deal labor policy, writes, "The Roosevelt administration, far from holding a clear vision of an enlarged labor movement . . . played a vacillating and ambiguous role . . . up to and including the passage of the Wagner Act."[16]

unions. Although the immediate effects of these laws were not dramatic, in the long run, they had an enormous impact. It is also possible to demonstrate Nazi concern for industrial workers. The "battle against unemployment" had first priority in Germany in 1933, and it was won remarkably swiftly. By 1936 something approaching full employment existed. Soon thereafter an acute shortage of labor developed. Of course the military draft siphoned thousands of men out of the German labor market. But this was also true in the United States after 1940. Full employment was never approached in America until the economy was shifted to all-out war production. As late as March 1940, unemployment in the United States stood at 7.8 million, almost 15 percent of the work force.

Moreover, Nazi ideology (and Hitler's prejudices) inclined the regime to favor the ordinary German over any elite group. Workers—as distinct from "Marxist" members of unions—had an honored place in the system. To the extent that the Nazis imposed restrictions on labor, they did so to benefit the state, not employers.

The Nazis created what were called Courts of Social Honor. These courts may be compared with the New Deal National Labor Relations Board. They did not alter power relationships between capital and labor the way the National Labor Relations Board did in the United States; they represented the interests of the Nazi party rather than those of labor. But they did adjudicate disputes between workers and bosses, and there is considerable evidence that the Courts of Social Honor tended more often than not to favor workers in these disputes. Furthermore, the very existence of the courts put considerable psychological pressure on employers to treat labor well. One historian has referred to the Nazi system as a "gigantic State Prison" in which the Nazis locked up workers and bosses and made them cooperate with each other.[17]

It is beyond argument that the Nazis encouraged working-class social and economic mobility. They eased entry into the skilled trades by reducing the educational requirements for many jobs and by expanding vocational training. They offered large rewards and further advancement to efficient workers. In the *Kraft durch Freude*

(KdF) Strength Through Joy movement, they provided extensive fringe benefits, such as subsidized housing, low-cost excursions, sports programs, and more pleasant factory facilities. It was under Hitler that the famous Volkswagen ("the Bug") was developed as part of the *Motorisierung* policy. The name of course means "people's automobile." At the same time it was called the *"KdF Wagen."* In a speech at the Berlin Motor Show in 1934, Hitler promised that besides "giving bread and work to thousands of men," *Motorisierung* would "offer ever greater masses of our people the opportunity to acquire this most modern means of transport."[18]

Eventually the Nazi stress on preparation for war meant harder work, a decline in both the quantity and quality of consumer goods, and the loss of freedom of movement for German workers. But because of the need to win and hold the loyalty of labor, the hierarchy imposed these restrictions and hardships only belatedly and with great reluctance. If the question is: "Did the Nazi system give workers more power?" the answer is that it did not. But that question, albeit important, has little to do with the economic position of workers or with the effectiveness of the Nazi system in ending the depression.

New Deal and Nazi methods of dealing with the agricultural depression also had much in commmon. Both sought to organize commercial agriculture in order to increase farm income. The New Deal Agricultural Adjustment Act set up supposedly democratic county committees to control production. In Germany the centralized Estate for Agriculture (*Reichnäherstand*) did the job. The purpose was to raise agricultural prices and thus farm income through a system of subsidies, paid for in each instance by processing taxes that fell ultimately on consumers. Both governments also made agricultural credit cheaper and more readily available, and they protected farmers against the loss of their land through foreclosures.

These similarities are not remarkable. I have already shown how, under the impact of the depression, farmers everywhere, large and small alike, were expressing the same resentments and demands and how these affected governments in related ways. What *is* remarkable, given the profound differences between American and German agriculture, is the attitude of the two governments toward the place of farmers in society.

Both Roosevelt and Hitler tended to idealize rural life and the virtues of an agricultural existence. Each hoped to check the trend of population to the cities and to disperse urban-centered industries. Roosevelt spoke feelingly of the virtues of close contact with nature and of the "restful privilege of getting away from pavements and from noise." Only in the country, he claimed, did a family have a decent chance "to establish a real home in the traditional American sense." Roosevelt did not deny the attractions of city life. He reasoned that electricity, the automobile, and other modern conveniences made it possible for rural people to enjoy these attractions without abandoning their farms.

While governor of New York, Roosevelt set up a program for subsidizing the settlement of unemployed city families on farms so that "they may secure through the good earth the permanent jobs they have lost in overcrowded industrial cities and towns." "Is it worthwhile," he asked in a radio address late in 1931, "for us to make a definite effort to get people in large numbers to move out of cities . . . ? It seems to me that to that question we must answer an emphatic YES."[19]

Because they were property owners, had large families, and were, in general, good Nazis, Hitler called the German peasants "the foundation and life source" of the state, "the counterbalance to communist madness," and "the source of national fertility." The superiority of rural over urban life was a Nazi dogma—especially the life of the self-sufficient small farmer, free from the dependency and corruption of a market economy. "The fact that a people is in a position to nourish itself from its own land and through that to lead its own life independent of foreign nations has always in history been significant," a Nazi agricultural expert wrote in 1935. To make sure that the peasants remained as they were, a law of 1933 (the *Erbhofgesetz*) forbade the sale or mortgaging of farms of a size "necessary to support a family . . . independent of the market and the general economic situtation." About a third of the farms in

Germany were thus entailed. As the historian J. E. Farquharson notes, this law, along with Nazi agricultural price supports, made the possessor of an Erbhof a member of "a privileged class, sheltered from all the worst effects of free market forces."[20]

Nazi leaders described Berlin as a den of iniquity and deplored the influx of Germans from the east into the capital. Nazi housing policy sought to stimulate suburban development in order to bring industrial workers closer to the land and to reduce urban crowding. They placed all construction under government control and made funds available for low-interest, state-guaranteed mortgage loans.

The New Deal Tennessee Valley Authority and the rural electrification program made important progress toward improving farm life, but efforts to reverse the population trend in the United States yielded limited results. Despite Roosevelt's dreams of decentralizing industry and relocating millions of city dwellers on farms, during the whole of the New Deal, his Resettlement Administration placed fewer than 11,000 families on the land. The Resettlement Administration had a Greenbelt Town program for planned suburban development. It produced minuscule results—only three of the 60 originally planned greenbelt towns were built.

Nazi rural resettlement efforts proved equally disappointing. Between 1933 and 1938, the Nazis resettled about 20,000 families, but this was barely more than half the number that the Weimar government had managed to relocate between 1927 and 1932. In both the German and American cases, efforts to check the movement of people to the cities foundered on the opposition of real estate and construction interests. The unwillingness of the politicians to allocate sufficient funds to enable much progress to be made was another reason for the failure of rural resettlement, and so were the frequently conflicting objectives of government policy makers. In Germany, for example, the new factories constructed under the Four-Year Plan pulled labor *into* the cities.

There were significant differences between the objectives of American and National Socialist agricultural policies: the former, plagued by surpluses, sought to limit output; the latter, seeking to become self-sufficient, sought to increase it. All in all, the New Deal was the more successful in solving farm problems; far less was accomplished in Germany toward modernizing and mechanizing agriculture during the thirties. On the other hand, Nazi efforts on behalf of farm laborers were more effective than those of the New Deal. As is well known, the AAA programs actually hurt many American agricultural laborers and also tenants and sharecroppers. In both nations, agricultural relief brought far more benefits to large land owners than to small.

Where trade and finance were concerned, both Germany and the United States adopted policies of economic nationalism, seeking to improve the competitive position of their export industries. Both paid most of the costs of their recovery by deficit financing but ignored the newly developing Keynesian economics and remained inordinately fearful of inflation.

Most Nazi and New Deal economic policies were narrowly nationalistic. In this respect, they were not essentially different from those of other industrial nations. They adopted them sooner, however, and pursued them more vigorously than, for example, the British or the French. The best-known American example occurred when Roosevelt decided against seeking an international agreement on the stabilization of foreign exchange rates at the London Economic Conference in 1933. The British and French were bitterly disappointed. They said that Roosevelt had "torpedoed" the conference. But the Germans were delighted. Roosevelt had announced in his "bombshell message" that "the sound internal economic situation of a nation is a greater factor in its well-being than the price of its currency." That principle was Nazi orthodoxy. In a radio message beamed to the United States at the time, the German foreign minister, Konstantin von Neurath, praised Roosevelt's "fearlessness" and spoke of the "heroic efforts of the American people . . . to overcome the crisis and win a new prosperity." Reichbank president Hjalmar Schacht told a *Völkischer Beobachter* reporter that FDR had adopted the philosophy of Hitler and Mussolini: "Take your economic fate in your own hand and you will help not only yourself but the whole world."[21]

A chronic shortage of hard currency and the equally chronic

German fear of inflation, which caused the government to overvalue the mark, made economic nationalism a political necessity for the Nazis rather than a choice. Trade treaties with Hungary, Yugoslavia, and Rumania in 1934 and 1935 provided for bartering German manufactures for grain and other food products (and in the Rumanian case, oil) without recourse to hard currencies. These treaties resulted in a modest increase in German commerce with Eastern Europe.

By 1935 the decline of unemployment and the revival of the economy caused German food consumption to rise rapidly. The Germans' hope of achieving agricultural self-sufficiency evaporated. Fearful of a possible domestic crisis should a food shortage develop, Hitler expanded the barter system. His Four-Year Plan in 1936 involved exchanging German manufactures, especially arms, for large amounts of grain and other food products from Eastern Europe.[22]

In the early months of the New Deal, Roosevelt toyed with the idea of stimulating exports by means of similar barter agreements. A mighty behind-the-scenes battle was fought within the Roosevelt administration in 1933 and 1934 between supporters of this approach and those who believed in lowering tariff barriers by making reciprocal trade agreements. The president—after one of his typical attempts to get the protagonists to reconcile the irreconcilable—finally sided with the low-tariff faction. He nevertheless continued for some time to flirt with the idea of bilateral agreements. He was really tempted by one suggested by the German economic czar, Hjalmar Schacht, involving 800,000 bales of American cotton.

The rejection of this and similar proposals resulted more from Roosevelt's growing political and moral distaste for Hitlerism than from economic considerations. But despite Roosevelt's antifascism and the internationalist, free-trade rhetoric of the reciprocal trade program, New Deal foreign policy was as concerned with advancing national economic interests as was German policy. State Department alarm at Nazi "penetration" of Latin America, publicly expressed in strategic and moral terms, had a solid base in lost and threatened markets for American exports resulting from Nazi barter agreements with Argentina and other nations in the Western Hemisphere that were short on foreign exchange.

There is still another way in which New Deal and Nazi practices were similar, and different in degree from those of other industrial nations. This was in the way the two governments tried to influence public opinion. The Nazi use of parades, banners, rallies, and of every instrument of propaganda are well known. During the New Deal, the American government never went so far, but it did make efforts to sell its policies to the public that were unprecedented in peacetime. The NRA slogan "We Do Our Part" served the same function as the Nazis' incessantly repeated *Gemeinnutz geht vor Eigennutz* (the public interest before the individual's interest). With Roosevelt's approval, General Hugh Johnson, head of NRA and designer of its Blue Eagle symbol, organized a massive campaign to muster support for the NRA. Like the Nazi swastika in the Reich, the Blue Eagle was plastered everywhere—on billboards, in shop windows, even on cans of beans and applesauce. Johnson's office blanketed the land with posters, lapel buttons, and stickers. He dispatched volunteer speakers across the country and published *Helpful Hints* and *Pointed Paragraphs* to provide them with The Word.

This was the positive side of the NRA campaign. There was also a negative side. "Those who are not with us are against us," Johnson orated. "The way to show that you are part of this great army of the New Deal is to insist on this symbol of solidarity." He denounced opponents of NRA as "chiselers" and "slackers," thereby suggesting that disagreement was equivalent to criminality and cowardice. President Roosevelt himself, in a fireside chat, compared the Blue Eagle to a "bright badge" worn by soldiers in night attacks to help separate friend from foe.[23]

Placed beside the overpowering Nazi displays at Nuremburg, even the ten-hour, 250,000-person NRA parade up Fifth Avenue in September 1933 would not appear especially impressive. But it and other NRA hoopla were designed to serve the same functions: rousing patriotic feelings and creating in the public mind the impression of support for government policies so extensive as to make disagreement appear unpatriotic. As Johnson himself explained, the purpose was to "put the enforcement of this law into the hands of the *whole* people."[24]

Another example of New Deal propaganda is provided by the efforts of the Resettlement Administration and the Farm Security Administration. Pare Lorenz's documentary films, *The Plow That Broke the Plains* (1936) and *The River* (1938), and the still photographs of sharecroppers taken by Dorothea Lange, Walker Evans, Margaret Bourke-White, Gordon Parks, and others were aesthetic achievements of the highest order. They were also a form of official advertising designed to explain and defend the New Deal approach to rural social and economic problems. They differed from Leni Riefenstahl's *Triumph of the Will* (also a cinematic masterpiece) and the annual volumes of photographs celebrating National Socialism chiefly in style—"soft" rather than "hard" sell—and point of view.

New Deal efforts at mass persuasion reflect the attitude of Roosevelt's government—an attitude shared by Hitler's government—that the economic crisis justified the casting aside of precedent, the nationalistic mobilization of society, and the removal of traditional restraints on the functions of the state, as in war. The two regimes also agreed that the crisis called for personal leadership more forceful than that needed in normal times. That all these attitudes were typical of Hitler goes without saying, but Roosevelt held them too. When we think of Roosevelt's first inaugural nowadays, we tend to remember his fatherly reassurance, "the only thing we have to fear is fear itself." But he also said:

Our true destiny is not to be ministered unto but to minister to ourselves. . . . I assume unhesitatingly the leadership of this great army of our people. . . . In the event that the Congress shall fail . . . I shall ask the Congress for the one remaining instrument to meet the crisis—broad Executive power to wage a war against the emergency, as great as the power that would be given to me if we were in fact invaded by a foreign foe.

This last sentence evoked the loudest cheering that Roosevelt's speech produced. Eleanor Roosevelt found the response "a little terrifying." Commenting on it later, she said, "You felt that they would do *anything*—if only someone would tell them *what* to do."[25]

Roosevelt was neither a totalitarian nor a dictator, real or potential, but his tactics and his rhetoric made it possible for anti-New Dealers and outright fascists to claim that he was both. Many of the accusations of both conservatives and communists in the United States were politically motivated, as were, of course, Nazi comments on the president. But during the first years of the New Deal German newspapers praised him and the New Deal to the skies. Before Hitler came to power, he was contemptuous of the United States, which he considered an overly materialistic nation dominated by Jews, "millionaires, beauty queens, stupid [phonograph] records, and Hollywood."

Nevertheless, Hitler and the Nazi party hierarchy were impressed by Roosevelt's success during the Hundred Days in dominating Congress and pushing through the New Deal depression policies so swiftly. "Mr. Roosevelt . . . marches straight toward his objective over Congress, over lobbies, over stubborn bureaucracies," Hitler told Anne O'Hare McCormick of the *New York Times* in July 1933. The *Völkischer Beobachter* announced smugly that Roosevelt's leadership proved that representative government, which the paper described as "government without a head," had "outlived its usefulness generally, not only in Germany." By July 1934, that newspaper was describing Roosevelt as "absolute lord and master" of the nation, his position "not entirely dissimilar" to a dictator's. Roosevelt's collected speeches, *Looking Forward* (1933) and *On Our Way* (1934) were translated into German and enthusiastically reviewed, the critics being quick to draw attention to parallels in New Deal and National Socialist experiences.[26]

A friendly German biography, *Roosevelt: A Revolutionary with Common Sense*, by Helmut Magers, appeared in 1934. Magers described the New Deal as "an authoritarian revolution," a revolution "from above," and pointed out what he called the "surprising similarities" it bore to the Nazi revolution. That there appeared to be some basis for this view at the time is suggested by the fact that the American ambassador to Germany, William E. Dodd, wrote a foreword to Magers's book in which he praised the author's "outstanding success" in describing both conditions in the United States and the nation's "unique leader." Dodd also mentioned what he called the "heroic efforts being made in Germany and the United States to solve the basic problem of social balance."

Dodd was vehemently anti-Nazi, but like many other well-meaning people, he hoped that German moderates would be able to overthrow Hitler or at least restrain him. He considered the Magers volume an "excellent, friendly, unpartisan book . . . without a sentence that could have been quoted to our disadvantage" and allowed his foreword to be published despite State Department objections.[27]

For their part, the Germans went out of their way to welcome Dodd as ambassador. A throng of reporters and Foreign Office officials greeted him when he arrived in Berlin. He was put up in the six-room royal suite of the Esplanade Hotel and charged only ten dollars a day. He was invited to lecture at the University of Munich. Hitler assured him that Germany had no warlike intentions. When he criticized authoritarian rule and economic nationalism in a speech, the German press reported his remarks accurately.

At the end of Roosevelt's first year in office, Hitler sent him a private message through diplomatic channels offering sincere congratulations for "his heroic efforts in the interests of the American people. The President's successful battle against economic distress is being followed by the entire German people with interest and admiration," Hitler claimed. In November 1934, the *Völkischer Beobachter* characterized Democratic gains in the Congressional elections as an "exceptionally personal success" for Roosevelt. The tone of this article was almost worshipful, the rhetoric hyperbolic. The president was a man of "irreproachable, extremely responsible character and immovable will." He had shown himself to be not only an energetic politician but a "warmhearted leader of the people with a profound understanding of social needs."[28]

This friendly attitude ended in 1936, although even after Roosevelt made his famous speech denouncing the dictators and calling for a "quarantine" of Germany and Italy, the Nazi propaganda machine refrained for tactical reasons from attacking him personally. It is clear, however, that New Deal depression policies seemed to the Nazis essentially like their own and the role of Roosevelt not very different from the Führer's.

So far as the Great Depression is concerned, Roosevelt and Hitler, the one essentially benign, the other malevolent, justified far-reaching constitutional changes as being necessary for the improvement of economic conditions in a grave emergency. But they used change also as a device for mobilizing the psychic energies of the people. Both their administrations were plagued by infighting and confusion, partly because of genuine conflicts of interest and philosophy within the two diverse societies and partly because of ignorance. No one really knew how to end the depression or even how best to serve the different interests that the governments presumed to represent. Time after time, major American and German policies produced results neither anticipated nor desired. Some of them were directly contrary to the leaders' intentions—the effect of New Deal farm policy on sharecroppers and of its public housing policy on racial segregation, and that of Nazi rearmament on urban concentration, for example.

Hitler papered over confusion, doubts, and rivalries with the *Führerprinzip*, command from above, unquestioning obedience to one's leader, who was presumed to know what was best. Roosevelt, on the other hand, made a virtue of flexibility and experimentation. Both, however, masterfully disguised the inadequacies and internal disagreements in their entourages and to a remarkable extent succeeded in convincing ordinary citizens of their own personal wisdom and dedication.

The differences in the degree and intensity with which psychological pressures were applied by Nazis and New Dealers were so great as to become differences in kind. Nevertheless, the two movements reacted to the depression in similar ways, distinct from those of other industrial nations. Of the two, the Nazis were the more successful in curing the economic ills of the 1930s. They reduced unemployment and stimulated industrial production faster than the Americans did. Considering their resources, they handled their monetary and trade problems more successfully, certainly more imaginatively. By 1936 the depression was substantially over in Germany but far from finished in the United States.

This was partly because the Nazis employed deficit financing on a larger scale. Between 1933 and 1939 the German national debt nearly quadrupled, the American rose by less than 50 percent. It was also partly because the Nazi totalitarian system better lent itself to the mobilization of society, both by force and by persuasion. There was no German parallel to the combination of timorousness and stubborn resistance to change characteristic of American business interests. Unlike the New Dealers, the economist H. W. Arndt wrote while Hitler was still in power,

> the Nazi Government . . . was not hampered in its expansionist policy by 'low business confidence'. . . . German business which, rightly or wrongly, had thought itself threatened by imminent social revolution, breathed again under a government which . . . appeared as the saviour and benefactor of private property. . . . During the later years of the Nazi régime when profit expectations of a good many business men must have been low, State control of investment insured that private investment absorbed what factors of production and savings were not required by the demands of the State.[29]

Yet neither regime solved the problem of maintaining prosperity without war. The German leaders wanted war and used the economy to make war possible. One result was "prosperity": full employment, increased output, hectic economic expansion. The

Americans lacked this motivation. But when war was forced upon them, they took the same approach and achieved the same result.

A NOTE ON AMERICAN FASCISM

By emphasizing the similarities of American and German reactions to the Great Depression, I have perhaps created the impression that there was a large fascist element in the New Deal. This was certainly not so, but it raises the question of how various American groups responded to fascist movements in the thirties.

Most American conservatives thought of themselves as laissez-faire individualists. They found totalitarian movements distasteful because the totalitarian glorification of the state justified placing restrictions on their freedom to run their businesses as they saw fit. They disliked the New Deal because of the expansion of the scope of the federal government that it brought about, and they tended when roused to call Roosevelt either a fascist or a communist. In each case, of course, they used the term as a pejorative.

At first American communists confined themselves to denouncing Roosevelt as a tool of Wall Street and the New Deal as a "desperate mobilization . . . to save finance capital." But in the autumn of 1933, in response to criticism by the Comintern, the Communist Party began to describe the New Deal as fascistic. "All roads of the New Deal lead to fascism and to war!" the *Daily Worker* claimed repeatedly. The superficial resemblance of NRA and New Deal unemployment relief programs to Italian and German policies provided the communists with ammunition for these attacks.

However, after the Supreme Court declared the NRA unconstitutional, the communists changed their tune. By the time of the 1936 presidential election the growing tendency of business leaders to criticize New Deal policies, and Roosevelt's increasingly harsh denunciations of Nazi and Italian aggression, had, along with a new Soviet policy of seeking to make a "popular front" with the western powers to resist the fascist threat, had put an end to the communists' association of the New Deal with fascism.

There was a small native fascist movement in the United States

209

and a number of nondescript fascist organizations emerged during the depression. They bore names such as Khaki Shirts and American Vigilantes. Without exception, these groups were anti-New Deal and anti-Roosevelt. All were controlled, in the words of the historian Arthur M. Schlesinger, Jr., by "two-bit demagogues, part racketeers, part prophets, [who] preyed on simpletons and deadbeats."

A few American intellectuals found fascist ideas appealing. The poet Ezra Pound was probably the most notorious of these. The architect Philip Johnson was another prominent American who was attracted by fascist ideas. But none of the American fascist intellectuals had political influence or even political pretensions.

One such person, Lawrence Dennis, a former diplomat and banker who had become critical of the American financial establishment and who admired Hitler, published *Is Capitalism Doomed?* in 1932. Four years later, in *The Coming American Fascism*, he argued that the continuing depression was proof that just as feudalism had given way to capitalism, now capitalism was also finished. The choice was between communism, fascism, and anarchy. Communism, Dennis wrote, involved class conflict, whereas "the driving force of a consciousness of group solidarity and common group objectives is needed to run the social machinery. . . . This force fascism develops by intensifying the national spirit and putting it behind the enterprises of public welfare and social control."

Dennis claimed that the United States was ideally suited for a fascist system. He would nationalize the banks, increase government spending in order to get rid of unemployment, and set up government-controlled industrial monopolies modeled on Italian and Nazi corporate organizations. He would also encourage employed women to get out of the work force. "If a woman is looking for the best chances of finding wealth and power . . . or simply personal happiness," he wrote, "marriage is her best bet."[30]

Dennis greatly admired Huey Long. He realized that Long was not a fascist but considered him "the nearest approach to a national fascist leader" America had yet produced. "I have no ambitions," Dennis said. "It takes a man like Long to lead the masses."

After Long was assassinated, Dennis had great difficulty thinking of anyone to replace him as the future fascist dictator of America.[31]

Although some Americans found good things to say about Italian fascism, few persons of influence or stature had much respect for Hitler, at least not after the character of his regime began to be understood. The newspaper tycoon William Randolph Hearst was for a time impressed by the Nazi movement. In 1934 he went to Germany and had an interview with Hitler. If he had ever been forced to choose between fascism and communism, he would not have hesitated for a moment. But Hearst objected bitterly to NRA because he thought it violated the rights of businessmen such as himself. He would have objected even more vehemently to the kind of controls the Nazis placed on business. In this respect, he was surely typical of most conservatives in the United States.

CHAPTER IX

BRITISH AND FRENCH
POLICIES

A lthough it would be incorrect to say that the course of the
Great Depression in Great Britain and France or, for that
matter, in other parts of the world, would have been basically
different if the New Deal and the Nazi revolution had not occurred,
the events that took place in the United States and Germany beginning in 1933 had a great deal of influence on the policies of other
nations.

At the start, the New Deal "experiment" attracted a considerable amount of attention in Great Britain. That old liberal war-
horse, David Lloyd George, listened to Roosevelt's inaugural via
short-wave radio with a group of friends. According to one of the
group, he was "terrifically excited" by it. The address was "most
remarkable," Lloyd George said, the kind of speech politicians make
before an election, not after taking office. Early in 1934, John
Maynard Keynes described Roosevelt as "the trustee of those in
every country who seek to mend the evils of our condition by reasoned experiment within the frame-work of the existing social
system. If he fails, rational change will be gravely prejudiced

throughout the world, leaving orthodoxy and revolution to fight it out." Later that year, Winston Churchill compared the president to "an explorer who has embarked on a voyage as uncertain as that of Columbus, and upon a quest which might conceivably be as important as the discovery of the New World." In 1934 John Strachey described the New Deal as a "decisive attempt to reform and reconstruct the Capitalist system." He believed it so important that he issued a revised edition of *The Coming Struggle for Power* with an additional chapter on "the striking events which have taken place in America."[1]

Strachey, as might be expected, concluded that the New Deal was doomed to failure. With the passage of time most other British observers took a less apocalyptic view, but the most common conclusion was that Great Britain had little to learn from American depression policies. In 1936 the editors of *The Economist* published a detailed appraisal of the achievements of Roosevelt's first term. They admitted that a "gigantic experiment" had taken place. Compared to what had been accomplished in other countries, the New Deal "comes out well," they reported. But the best they could say for Franklin Roosevelt was that he asked the right questions. More often than not, in their opinion, he had supplied the wrong answers to these questions.

As for specifics, although New Deal make-work programs displayed an "admirable elasticity" and a "worthy humanitarian impulse," they were wasteful and inefficient. No doubt influenced by the fact that the British had not instituted any extensive work-relief programs, they concluded that "only a rich country . . . can afford to deal with its unemployment in this expensive, unremunerative way." The New Deal had done little about improving the housing of the poor and less than nothing for sharecroppers and other impoverished farm workers, they claimed. The NRA was "more of a muddle than a policy"; the law contained "more divergent economic and social theories [in] a single enactment than any other piece of legislation ever known." All in all, the editors concluded, "the bold improvisation of 1933 has become rudderless instability."[2]

The Economist's lack of enthusiasm for the New Deal and for

President Roosevelt was similar to the attitude of many liberal Americans in 1936. It was also influenced, however, by the fact that much of what the New Deal had accomplished did not seem particularly unusual to the average Briton. After Great Britain abandoned the gold standard in 1931, the economy began to pick up. Low interest rates contributed to a housing boom of major proportions. During the thirties, 2.7 million units were constructed, nearly double the number built in the previous decade. Industrial output, led by chemicals, automobiles, and other "new" products, was 46 percent higher in 1937 than it had been in 1932 and nearly 25 percent higher than in 1929. Steel production had more than doubled from its low point in 1931, and unemployment, which had peaked in 1933 at about 3 million, was down to 1.6 million in 1937.

During these years, Parliament had been almost as active as the American Congress in passing laws aimed at reviving the economy. Besides helping British farmers in ways already mentioned, it had adopted tactics designed to stimulate industrial recovery that were strikingly similar to those of the NRA. The Coal Mines Act of 1930 allowed coal operators to limit and allocate output, fix prices, and amalgamate companies. The government encouraged cotton textile manufacturers to scrap obsolete machinery, and the steel industry to form a cartel, the British Iron and Steel Federation. The Central Electricity Board helped utility companies to consolidate their activities in the interest of efficiency. The automobile industry received subsidies, and the North Atlantic Shipping Act of 1934 made possible, among other things, the completion of the liner *Queen Mary*, which the Cunard company had mothballed, half-built, for lack of funds. In addition, the merger of the Cunard and White Star lines was facilitated. These measures probably had no more direct effect on the recovery than the related American policies, but they help to explain British attitudes toward the New Deal.

The British government had also done a great deal to improve the lot of the poor and the unemployed during this period—so much, indeed, that an authority on the subject, Bentley B. Gilbert, writes in his study of *British Social Policy, 1914–1939* that by 1939 "the

216

British State had committed itself to the maintenance of all its citizens according to need as a matter of right."

The Unemployment Act of 1934 put the insurance system on a sounder financial basis and created an Unemployment Assistance Board, freed from political pressures and financed by general taxation. The change did away with the demeaning aspects of the dole and still gave support to persons not covered by national insurance. Two years later, agricultural laborers were brought into the insurance system, something the New Deal never did. Other laws provided aid to persons moving from the north and west, where jobs were scarce, to the more prosperous southeastern part of the country. At the same time, manufacturers willing to build factories in the depressed areas were given government subsidies.

Recovery was thus accompanied by considerable social reform. Economists estimate that by 1937 the combination of a progressive tax structure and extended social services was transferring 5 or 6 percent of the national income from rich to poor. This transfer raised the real income of the working classes by more than 10 percent between 1929 and 1938. By way of contrast, New Deal legislation, including the so-called Wealth Tax Act of 1936, had almost no effect on the distribution of wealth in the United States.

Yet despite this excellent record, most people in Great Britain apparently had no sense of living in a new era. The social reforms, Bentley Gilbert remarks, were conceived and put into effect "in a fit of absence of mind."[3] It seems clear (although such things are difficult to measure) that the national mood remained depressed, despite economic recovery. No political leader was able to generate a sense of common involvement in an organized struggle to overcome the depression. When Lloyd George announced a plan for a "New Deal for Britain" in 1935—a plan that was little more than a rehash of proposals he had made repeatedly in the 1920s—Prime Minister MacDonald's cabinet was thrown almost into a panic. MacDonald gave serious consideration to inviting both Lloyd George and Winston Churchill to join the government. But in the end, the cabinet did not act. Chancellor of the Exchequer Neville Chamberlain wrote in his diary at this time, "The P[rime] M[inister] is ill and tired, S[tanley] B[aldwin] is tired and won't apply his mind to problems." When Chamberlain wrote this, Baldwin was about to become prime minister! Contrast this state of mind with the mood in government circles in Washington and Berlin in 1935.

"It is certainly time there was a change," Chamberlain also wrote, having himself in mind as the person to make it. But under Baldwin, and under Chamberlain himself, who replaced Baldwin as prime minister in 1937, the national mood remained lethargic. Chamberlain was a conservative of the finest type, a man whose reputation has been unfortunately distorted by his connection with the appeasement of Hitler. He was hard working and public spirited; no one in Great Britain contributed more to social reform in the interwar period than he. But by this time, Chamberlain was also aging and ailing—unable to inspire public enthusiasm. As he said of himself, he could not "unbutton."

Thus the 1930s passed into memory in Great Britain as a time of inactivity and decline—the Great Slump. "The man in the street's view of Britain's economic experience . . . is that activity was stagnant and very depressed," the economic historian Harry W. Richardson writes—this even though "any glance at the evidence shows it to be a misconception."[4]

This state of affairs helps explain why the Nazi example, or at least the general European fascist example, had a considerable influence in Britain despite the recovery, the deep commitment of the country to democracy, and the serious and immediate threat to British security that the Nazis posed.

The key figure in the history of British fascism was Sir Oswald Mosley, one of the most fascinating figures of the depression decade. Mosley came from a wealthy upper-class family. His grandfather was said to be the original of the cartoon character, John Bull. After serving in the Great War as a pilot, he was elected to the House of Commons as a Conservative. By 1924, however, he had shifted to the Labour Party.

In Parliament Mosley devoted most of his attention to the unemployment problem. He advocated higher wages, more government spending on such things as slum clearance, and, in general, the idea of a planned economy.

Although he was at this time a close friend and political associate of John Strachey, the future author of *The Coming Struggle for Power*, Mosley was too fervent a nationalist to embrace communism. He favored protective tariffs, for example, and in his speeches made frequent use of the term "socialist imperialism." When the Labour Party came to power in 1929, Ramsay MacDonald gave him a cabinet post. Although still in his early thirties, he was widely perceived of as a future prime minister.

Mosley soon became exasperated by the MacDonald government's unimaginative, financially conservative approach to the depression, which he described accurately enough as the "economics of the last century." He favored a large public works program to deal with the jobless problem, and concentration on the home market rather than on exporting as a way of stimulating industrial recovery. "This nation must to some extent be insulated from the electric shocks of present world conditions," he said. Instead of trying to sell steel in Iraq and Argentina, it should put people to work building roads in Great Britain itself. Mosley urged the government to keep children in school for an additional year and grant pensions to older workers to get them out of the labor market. He claimed that all told, his proposals would create jobs for 700,000 people.[5]

When the cabinet rejected his plan in May 1930, Mosley resigned. He appealed over the government's head to the House of Commons but got nowhere. Then in 1931, he formed what he called the New Party in an effort to rally members of varying viewpoints who were dissatisfied with the status quo. The New Party offered only a vague program involving the corporatist principle of cooperation between the classes. Britain should become "a society working with the precision and harmony of a human body. . . . Every individual [should be] subordinate to the overriding purpose of the nation."

Mosley's biographer, Robert Skidelsky, has suggested that if Mosley had still been a member of the Conservative Party in 1930, he would have moved to the left when his proposals were rejected. Beginning from a socialist position, he moved to the right. "The fact that the party of radical transformation had itself been helpless before the crisis . . . launched him on his perilous journey towards fascism."[6]

In the 1931 general election, Mosley, along with John Strachey and all the other New Party candidates for the House of Commons, was defeated. This was the crucial turning point in his career. Early in 1932, he went to Italy "to study fascism at first hand." From Italy he traveled to Munich, where he met with high Nazi officials. Upon his return to England, he began to contact the leaders of fringe fascist organizations, most of them, in the words of one historian of British fascism, reactionaries who "had never adjusted themselves to the death of Queen Victoria."[7] The outcome of all this was the creation of the British Union of Fascists, headed by Mosley.

Like most other fascist groups, Mosley's uniformed Black Shirts were anti-Semitic, violence prone, and intolerant of anyone who disagreed with them. The party's economic program was modeled on Hitler's—a corporate industrial and agricultural structure, public works to reduce unemployment, labor camps for youth, and national, or in Britain's case, imperial self-sufficiency.

Mosley's Union of Fascists attracted a large following, and its parades and mass meetings often ended in street riots. Finally, in 1937, the government cracked down. It banned the wearing of uniforms and used large numbers of police to maintain order at fascist meetings. The threat of war with Germany acted as a severe check on the movement's growth, and the war itself ended it. But it is an open question what would have happened if Hitler had found some way to attack the Soviet Union in 1939 without attacking Poland, a nation the British were committed by treaty to defend.

The reaction of the French to the New Deal and to Nazi policies was both similar to and different from the British reaction. Fascist movements in France antedated those in Germany and Italy. But French fascists, being intensely nationalistic, were anti-German and thus anti-Nazi. And whereas Mosley and his followers had no trouble accepting the Nazis' vicious racial policies, French fascists, while not troubled by Hitler's anti-Semitism, found his nonsense about Aryan superiority difficult to swallow, because of their own "Latin" origins.

On the other hand, fascism appealed to a considerable number of conservative French intellectuals. The popularity of corporatism in France made the economic policies of the Italian and German governments attractive to business interests. The low opinion of representative democracy that many French people had developed because of the ineffectuality of the governments of the period was another reason why fascism found many converts among "respectable" elements in the country.

France and the United States had long been what were called "traditional" allies. However, from the end of the Great War until the time that Roosevelt became president, the French had found much about America to criticize. The failure of the United States to join the League of Nations and the retreat of the nation to isolationism in the 1920s annoyed and alarmed the security-minded French. American insistence on the full payment of the Allied war debts was an additional source of resentment. When the depression struck, most French economists put the blame on the Wall Street stock market crash. Then came the Hoover moratorium, which angered nearly all French commentators. Although they were happy to accept this respite from paying their own obligations, the idea that Germany would not be paying reparations appalled them.

During the early stages of the depression, just about the only aspect of American policy that the French liked was the maintenance by the United States of the gold standard. While many French people, like other Europeans, were deeply influenced by American movies, music, and other aspects of popular culture and were fascinated by American technology and business efficiency, they tended to complain that American materialism was contemptible and a threat to French values. Georges Duhamel's diatribe on the subject, *Scènes de la vie future*, was a big success in France.[8]

Yet most people in France seem to have been pleased by Roosevelt's victory in the 1932 presidential election. He was seen as a Wilsonian internationalist. (After all, he had been Assistant Secretary of the Navy in Wilson's cabinet and had campaigned for the League of Nations while going down to defeat as the Democratic vice-presidential candidate in 1920).

The swift unfolding of Roosevelt's New Deal, however, startled French observers. Opinions varied, but that the changes were revolutionary was a common reaction. Conservative press opinion during and after the Hundred Days was uniformly negative. The New Deal seemed a "dangerous experiment in state socialism," almost as threatening to the capitalist world as what was going on in the Soviet Union. Like the Germans, the French thought the early New Deal resembled the Nazi "revolution"; one conservative paper claimed that the difference between Roosevelt and Hitler was "the form [rather] than the heart of the matter." Roosevelt's inflationary policies and the NRA code system seemed particularly dangerous.

French socialists did express some interest in New Deal public works pump-priming, and in the minimum-wage rules embodied in the NRA codes. The communists, on the other hand, labeled the New Deal approach fascism. When Roosevelt took the United States off the gold standard and caused the collapse of the London Economic Conference, the response in France was almost universally negative. One journal compared American policy to trying to cool off on a hot day by changing the calibration on one's thermometer.[9]

This was a low point in the history of French opinion of Roosevelt and the New Deal; thereafter more friendly attitudes prevailed. The American reciprocal trade program seemed a step in the direction of internationalism. When the National Industrial Recovery Act was declared unconstitutional in 1935, that source of dislike was removed. As time passed, it became clear to all but the most obtuse that Roosevelt was *not* like Hitler, that he was not a dictator and did not wish to become one. "He is perfectly conscious of the immense responsibility that weighs on his shoulders," one French correspondent wrote, "but this does not incite him to adopt the attitude of a Hamlet or a Napoleon. He does not believe that fate has assigned him the task of saving his country."

Strangely enough, the so-called Second New Deal, which to Americans seemed a shift to the left, was generally praised in France, even by conservatives. The Wagner Labor Relations Act and the Social Security Act were, according to one French editorialist, "negative interventions in the economy rather than the measures of an economic police" such as NRA and AAA.[10]

When Roosevelt was overwhelmingly reelected in 1936, the whole spectrum of French political opinion expressed approval. Now the conservatives decided that he was a great leader, the person who had rallied diverse interests behind a common national purpose, something France badly needed. French socialists, and in particular their leader, Léon Blum, admired Roosevelt's policies, especially the idea that the way to turn the economy around was to increase the purchasing power of consumers. Even the communists saw FDR as preferable to Alfred M. Landon, his Republican opponent, whom they considered quite unfairly to be the very embodiment of capitalism—a tool of Wall Street and the munitions industry.

The full impact of the New Deal on France, however, came in 1934, when the Communists and Socialists formed a coalition and agreed to cooperate with centrist parties in an effort to check the growing threat of fascism in France. The idea was to create a Popular Front, to make, as Maurice Thorez, leader of the French Communists, said, "a contract between the working class and the middle class."[11] In the summer of 1934, the depression was approaching its nadir in France. Farm prices were collapsing, and industrial output was down sharply. Unemployment was rising, and wages, although on the average lower than wages in other industrial nations, were falling still lower.

Faced with this crisis, a succession of governments failed to make even an attempt to develop new ideas. In February 1935, for example, Premier Pierre-Etienne Flandin told the National Assembly that direct relief payments to the unemployed would be impractical because unemployment was so large that the payments would unbalance the budget. As for a public works program on the American model, that would be impractical. To begin with, France lacked the resources, and the country was too deeply in debt to borrow for such a purpose. Besides, Flandin added (he was apparently addicted to overkill), France did not need more public works.

In other words, while Flandin recognized the seriousness of the problem and professed to be agonizing over it endlessly, he had nothing to suggest about how to deal with it.[12]

By the summer of 1935, the center-left coalition was complete. Communists, Socialists, and the Radical Party of Edouard Daladier formed the *Rassemblement Populaire*, a step confirmed by an enormous parade and demonstration in the working-class section of Paris.

During the French election campaign in the spring of 1936, Popular Front orators denounced the 200 Families and the fascists and demanded a long list of economic reforms. Léon Blum hit hard at the deflationary policies of past governments and promised measures that would "breathe life again into the economic organism." The election produced a resounding victory for the Popular Front. The coalition won a majority of the seats in the National Assembly. Blum became premier.

The Popular Front program had many elements that resembled important New Deal policies. These included guarantees to labor such as old-age and unemployment insurance, enforcement of the right of workers to organize and bargain collectively, and a 40-hour work week. Blum also promised a public works program to stimulate the economy and create jobs, an end to deflationary financial policies, greater government control of the banking system, and agricultural price supports.

From the start of his tenure as premier, Blum set out consciously to imitate Roosevelt's approach. "What inspires me at the present moment is the example of Roosevelt," he told a prominent French labor leader, "especially his boldness, which has enabled him to change his methods when he realizes that they are not working out as planned."[13] That autumn, when news of Roosevelt's landslide reelection reached Paris, Blum went personally to the American embassy to congratulate Ambassador William C. Bullitt —an unprecedented action for a premier. Casting aside hat and coat, he bounded up the stairs to where Bullitt was standing and kissed him vigorously on both cheeks. It was "as genuine an outpouring of enthusiasm as I have ever heard," Bullitt reported to the president. By 1937 it was possible for an observer to write an article about the Blum government entitled "A New Deal in France."[14]

Blum's Popular Front victory was greeted with an outpouring of popular support, and the government responded with a burst of legislation even more remarkable than that which had occurred in the United States during the Hundred Days. The explosion was sparked by a spontaneously generated wave of sit-down strikes that brought the economy to a standstill and so alarmed the leaders of French industry that they abandoned all resistance to reform.

The first occupation of a factory, triggered when two workers were discharged for not coming to work on May Day, the Socialist Labor Day, took place in the channel port of Le Havre. It attracted little notice, even though the company promptly agreed to rehire the workers. Two days later, a similar strike occurred far to the south in Toulouse. Soon came the first occupations of Paris factories. Then, overnight it seemed, the sit-down movement swept the country.

Neither the socialists nor the communists nor the trade unions had anything to do with organizing most of the strikes. Workers who had never been unionized or displayed the slightest signs of militancy—even the young women sales clerks in the big Paris department stores—sat down in their work places and refused to leave until their demands were met. The excitement was so great that workers often took over the plants before they had decided exactly what to demand of their employers as the price of returning to work.

By early June, nearly a million workers were occupying their plants. Even members of the conservative Catholic union, which had held aloof from the Socialists and Communists when the Popular Front was formed, joined in large numbers.

This enormous, obviously heartfelt outpouring of worker dissatisfaction took place in an atmosphere of celebration rather than resentment. In many places, a carnival atmosphere prevailed. The workers sang and danced to pass the time; friends and relatives stopped by with supplies of food and drink. There was remarkably little violence and almost no damage to property. The workers at

225

the Galeries Lafayette department store in Paris slept on the floors rather than make use of the beds in the store's large furniture department. They felt it would be wrong even to sit on chairs that did not belong to them.

Blum took office in the midst of this eruption. It was obvious that the Popular Front victory and the expectations it had aroused had much to do with the strikes. Blum went on the radio even before he was sworn in as premier and promised to "act with decision and rapidity" in order to obtain "the principal reforms demanded by the working class." These he defined as the 40-hour week, paid vacations, and the right of collective bargaining. He appealed for calm, but he did not ask the strikers to leave the factories.[15]

Once formally installed, Blum made good on his promises. He admitted that the sit-down strikes were technically illegal. But he justified not using force to eject the strikers on the ground that the occupations were understandable. With so many people unemployed, the workers were afraid that if they merely went out on strike in the conventional manner, employers would easily fill their places.

French employers were, as a class, terrified by the sit-down strikes. One observer later wrote that the employers "seemed to be living in an unreal atmosphere, not in a nightmare but in a dream, as in a Pirandello play." At the time, *nightmare* is the word most employers would surely have used. They were desperate to end the seizures, which they feared would lead either to destruction of their property or to a real revolution. As a result, they suggested a meeting with union representatives under government sponsorship.

Union, management, and government leaders met at Blum's office in the Matignon Palace on June 7. In one day, they reached an accord that revolutionized the working conditions of French labor. The employers agreed not to try to prevent workers from joining unions and to bargain collectively with them. They granted wage increases ranging from 7 to 15 percent. In return, the union leaders agreed to see that the workers ended the sit-down strikes.

This Matignon Accord was attacked from both the right and the left. The conservative *Le Temps* warned its readers that moderates who supported the Popular Front were *"dupes éternelles"* and that the left-center coalition was going to end with the creation of a "dictatorship of the proletariat." Leon Trotsky, announcing gleefully that "the French Revolution has begun," reflected the feeling of the extreme left that the accord did not go nearly far enough. Still worse, the accord did not bring an immediate end to the occupations. Many strikers refused to leave the factories and shops, fearing that the group of employers who had negotiated and signed the accord were not speaking for all French employers.

For a time the situation was almost completely out of hand—the number of strikers soared well beyond the million mark. But Blum quickly pushed bills through the National Assembly granting workers paid vacations and a 40-hour work week, and restoring pay cuts imposed on government employees by previous administrations. Union leaders, government officials, and prominent members of the Communist Party joined in urging the strikers to go back to work. The key plea was made by Maurice Thorez. This was not the time for revolution, the Communist Party leader told the strikers. By continuing the occupations, "we risk alienating sympathetic elements among the bourgeoisie and the peasants." Compromise is sometimes necessary, he added. "It is necessary to know how to end a strike when satisfaction has been obtained." This advice had its effect and the sit-down movement petered out.[16]

Blum was then able to carry forward the rest of his reform program. A three-year, 20-billion-franc public works program was begun. The Wheat Office was created. The government made money available for loans to small businesses. The power of the notorious 200 Families over the Bank of France was reduced, though not entirely eliminated. While restrictions on foreign workers were not ended, they were liberalized; local officials were told not to expel aliens who were "temporarily" unemployed, and foreigners were allowed to move from one *département* of France to another in search of jobs. All this was accomplished not in 100 days but in 70.

Working people and their friends rejoiced. Jean-Paul Sartre

had not even bothered to vote in the election. But after the occupation of the factories, he and his companion, Simone de Beauvoir, contributed generously when supporters went through the streets collecting money for the strikers. As Beauvoir wrote later (the expression is difficult to translate), the Matignon Accord "put our hearts en fête," in a holiday mood.[17]

Higher hourly wages produced an immediate if not necessarily permanent increase in workers' living standards. More significant in the long run was the agreement of the employers to bargain collectively, a change as important as that accomplished in the United States by the Wagner Act. Union membership in France jumped from 1 million to 5.3 million.

In a way, however, the new system of guaranteed paid vacations was the most significant of the gains achieved by the Popular Front legislation. It gave birth to the annual August migration of the French from the cities to the countryside. The government railroads sold cut-rate tickets and put on extra excursion trains. In the first year, 500,000 of the special tickets were sold. More than any single thing, annual vacations put an end to the provincialism that had been characteristic of the lives of most French working-class people. Investigators along the Riviera that first August reported that 60 percent of the new vacationers had never before seen salt water.

The government-sponsored vacation idea was of fascist origin, similar to the Nazi Kraft durch Freude program. "Hitler has been very clever at that sort of thing," a Popular Front official told a reporter. "There is no reason why a democratic government should not do the same."[18] This was certainly Léon Blum's opinion. He was properly proud of the system. When he was put on trial by the Vichy authorities after the fall of France, he spoke of watching worker couples on the road experiencing for the first time "the idea of leisure." Besides getting them out of the cafes, he went on, "I have brought . . . some light into their hard lives" and "opened for them a perspective on the future, given them hope."[19]

Most of the other Popular Front achievements were short-lived or of minor importance. Instead of nationalizing the Bank of France or at least forcing it to adopt more liberal credit policies, Blum allowed the bank to operate largely as it always had. He feared instituting changes that would further antagonize already hostile financial and business interests and thus delay economic recovery.

However reasonable this decision may have seemed, it failed to accomplish Blum's objective. At their last meeting, the deposed directors of the bank issued a public statement. Besides insisting that they had always performed their duties "with perfect correctness and absolute integrity," they accused the Blum government of having undermined the security of the women and minor children who were dependent on the stock of the bank for their support. Ignoring the fact that only the 200 largest stockholders had had any say in making bank policy, the directors charged that 41,000 stockholders had been "dispossessed of their rights." Henceforth bank policy would be in the hands of the very interests that wanted to borrow money from the bank. Because of this, they added, "we envisage the coming times with great apprehension," and "we fervently hope that the new managers will not be submerged by the flood of demands for loans, and that the least possible damage to our money and the economy of France will emerge from the present tumult."[20]

Although Finance Minister Vincent Auriol promptly responded to this inaccurate and irresponsible (one might almost say traitorous) charge, the directors' statement contributed to the "sit-down strike of capital" conducted by French business and financial interests. Many of the well-to-do smuggled their wealth out of the country in the form of gold. Once they regained possession of their plants, employers tended to drag their feet about cooperating with labor in much the same way that American manufacturers had behaved in 1933–34 under the NRA codes. In August 1936, they formed a new employer organization, *La Confédération Générale de la Production Française*, with a committee devoted to preparing and distributing propaganda attacking the government's economic controls.

One Popular Front "gain" turned out quickly to be a loss. This was the reduction of the work week to 40 hours, which was put into effect rapidly, industry by industry. This measure, one of the workers' most urgent demands, was a prime example of the influence of the New Deal on the Popular Front. The trouble was that conditions in France were far different from those that had existed in the United States in the early 1930s. Because of the depression, the average work week in 1933 had been well below 40 hours in the United States. In France in 1936 it was in the neighborhood of 48 hours in many large manufacturing establishments. The sharp decrease in output and the corresponding increase in labor costs that resulted from the law had disastrous effects on the French economy. French coal production fell in 1937, and the amount of coal imported rose. As Alfred Sauvy writes in his history of the period, "The 40-hour week had the effect, in this sector, of shifting the work to foreign countries, giving it to English and German miners."

There was no rational justification for so steep and sudden a cut in the work week, Sauvy insists. Blum was a victim of "the well-known attraction for round numbers." Yet given the depth of workers' feelings about the 40-hour week in 1936, no Socialist government (probably no democratically elected government) could have failed to enact some such measure.[21]

In September the continuing flight of capital from France forced Blum to devalue the franc by about 30 percent. (He justified his change of policy by referring to Roosevelt's "courage" in being willing "to try something else until at last he found the method that succeeded.") For a time, the economy improved. But soon the reductions of output caused by the 40-hour week and the fear and resentment of so many French manufacturers stifled the expansion. Prices rose, but government revenues fell.

Blum then announced a "pause" in the reform movement. He surrounded himself with conservative economists. He cut a billion francs from the 1937 public works budget, turning it into what one historian has called "a mouse." It is the judgment of Sauvy that Blum surrendered to the financiers, that he adopted a kind of bookkeeper's mentality, *"l'optique de la caisse."*[22]

The surrender did Blum no good. The economy continued to

slide. Speculators drove the value of the franc lower and lower. His conservative advisers demanded that he reduce government expenditures still further and raise taxes. Finally, in June 1937, he was forced to resign.

Unlike his model, Franklin Roosevelt, Blum was unable to hold his coalition together when his program ran into difficulties. To what extent his personal inadequacies caused this inability to rally support is a difficult question. His performance can be criticized from two quite different perspectives. At the time, the left wing in his own Socialist Party believed that he had suffered a failure of nerve at the very start. The tidal wave of strikes had created a fluid situation, and the opposition was demoralized. According to these critics, Blum, a lifelong socialist, should have instituted basic changes, not simply tried to patch up French capitalism.

Although he had stressed reform within the system while running for office, he had also made clear his belief that more basic changes were necessary. He had vigorously defended his socialist beliefs. "The cause of our common miseries resides in an evil social system," he said in a radio address. He rejected halfway measures such as those based on the plan of Henri de Man. Back in 1934, he had argued that de Man's type of compromise would only delay "the process of capitalist evolution which, through steady concentration, readies it for socialization." But in 1936 he approved of nationalizing "key industries and credit" in order to "relieve misery, attenuate injustice, and establish within chaos a modicum of order and clarity."

The argument of the left was made most forcefully when the strikes were just beginning by Marceau Pivert, a physics and mathematics teacher who was a leader of the Left Revolutionary faction of the Socialist Party. Pivert published an article, *"Tout est possible,"* in the Socialist newspaper *Populaire de Paris* on May 26. "Stop singing us nursery rhymes," Pivert told Blum. "The people are now on the march towards a magnificent destiny. . . . *Everything is possible* to those who dare!" It was not true that the Radical Party would oppose the nationalization of the banks, public utilities, and "trusts," Pivert insisted. Nor would "our brothers the Communists" block a real social revolution because of "diplomatic considerations." (This was a reference to the Soviet Union's strategy of cooperating with capitalist parties because of the fascist threat.) There must be "a most vigorous anti-capitalist offensive."

> The masses are more advanced than you think. . . . They will not be content with an insipid cup of herb tea carried on slippered feet to the bedside of a sick mother. On the contrary they will agree to the most drastic surgery because they know that capitalism is in its death throes, and that it is necessary to build a new world if we are to put an end to the depression, fascism, and war. . . . Everything is possible with a party faithful to its . . . principles.[23]

Blum rejected Pivert's call to arms, and he was supported by most Socialists as well as by the Radicals and the Communists and the labor leaders who made up the Popular Front coalition. He did so on the honorable ground that the Popular Front parties, having campaigned on a platform calling for moderate reforms within the capitalist system, had no mandate for revolutionary change. "We are not a Socialist government," he said in a radio speech at the end of 1936. "We do not seek, either directly or insidiously, to put into effect our Socialist program." He felt obligated, he explained in later years, to "keep loyally, publicly, the promise that I had made."

But it can be argued that the upheavals of 1936 *were* revolutionary. "Faced by a powerful enemy," Pivert said at a Socialist Party meeting in 1937, Blum displayed "the elegance of a duelist in lace cuffs." Many years later, at a conference on the Blum regime, another reform-minded premier, Pierre Mendès France, pointed out that the election of 1936 was not a plebiscite for any particular reform but "an affirmation of a popular desire to see the country break out of its deflationary rut and conservative structures." Other Socialist critics, rereading some of Blum's modest and diffident comments about the responsibilities of his office, have been impressed by a "crushing masochism" in his character, a defeatist attitude, an exaggerated concern for punctilio. Blum was too much the "grand bourgeois," Pivert recollected, "too subtle, too refined to be a revolutionary leader."[24]

Pivert was perhaps too committed to his own position to be objective about Blum. But Pierre Cot, a Radical Party member of Blum's Popular Front government, made essentially the same point at the conference. After praising Blum's lucidity, intelligence, graciousness, and "mixture of charm and firmness," Cot added that in politics the premier was "not a man of the corridors." He did not have "*le toutoiement facile,*" Cot recalled, the ability to deal informally and familiarly with his political associates.[25]

In any case, Blum did not go beyond what he had promised to do during the campaign. Who can say whether or not he should have? What remains beyond argument has been well expressed by Georges Lefranc, a participant in and one of the leading historians of the events of 1936. Perhaps everything was not possible, Lefranc wrote three decades later. "But can one say that everything that was possible was tried?"[26]

Which of these positions is correct is hard to determine. It is clear, however, that Blum did not build upon the reforms of 1936, and he failed to protect the reforms adequately against counterattack. The difficulties were admittedly staggering—the antediluvian mentality of French industrialists, the doctrinaire rigidity of union leaders, the slavish commitment of the Communists to the policies of the Soviet Union, the tragic divisions resulting from the Spanish Civil War, the noisy rightist "patriots," the sometimes perverse individualism of nearly everyone in France. Probably no political leader could have overcome the shortsighted selfishness and inertia, or resisted the splintering factionalism that plagued French society in the late thirties.

Yet Blum's efforts were pitifully inadequate, no better or worse than those of the uninspired premiers who preceded and followed him. Long years of balancing his socialist principles against his political ambitions and responsibilities made him in biographer Joel Colton's words, a "tightrope-walker." Before the formation of the

Popular Front, when forced to make a choice, he had always put his socialist principles above political accommodation. After he finally made the other choice in 1936, he became too much the accommodator, telling the striking workers, for example, that they must learn "moderation and patience."

Marceau Pivert, who had responsibility for the government radio in Blum's cabinet and who "brought a breath of fresh air" to programming by increasing the amount of time devoted to social and economic issues, complained that he could not do as much as he wished because technicians hostile to the government remained in key posts. Pivert wanted to replace them with unemployed socialists, but Blum would not allow him to do so. No "unjustified discharges" would be permitted.[27]

Alfred Sauvy has written that Blum's ignorance of economics was matched only by his sincerity. Even if so, that is not of central importance. After all, Roosevelt was no economist, and neither was Hitler. Blum's problem was that he could not muster either Roosevelt's flexibility or Hitler's ruthlessness.

Blum got a second chance to run the government in 1938, again as head of a Popular Front coalition. This time, with the assistance of George Boris, a treasury official who had written an admiring book on the New Deal, *La Révolution Roosevelt* (1934), and who was one of the few people in France who was in sympathy with the new Keynesian economics, he drafted a comprehensive reform program, including tax relief and government credits for defense industries, tax relief for the construction industry and small business, suspension of efforts to reduce the national debt, a special capital levy on the rich, and a more progressive income tax. He even called for rudimentary exchange controls, the American and British governments having given him confidential assurances that they would not object. A massive national effort was necessary, he said, to build up French defenses against the fascist threat, to expand production, and to maintain "social solidarity."

Blum later admitted that in drafting this elaborate program, he drew upon the Soviet Five-Year Plans and National Socialist economic techniques as well as the New Deal for ideas. "In the grim world of 1938," writes Colton, "[Blum] demonstrated his understanding and acceptance of the needs of the nation. . . . He had reconciled in his own mind all possible contradictions between his patriotism and his socialism."[28]

The National Assembly supported Blum's program, but when, as expected, the conservative Senate voted it down, he meekly resigned. He did not even demand a vote of confidence. If he had appealed to the people over the Senate's head he might have forced the opposition senators to yield. He could also, no doubt, have forced new elections that would at least have put his program before the country.

Back in 1935, when he was campaigning for the new Popular Front, he raised the question of what such a government could do if the banks used their power to prevent reform. Its duty, he said, "would be to demand immediately of the nation so defied the means to break the artificial resistance to its will."[29] But that was before he became premier.

In power, to quote Joel Colton again, "it was part of Blum's temperament to recoil from strong measures." It is hard to see how a socialist with any political experience could have expected ever to install such a system without *some* stretching of executive power, some rocking of the boat.

Later events were to demonstrate beyond argument that Léon Blum was no coward. What he lacked was confidence in the soundness of his own proposals and the daring to step beyond the comfortable security of conventional political procedures. After his second retirement, he confessed, "Perhaps, if I committed errors it was because of not having been enough of a leader."[30]

CHAPTER X

HOW IT ENDED

I n Léon Blum's problems and in the policies he put forward during
his brief second period as premier lay the seeds of the economic
recovery that ended the Great Depression in France and elsewhere
in the world. Blum's problems in 1938 were related to the need to
spend large sums on arms to meet the growing threat of war with
Germany. His policies were at least indirectly influenced by John
Maynard Keynes's *General Theory of Employment, Interest, and
Money*, which was published in 1936.

Blum saw the connection between the problems and the recovery that everyone was seeking, but he lacked enough confidence
in the policies to fight for them effectively. Neither he nor, so far
as is known, any other head of state in 1938 (certainly not Roosevelt
or Hitler or the British prime minister, Neville Chamberlain) had
read Keynes's new book.* But this does not mean that they had
escaped its influence. It is true that the reviews of the *General
Theory* tended to be critical and that many reviewers did not grasp

---

* Swedish Finance Minister Ernst Wigforss is a possible exception.

the significance of what Keynes was saying. Among the Americans, Professor Alvin Hansen felt so strongly that he reviewed the book in both the *Journal of Political Economy* and the *Yale Review*, where he hoped to reach a more general audience. He dismissed it as a mere symptom of the depression. The theoretical sections were without merit, he declared, logically flawed. Another American reviewer dismissed the book as "an interesting exhibit in the museum of depression curiosities." The reviewer in the leading French professional journal, the *Revue d'économie politique*, described the work as muddled, in parts absurd. The German economists of the "Reformer" group, who favored work creation projects, were more sympathetic because Keynes's practical proposals were similar to their own. But his lighthearted way of dealing with the dangers of inflation alarmed them. One prominent German economist, Wilhelm Lautenbach, saw considerable merit in the general theory but was disturbed by Keynes's failure to pay attention to the work of the Swedish economist Knut Wicksell. Lautenbach was also annoyed by the tone of the book, especially Keynes's *"Sarkasmus"* when pointing out the inadequacies of the classical economists.*

The English economist A. C. Pigou, normally an impenetrably dull writer, concluded his review of the *General Theory* with the line, "We have watched an artist firing arrows at the moon," and a German economist quipped that while some of what Keynes said was new and much of what he said was good, what was new was seldom good, and what was good was not always new *("was er Neues sagt, kaum immer gut, und das, was er Gutes sagt, nicht immer neu genannt werden kann")*. Keynes's hyperbolic, epigrammatic style was evidently contagious.[1]

The negative tone of so many of the reviews of the *General Theory* can be deceptive if the reviews are used to judge the impact of Keynes's ideas. When reviewing theoretical works, especially ones as novel as Keynes's, professionals tend to look for flaws and logical inconsistencies, to deny that the ideas are really new, and

---

* For example (*General Theory*, p. 192): "Ricardo offers us the supreme intellectual achievement, unattainable by weaker spirits, of adopting a hypothetical world remote from experience as though it were the world of experience and then living in it consistently."

to stress their doubts and disagreements. The number and length of the reviews—the French review mentioned above filled more than 30 closely printed pages—and the importance of the reviewers testify to the seriousness with which the scholarly world received the book. By 1937 articles about it were being published in professional journals; by 1938 books were being published. Not long thereafter, it became the subject of doctoral dissertations. Even in the Soviet Union, where Keynes was scorned for his attempts to make "repair patches on capitalism" and vilified for his disparaging remarks lumping Karl Marx with Silvio Gesell, an obscure economist, and Major C. H. Douglas, a muddle-headed amateur, his theory was attracting comment by 1938.[2]

Economists who disagreed with Keynes's reasoning were nonetheless affected by it. Within a year of writing his hostile reviews of the *General Theory*, Alvin Hansen had begun to change his mind and soon thereafter he became a thorough Keynesian. So did many, many others.

Through such converts and especially through those of them who were directly or indirectly involved in government service, Keynes's theory became known to, if not necessarily understood by, the politicians. In France Georges Boris read the *General Theory* in the summer of 1937. According to both Boris and Pierre Mendès France, he used its reasoning to persuade Léon Blum to make increased public spending part of his 1938 program.[3]

In the United States, Marriner Eccles of the Federal Reserve Board, a longtime advocate of deficit spending during depressions, found Keynes's policy recommendations attractive, although he had not yet read the *General Theory* or Keynes's other theoretical writings. The New Deal officials whose policy recommendations were similar to Eccles's reacted in the same way. When he first read it, Lauchlin Currie, who was assistant director of research for the Federal Reserve Board, found the *General Theory* less convincing as a theory than its author imagined. The parts that seemed persuasive had been "purchased at the expense of reality." Nevertheless, Currie entirely agreed with the policies Keynes had recommended and prepared a detailed, if noncommittal, summary of the *General Theory* for the Board of Governors of the Federal Reserve.[4]

What added political weight to the arguments of these New Dealers was the terrible, unexpected recession of 1937–38. In late 1936 and early 1937, the depression seemed to be ending nearly everywhere. In Germany the Nazis, now engaged in full-scale rearmament, had launched their Four-Year Plan. The economy was expanding rapidly, and unemployment had almost disappeared. In other countries, the recovery was spotty, and unemployment remained disturbingly high, but most economic indicators were on the rise. Production had reached or exceeded 1929 levels in all the major industrial nations except France, and in France it was also rising rapidly—up 12 percent in the last three months of 1936. The annual League of Nations *World Economic Survey* published in 1937 reported that the industrial countries were "rapidly emerging" from the long slump.[5]

Nowhere were spirits more ebullient than in the United States. A group of New Deal liberals who met in October 1936 at the home of Marriner Eccles were so confident that the depression was over that their talk turned to how to avoid *future* depressions. The authors of an analysis of the agricultural situation published some months later wrote of "the present tide of returning prosperity," and in a book ghost-written by a young economist named John Kenneth Galbraith, four liberal American businessmen treated "the depression of the 1930's" and its "lessons" in a way that suggested that they believed it was over. "America gives absolutely no impression of being in a depression," the French novelist Jules Romains wrote after a visit to the United States at this time. "When Americans speak of the Depression . . . they always use the past tense. 'During the Depression I did so and so. . . .' "[6]

The economic growth was of course welcome. But although the prices of all sorts of goods were still below 1929 levels in most countries, they were going up. At the end of 1936, Sir Frederick Phillips of the British Treasury predicted that the coming year would see the price level "as high as we care to see it."[7] Phillips's prediction proved to be an example of British understatement. The price of most raw materials soared between the summer of 1936 and the following spring. In 1937 the wholesale price index (1929 = 100) climbed from 83 to 96 in Great Britain, from 80 to 93 in Italy, from 87 to 98 in Sweden, from 80 to 86 in the United States.

As soon as prices began to go up, the grinding deflation of the long depression was forgotten. Fears of inflation resurfaced. In France higher labor costs resulting from the new 40-hour-week law caused the wholesale price index to soar from 65 to 90 in 1937. This added to the worries of French businessmen and other conservatives already frightened by the economic and social upheavals of the previous year.

In Great Britain the Committee on Economic Information, which was charged with preparing reports for the government, reacted in a similar manner. Keynes was a member of this committee, and most of its reports reflected his thinking. By January 1937, he had become convinced that the British economy was overheating. A continuing building boom and a big rearmament program were pushing up prices at a rapid rate. Although he expected the economy to slow down of its own accord in a few years, he became so concerned about the risk of a boom-and-bust cycle if the pace of growth was not checked that he published a series of articles in the London *Times* on "How to Avoid a Slump." It might soon be necessary "to retard certain types of investment," he warned. Local governments should hold back on new public works projects. There was even, he added, "a risk of what might fairly be called inflation."[8]

The next month the committee issued a report warning that "the present level of investment activity . . . has already substantially affected the level of wholesale prices." It urged the government to raise taxes to cover a large percentage of the cost of rearmament and to postpone work on "road improvements, railway electrification, slum clearance," and other public works "which are not of an urgent character."[9]

In January 1937, somewhat alarmed by the trend of prices, the United States Federal Reserve Board announced an increase in member banks' reserve requirements. This caused American interest rates to rise. Soon thereafter, alarmed by what he saw as "unwarranted" price increases, Marriner Eccles warned President Roosevelt that although "a further increase in production" was desirable, "there is grave danger that the recovery movement will get out of hand, excessive rises in prices . . . will occur, excessive growth in profits and a boom in the stock market will arise, and the cost of living will mount rapidly. If such conditions are permitted to develop, another drastic slump will be inevitable."[10]

It did not take much of this kind of talk to revive President Roosevelt's concern about the federal budget deficit. He had learned to live with deficits but, in the words of the economist Herbert Stein, he regarded them as "an unfortunate by-product" of one or another necessary expenditure, such as the need to provide relief for people made destitute by the depression. While realizing that the deficits stimulated economic activity and thereby created new jobs, his basic approach to the unemployment problem was the same as the unions: he would reduce unemployment by redefining it, that is, by such policies as keeping young people in school longer, retiring workers at 65, and shortening the work week.

Early in March 1937, Roosevelt warned in a radio speech that "the dangers of 1929 are again becoming possible."[11] With advisers such as Secretary of the Treasury Henry Morgenthau urging him on, he ordered a big cut in public works expenditures and demanded that the members of his cabinet trim a total of $300 million from their departments' budgets. He vowed to balance the next federal budget and begin to reduce the national debt. At the same time, the Federal Reserve Board pushed interest rates still higher. Because of these and other measures, the federal deficit for 1937 was only $358 million, down from $3.6 billion in 1936.

These restrictive monetary and fiscal policies, along with the coincidental drain on consumers' disposable income occasioned by the collection of the new social security tax enacted in 1935, brought the recovery to a sudden halt. American industrial production slackened in the spring and summer, then plummeted in the fall. Unemployment, still far higher than 10 percent of the work force, began to rise. On the stock exchange, the shares of manufacturing corporations fell about 40 percent in less than two months. By June

243

1938, national income was down by 13 percent, more than 11 million workers were jobless, and business profits were running at less than a quarter of what they had been the previous September. It was, according to a student of the slump, a recession "without parallel in American economic history."[12]

The British economist Sir Dennis Robertson later remarked that when the United States sneezed, Europe caught pneumonia.[13] This was something of an overstatement. The American recession affected the economies of other countries, but in Great Britain, the recession, though sharp, was brief and relatively mild. This was also the case in Italy and Sweden, and the German economy did not falter at all. Of the major European countries, only France suffered a severe downturn in 1937. But most of the underdeveloped nations, particularly those accustomed to selling raw materials in the United States, were hard hit by the loss of much of their American business. The price of coffee, rubber, and many other products fell rapidly, and attempts to bolster prices by the employment of export quotas failed to check the slide.*

The sudden economic downturn in the United States caused Roosevelt's liberal advisers to urge him to resume deficit spending. He was hard to convince; in October 1937 he was still talking about balancing the 1939 budget, and he warned important congressmen not to let appropriations exceed his recommendations unless they provided additional revenues to cover the cost. A month later, the president was asking why, if reducing the deficit had been desirable in January, it was wrong to do so in November.

Keynes himself joined in the effort to persuade Roosevelt to change his mind. In a letter to the president, he admitted that an "error of optimism" had caused him to overestimate demand in 1936. At present more spending on public works, and particularly on housing was needed. "I should advise putting most of your eggs in this basket . . . and making absolutely sure that they are hatched without delay," he said. Keynes had other specific recommendations, but his main point was that "promoting large-scale investment . . . is an urgent necessity."[14]

* Cheaper food and raw materials moderated the effects of the recession in the industrial countries.

Roosevelt was unmoved by this argument. He told Secretary of the Treasury Morgenthau, a fiscal conservative, to draft a reply, which Morgenthau did with relish. The letter, which Roosevelt signed, thanked Keynes for his advice and for the kind things he had said about New Deal policies. But it ignored Keynes's central recommendation about government spending as a way of stimulating the economy.

The recession continued to deepen, however, and in late March, Roosevelt yielded to the spenders. His fear that the Democrats might suffer heavy losses in the 1938 congressional elections if the slide was not checked was an important consideration. And when he gave in, he succumbed completely. He asked Congress to appropriate an additional $1.25 billion for unemployment relief and $750 million more in other budget-breaking outlays.

At the same time, the Federal Reserve Board acted to lower interest rates. "We have been traveling fast this last week," Roosevelt explained to Morgenthau shortly before the public announcement of his change of policy. "You will have to hurry to catch up."

"Mr. President, maybe I never can catch up," Morgenthau replied. The spenders had "stampeded" FDR "like cattle," he told his subordinates at the Treasury Department next day.[15]

Because of the new spending, the American economy rebounded in the summer and fall of 1938, then grew more slowly in the following months. It did not get back to the level of early 1937, however, until the autumn of 1939, which meant that it was still far from full prosperity. The unemployment rate, for example, remained well over 10 percent.

What finally ended the Great Depression was the problem that Léon Blum faced during his brief second term as premier of France, the threat to peace imposed on the world by Nazi Germany. Blum had been a strong supporter of disarmament during the 1920s and early 1930s. But because of the aggressions of Germany and Italy, he had approved new defense appropriations while premier in 1936–37, despite his concern about the effect of these outlays on France's already unbalanced budget. In his call for still larger military ap-

245

propriations when he again became premier, he no longer found the budget deficit so alarming. Instead, he stressed the connection between rearmament and recovery. "Around the manufacture of armaments," he declared, "there will be coordinated an ecomomy which will be the basis for a more abundant production in all domains."[16]

Blum, of course, was right. No more effective way of reviving a stagnant industrial economy could be found. The manufacture of guns and munitions stimulated dormant heavy industry and the building trades. Since the government was the only buyer, the additional demand did not reduce consumer demand for civilian goods, and since the sums spent in order to make armaments put money into the pockets of hundreds of French employers and thousands of their workers, both investment and consumption expanded.

Although Blum's second government lasted only a few days, his proposals and the forces and ideas that had shaped them did not end with his resignation. The French government expended 72.7 billion francs in 1937 (up from under 50 billion in 1935), 82.3 billion in 1938, and no less than 150 billion in 1939.

A similar growth of government spending on arms occurred in other nations. British expenditures rose from £1 billion in 1938 to £1.4 billion in 1939, a large proportion of the increase going to the military. German expenditures also increased rapidly, though the proportion spent on armaments was not much larger than that of Britain or France. Italian outlays doubled between 1935 and 1939. The United States responded more slowly to the threat of war, but by 1938 national security expenditures were twice what they had been in 1934. Total federal spending rose from $6.8 billion in 1938 to $8.9 billion in 1939. (The big proportional increase came in 1941, when the rise was from $13 to $34 billion.)

These huge expenditures necessitated heavy borrowing and stimulated economic activity. Whether one argues that government spending per se ended the depression or whether the war is given the credit depends on how far back in the causal chain one wishes to go. Keynes's theory "explained" why spending was necessary in the 1930s. His reasoning was not fully assimilated until the war was over, but it is clear in retrospect that either because of conviction or the lack of any viable alternative, by the end of the thirties more and more economists were urging (and political leaders adopting) the tactics he was recommending. If the concessions made to Hitler at Munich had slaked his thirst for conquest and produced the generation of peace that Neville Chamberlain hoped for, the economic growth of the war and postwar years would perhaps have been less hectic, the Keynesian "lessons" less enthusiastically absorbed. But the Great Depression would have ended, when it did or not long thereafter.

Nearly all of the economists and historians who have discussed the question believe that the world will never again experience a depression as severe and prolonged as that which occurred in the 1930s. "Could it happen again?" Lester V. Chandler asked in *America's Greatest Depression* (1970). "The answer," he concluded, "must surely be, 'No.' " It was "almost inconceivable that depressions will again be allowed to become so deep and so prolonged."

Chandler offered several reasons why such an economic debacle was most unlikely, and his listing is typical of most such explanations. The reasons include "the growth of economic understanding" (knowledge of "the determinants that influence the behavior of employment, output, and prices"); a general acceptance of the responsibility of governments to promote economic stability; a large increase in the volume of economic activity carried out by governments, with a corresponding increase in the impact of government activity on national economies; and measures designed to maintain the income and protect the savings of consumers during cyclical downturns, principally unemployment insurance and bank deposit insurance.

Unlikely does not mean impossible, as any experienced student of history will testify. In 1955 John Kenneth Galbraith concluded his book on the 1929 stock market crash with a discussion of why such a collapse could not have much effect on the modern American economy. His explanation anticipated much of what Chandler was

247

to say 15 years later. Galbraith added, however, that it would be "unwise to expose the economy to the shock of another major speculative collapse" because the new "reinforcements" might fail and "fissures might open at other new and perhaps unexpected places." As a matter of fact, Chandler was equally cautious; his "no" was qualified, despite the array of arguments to the contrary that he presented. If a "political deadlock" prevented governments from taking "the actions that we now know can shorten a depression and induce recovery," he wrote, big trouble could result.[17]

Galbraith's use of the word "fissures" and Chandler's concern about a possible international "political deadlock" are reminders that the marshaling of the "reinforcements" and the application of the new "economic understanding" that emerged from the Great Depression depend almost entirely on the decisions of individual nations. So long as rivalries exist between nations and so long as groups with conflicting interests contend for control of decision making within nations, national policies will not always harmonize, one with another. Then too, decades of experience indicate that most political leaders (responding, it is true, to the inclinations of their constituents) seldom look beyond the ends of their noses when dealing with pocketbook issues. The Keynesian theorem that governments should spend in bad times has been so thoroughly proved as to be accepted as axiomatic, but its converse, that governments should run in the black in good times tends to be ignored.

Moreover, world economic relationships, already complex in the 1930s, are more multitudinous by far in the 1980s. While the received wisdom of the day cannot possibly be (to quote Galbraith again) as "invariably on the side of measures that would make things worse" as was the "wisdom" of the thirties, the best use of the modern tools of economic adjustment is seldom obvious in specific situations.[18] There has been no great depression since *the* Great Depression, and there may never be one because governments take the actions to "induce recovery" that Chandler mentions. But economically undesirable things occur—high unemployment, inflation, unstable currencies—and they persist despite what governments do to end them. Put differently, the ebb and flow of economic activity retains an element of mystery. Business cycles still follow their rhythmic courses; they can be influenced but not really mastered. Economics is a science, but one that, like history, explains how things got to be the way they are far more accurately than what they are going to be like at some future date. During the period of apparently endless growth that followed World War II, experts talked of "fine-tuning" the economy. Inflation and the oil crises of the 1970s have made them rather less ambitious.

Yet it seems reasonable to believe that barring some act of gross human folly, such as a nuclear war, depressions as deep and long-lasting as the Great Depression of the 1930s are a thing of the past. If this is true, then not the least of the many things the Great Depression put an end to was great depressions.

Another result of the depression was to lead nations, such as the United States, that did not have unemployment insurance and well-defined public welfare systems to create them. This would have happened before very long even if the depression had been no more than a minor dip in the business cycle; such systems existed and despite their flaws had demonstrated social benefits that even in the prosperous twenties were attracting increasing amounts of attention and support. Throughout history, societies have always assisted their unfortunates, and they have usually adjusted their methods of doing so to changing conditions, albeit not without controversy and not always as generously as might be desired.

The changes that occurred during the depression in this field appear to have been permanent ones. The pressures of recent recessions and the exposure of flaws and loopholes in public assistance systems have led to cutbacks in the size and scope of some programs, but not to serious attempts to eliminate them. The Great Depression seems sure to merit at least a chapter in any future history of public assistance. But the depression was only a milestone in this area, neither the beginning nor even a major turning point in history.

More ephemeral was the nearly universal commitment of nations after World War II to maintaining full employment. The commitment was a product of the Great Depression, though, as has been said, it took the experience of wartime deficit financing to convince governments that they could fulfill such a promise. Even the United Nations Charter contained a clause (Article 55) that made full employment one of the objectives the organization was committed to advancing.

The reasoning that led to the worldwide belief that governments could make full employment possible was Keynes's chief contribution. The commitment was ephemeral, though not in the sense that interest in full employment waned. If anything, concern about employment grew more intense with the passage of time. But maintaining full employment in peacetime proved far more difficult than it seemed to be in the immediate postwar years. What was permanent and clearly a product of the depression experience was the belief that governments should treat *reducing* unemployment, not merely caring for the jobless, as a major responsibility.

Another change brought about by the depression was the awareness that to control economic activity intelligently, governments must know a great deal more about what is going on than they did in the 1930s. Since then, the collection and publication of statistical information has expanded almost infinitely. Some of the statistics, such as Gross National Product, did not exist as government-produced measurements during the depression, though the information now used to estimate GNP was available in most western nations. Other data (unemployment being an important example) that were compiled, were collected almost haphazardly, differently in different countries, and often only by nongovernmental agencies. Unemployment statistics are now gathered systematically everywhere, though still not by the same method in every case.

The problem—if there is a problem—with the present abundance of information is that small changes in the volume and direction of economic activity are sometimes interpreted as heralding trends, when in fact they are only minor fluctuations of no long-range significance. At times the flood of data serves to confuse rather than to enlighten. Nevertheless, the information that is constantly being generated and analyzed has become indispensable to

250

producers and consumers as well as to government policy makers and legislators.

The flow (or flood) of economic data is related to another result of the depression, the further discrediting of laissez-faire as an important economic theory. The great stress that reformers placed on planning during the depression, already discussed, produced many statements to this effect while the depression was in progress. Two examples that refer to the demise almost as a truism should suffice. In *Markets and Men* (1936), J. W. F. Rowe called attention to the "sudden and widespread substitution of conscious artificial control for the unconscious control of a *laissez-faire* system." Another commentator, writing in the *International Labour Review*, put it this way:

> The fundamental issue . . . is not, as is sometimes still supposed, between economic planning and *laissez-faire*. That question was decided in the years following the collapse of 1929. For good or ill, Governments are already exercising and must continue to exercise an active influence in economic affairs.[19]

The triumph of Keynesian economics after World War II heaped still more earth on the grave of laissez-faire. One must distinguish, of course, between laissez-faire as a theory and the actual practice of governments. Pure laissez-faire never existed, even in the heyday of classical economics, and it certainly never will in any economy as large and complex as now exists or is likely to exist in any imaginable future. Nevertheless, the Great Depression did result in a decided shift toward more regulation of economic matters by governments. A few crackpots aside, those who talk about "restoring" individual enterprise and "relying" on free markets to order economic affairs really seek no more than to reduce state regulation so as to take more advantage of people's acquisitive instincts.

The depression did put an end to the use of gold or any particular commodity as the basis for national monetary systems. The stimulating effects that resulted during the depression when any nation devalued its currency by going off the gold standard were repeatedly demonstrated. By the end of the 1930s, most nations had taken the lesson to heart. Great economic growth resulted, during World War II and continuing thereafter. By comparison to the Great Depression, the interruptions that occurred during the postwar recessions were minor indeed.

But endless inflation also resulted from the abandonment of the gold standard and thus from the Great Depression. It was to be expected that after the grinding, debilitating deflation of the depression years, an inflationary period would follow. This inflation, however, was without precedent—of a different order from any in the past. There had been times when the depreciation had been greater and nearly as widespread, most recently in the period following World War I. Always in the past, however, the inflation had been conceived of by economists, statesmen, and the general public as being part of a cycle of some sort. It is true that Keynes wrote of the tendency of money to depreciate throughout history, and of "the social advantages" and "the psychological encouragement" that continually rising prices produce. But the general expectation was that the value of money could and would increase as well as go down. Even Keynes, despite his fondness for hyperbole, did not deny this. "The very long-run course of prices has *almost always* been upward," was as far as he would go, at least in his more serious publications.[20]

It no longer seems to be the case that price levels are expected to move in both directions. The expectation now is that while the cost of particular items may go down from time to time, the general price level will go up constantly. Only the rate of inflation will fluctuate.

How much inflation is considered dangerous is now thought to depend on the speed at which the inflation rate is rising more than on the rate itself; if prices were doubling every year, even an 80 percent rate might seem low. Certainly when the rate is 10 percent, 7 percent seems close to ideal. Yet there have been times since the war when a 3 percent inflation rate caused economists in some countries to worry. In the 1970s, President Richard Nixon imposed price controls on the country when the American rate of inflation had risen to a little over 4 percent.

The relation between inflation and employment had long been recognized by economists, and the Great Depression drove this lesson home with force. When prices fell, unemployment rose; when prices went up, unemployment tended to decline. In 1958 the English economist A. W. Phillips reduced this relationship to a formula—the Phillips curve. After studying a century of British wage and unemployment statistics, Phillips concluded that the maintenance of stable prices required an unemployment rate of about 5.5 percent. The converse, however, was that to eliminate unemployment, one must learn to live with a certain amount of inflation.

Because of the disastrous unemployment of the depression years, the tendency during the postwar period was to "buy" jobs by "tolerating" inflation. (Another way of describing the situation would be to say that so long as a relatively low inflation rate appeared to keep the number of unemployed workers low, the inflation did not cause much public alarm.)

The mechanism driving the Phillips curve was economic growth. Inflation encouraged investment, which resulted in more employment, which led to more consumption, which further stimulated investment, and so on. Another legacy of the depression, therefore, was the stress on growth as essential not merely to economic prosperity—that had long been recognized—but to social harmony and social justice. When the economy expanded, when more goods were produced and more services rendered, the rich would no doubt get richer, but far more important, opportunities would open up for those lower on the social and economic ladder. Best of all, the process seemed capable of almost infinite extension. Witness the flood of new technologies ranging from the taming of the atom to the development of computers and jet airplanes, and the discovery of penicillin and other antibiotics.

The contrast with the glum view of the world prevalent in the 1930s escaped no one. Alvin Hansen, a leading stagnationist during the depression, became an apostle of growth and a defender of inflation in the 1950s. When alarmists became concerned about rising prices, Hansen warned against "making a fetish of rigid price stability."[21] Whereas during the depression farmers the world over had been so burdened by unsalable surpluses that they destroyed their crops unharvested and cut back on production, now, thanks to prosperity, a rapidly expanding world population, and the "green revolution" that vastly increased crop yields, they were increasing the production of food at an enormous rate.

Inflation seemed a small price to pay for such a profusion of happy results. But trouble developed in the 1970s, when the moderate inflation that was supposed to make investors optimistic and loosen the purse strings of consumers accelerated. When the inflation rate passed 10 percent, a new term, "double-digit inflation," was invented that had ominous, frightening overtones. For some reason, double-digit inflation did not produce enough growth to keep unemployment down and the door to social advancement open. More inflation began to cause less of what was good and more of what was bad. A strange combination of rising prices, high unemployment, and little or no growth called "stagflation," a condition unanticipated by and almost inconceivable to orthodox Keynesian economists, became reality.

The stagflation of the 1970s was to a considerable extent caused by political events. The first was the war in Vietnam. The large American budget deficits resulting from the failure of the government to raise taxes enough, and the financing of much of this debt by creating new money, pumped huge sums into the economy, which caused prices to go up in the United States and, because of the size of the American economy, in other parts of the world as well. Next came the 1973 Arab-Israeli war, which led to the cutting off of petroleum exports by the Arab states and then to skyrocketing energy prices as the OPEC countries drove the price of petroleum higher and higher. These events sent the American consumer price index up 50 percent between 1970 and 1977. Nations everywhere suffered similar rises, in some cases even more substantial ones. Prices in Japan, which was totally dependent on imported oil, doubled in these years; those in Great Britain rose at an even faster rate.

254

The world gradually adjusted to these shocks. Although the euphoria of the postwar era, with its combination of rapid growth, high employment, and low inflation, did not return, the world economy again expanded, though hesitantly in many places. The climate of opinion, however, was far different in the early 1980s from what it had been for a generation after World War II. Stagflation and double-digit inflation had sobering effects. Indeed, some attitudes turned full circle. Inflation now seemed more dangerous than unemployment—at least to persons who had jobs. Big, inflation-producing government deficits seemed particularly threatening, despite their reputation as engines of expansion and prosperity. Politicians and economists began to talk about the need for less government rather than more, and about balancing national budgets. One might almost think that Keynes had never written a line and that Herbert Hoover, Ramsay MacDonald, Heinrich Brüning, and one or another of the French premiers of the early 1930s were again holding the reins of government in the industrial nations.

This reversal does not mean that the "lessons" of the Great Depression have been forgotten or that the influence of the depression has ended. In the world of ideas, success often leads to failure, first because the very success of an idea tends to change the circumstances that caused the idea to be conceived, and then because people tend to rely too long on successful ideas after the circumstances change. If someone invented a sure-fire way to win at roulette, the immediate effect for those who used it would be most rewarding. But once the method became public knowledge, the casino owners would change the rules of the game, and those who used the method would be back where they started from.

Keynes's brilliant insights into the workings of the world economy of the 1930s had an effect something like this. His grasp of the psychological effects of inflation and his persuasive explanations of the productive power of deficits, for example, changed the way people and governments acted. For a time, however, old beliefs also continued to influence popular behavior. Because of Keynes's ideas, inflation resulted, but the fear of inflation subsided. Yet because people still believed in their hearts that the price level could be expected to go down eventually, nominal interest rates remained low. In Keynesian terms, the inflation had relatively little effect on the inclination of people to keep their wealth in the form of cash.*

With the passage of time, however, the persistent inflation brought home to both investors and consumers the fact that prices were not likely to fall. They began to anticipate inflation. Investors demanded higher rates of return, and workers demanded wage increases not merely to cover past rises in the cost of living but the rises yet to come. Consumers began to buy goods in advance of need in the belief (usually correct) that if they waited, prices would be higher still. In technical terms, the liquidity-preference of nearly everyone decreased, and that caused nominal interest rates to rise.

During the Great Depression, overconfidence in the automatic functioning of free markets, worry about the danger of runaway inflation, and the conventional belief in the desirability of husbanding one's resources in hard times led to policies that are now universally recognized to have been counterproductive. In more recent times, awareness of the errors of the past, and overconfidence in the ability of economists to design and statesmen to carry out policies that would stimulate economic growth and prevent depressions, have combined to lessen the effectiveness of Keynesian techniques. To change the metaphor, the pendulum had swung too far to the left, now it was swinging back to the right.

Of course the fact that Keynesian policies did not produce the results his admirers had come to expect does not mean that Keynes was "wrong" in his understanding of the economy of the 1930s or of how the people of that time viewed the world. Keynes's theory was and is sound, though (as some of his critics claimed back in the

---

* Keynes was well aware that supply and demand factors did not alone determine interest rates. In the *General Theory* he wrote (p. 203): "The rate of interest is a highly conventional . . . phenomenon. For its actual value is largely governed by the prevailing view as to what its value is expected to be. *Any* level of interest which is accepted with sufficient conviction as *likely* to be durable *will* be durable."

1930s) it no longer appears to be a *general* theory. Neither, for that matter, were the great classical economists "wrong" about how the nineteenth-century British economy functioned, despite Keynes's waspish remark that classical economics "cannot solve the economic problems of the actual world."[22] Their error, like Keynes's, was in assuming that they had discovered universal truths about human economic behavior. If Keynes had written "present world" instead of "actual world," his criticism would have been closer to the mark.

Keynes and his predecessors increased our knowledge of how economies function; their ideas remain vital, their teachings essential for understanding contemporary conditions even if they do not provide answers to every current question or solutions to every economic problem. Similarly, the Great Depression continues to be of use in dealing with the modern world even if some of the specific "lessons" of the depression seemed to have been forgotten.

NOTES

CHAPTER I

1. Arthur Salter, *Political Aspects of the World Depression* (Oxford, 1932), p. 5.
2. Herbert Hoover, *Memoirs: The Great Depression* (New York, 1952), pp. 2–16, 61–62, 79.
3. Robert Skidelsky, *Politicians and the Slump* (London, 1967), p. 241; Wilhelm Grotkopp, *Die grosse Krise* (Dusseldorf, 1954), pp. 18–19.
4. Alfred Sauvy, *Histoire économique de la France entre les deux guerres* (Paris, 1965–67), vol. 1, p. 115, vol. 2, p. 365.
5. Jacques Chastenet, *Les années d'illusions: 1918–1931* (Paris, 1960), pp. 184–85; Richard Lewisohn, *Histoire de la crise* (Paris, 1934), p. 32; Robert Sobel, *The Great Bull Market: Wall Street in the 1920s* (New York, 1968), p. 147.
6. Michel Tougan-Baranowsky, *Les crises industrielles en Angleterre* (Paris, 1913), p. 303.
7. Stuart Chase, *A New Deal* (New York, 1932), p. 117.
8. Quoted in Joseph Dorfman, *The Economic Mind in American Civilization*, vol. 3 (New York, 1949), p. 463.

259

9. Gottfried Haberler, *Prosperity and Depression: A Theoretical Analysis of Cyclical Movements* (Geneva, 1941), p. v.
10. *Encyclopedia of the Social Sciences*, vol. 4, pp. 595–99; J. R. Bellerby, in R. L. Smith, ed., *Essays in the Economics of Socialism and Communism* (London, 1964), p. 331; Grotkopp, *Grosse Krise*, pp. 18, 22–23.
11. Gaëtan Pirou, *La crise du capitalisme* (Paris, 1936), p. 32.
12. Bertil Ohlin, *The Course and Phases of the World Economic Depression* (Geneva, 1931).
13. Paul Einzig, *The World Economic Crisis: 1929–1931* (London, 1931), pp. vii–viii, 78.
14. H. V. Hodson, *Economics of a Changing World* (London, 1933), p. 280.
15. Lionel Robbins, *The Great Depression* (London, 1934), pp. 114, 190; C. C. Cox, "Monopoly Explanations of the Great Depression and Public Policies toward Business," in Karl Brunner, ed., *The Great Depression Revisited* (Boston, 1981), pp. 174–207.
16. Eugen Varga, *The Great Crisis and Its Political Consequences* (New York, 1934).
17. Haberler, *Prosperity and Depression*, pp. 2, 6–7, 168–69.
18. J. A. Garraty, *Unemployment in History: Economic Thought and Public Policy* (New York, 1978), pp. 167–70.
19. J. R. Moore, "Sources of New Deal Economic Policy," *Journal of American History* 61 (1974): 730.
20. D. H. Aldcroft, *From Versailles to Wall Street* (Berkeley, 1977), p. 383; C. B. Schedvin, *Australia and the Great Depression* (Sydney, 1970), p. 94; Sauvy, *Histoire économique*, vol. 2, 360, 469–70; Milton Friedman and A. J. Schwartz, *A Monetary History of the United States* (Princeton, 1963), pp. 247, 408, 411.
21. H. W. Arndt, *The Economic Lessons of the Nineteen-Thirties* (London, 1963), p. 254.
22. Susan Howson and Donald Winch, *The Economic Advisory Council, 1930–1939* (Cambridge, Engl., 1977), p. 31.
23. A. U. Romasco, *The Poverty of Abundance: Hoover, the Nation, the Depression* (New York, 1965), p. 222; R. G. Tugwell, *In Search of Roosevelt* (Cambridge, Mass., 1972), p. 150.
24. *New York Times*, April 16, 1983; Samuel Rosenman, ed., *The Public Papers and Addresses of Franklin D. Roosevelt*, vol. 2 (New York, 1938–50), p. 50; A. M. Schlesinger, Jr., *The Coming of the New Deal* (Boston, 1959), p. 10.

25. Heinrich Brüning, *Memoiren* (Stuttgart, 1970), p. 173; Edouard Bonnefous, *Histoire politique de la Troisième République*, vol. 5 (Paris, 1962), p. 138.

26. Kozo Yamamura, "Japan's Economic Recovery," in Herman van der Wee, ed., *The Great Depression Revisited* (The Hague, 1972), p. 199; L. J. Louis and Ian Turner, eds., *The Depression of the 1930's* (Melbourne, 1968), p. 217.

27. H. B. Neatby, *William Lyon MacKensie King*, vol. 2 (Toronto, 1963), pp. 307, 361, 394; Kenneth McNaught, in J. M. S. Careless and R. C. Brown, eds., *The Canadians*, vol. 1 (Toronto, 1968), p. 247.

28. P. T. Ellsworth, *Chile: An Economy in Transition* (New York, 1945), pp. 6, 16; J. M. Young, *The Brazilian Revolution of 1930 and the Aftermath* (New Brunswick, 1967), p. 75.

29. Jack Taylor, *The Economic Development of Poland* (Ithaca, 1952), pp. 35–47; Joseph Harrison, "The Inter-War Depression and the Spanish Economy," *Journal of European Economic History* 12 (1983): 317–18; Z. P. Pryor, "Czechoslovak Fiscal Policies in the Great Depression," *Economic History Review* 32 (1979): 232, 238–39.

30. Sidney Pollard, "The Trade Unions and the Depression," in Hans Mommsen, ed., *Industrielles System und politische Entwicklung in der Weimarer Republik* (Dusseldorf, 1974), p. 245.

31. *Financial Times*, Sept. 14, 1931, quoted in Marguerite Perrot, *La monnaie et l'opinion publique en France et en Angleterre de 1924 à 1936* (Paris, 1955), pp. 76–77.

32. Quoted in L. V. Chandler, *American Monetary Policy, 1928–1941* (New York, 1971) pp. 118, 124–25.

33. Howson and Winch, *Economic Advisory Council*, p. 284; Chandler, *Monetary Policy*, pp. 125–26.

34. D. E. Moggridge, *The Return to Gold, 1925* (Cambridge, Engl., 1969), p. 69. But see also Aldcroft, *Versailles to Wall Street*, pp. 170–72, 202–3, where the effects of this are somewhat played down.

35. Sauvy, *Histoire économique*, vol. 1, pp. 95–99; L. V. Chandler, *Benjamin Strong: Central Banker* (Washington, 1958), pp. 371–72.

36. Hoover, *Great Depression*, p. 9.

37. Friedman and Schwartz, *Monetary Policy*, pp. 269, 289–92, 362–91; Aldcroft, *Versailles to Wall Street*, pp. 92–96, 277, 281–83, 300; Brunner, *Great Depression Revisited*, passim.

38. C. P. Kindleberger, *The World in Depression* (Berkeley, 1973), pp. 28, 294.

39. Ibid, pp. 299, 306; Kindleberger, "International Capital Movements

and Foreign-Exchange Markets in Crises: The 1930s and the 1980s," unpublished paper, preliminary session, International Economic History Conference (Budapest, March 1985), p. 6.

CHAPTER II

1. Quoted in D. R. McCoy, *Calvin Coolidge: The Quiet President* (New York, 1967), p. 392.
2. Robert Skidelsky, *Politicians and the Slump* (London, 1967), p. 83.
3. Alfred Sauvy, *Histoire économique de la France entre les deux guerres*, vol. 1 (Paris, 1965), pp. 107–8, 118.
4. R. L. Buell, *Europe: A History of Ten Years*, quoted in W. Halperin, *Germany Tried Democracy* (New York, 1965), p. 362.
5. J. K. Galbraith, *The Great Crash: 1929* (Boston, 1961), pp. 116–17; A. M. Schlesinger, Jr., *The Crisis of the Old Order* (Boston, 1957), p. 162; R. Dufraisse, "Le mouvement ouvrier français 'rouge' devant la grande dépression économique," in Denise Fauvel-Rouiff, ed., *Mouvements ouvriers et dépression économique* (Assen, Holland 1966), p. 175.
6. Schlesinger, *Crisis of the Old Order*, p. 231; Robert Sobel, *The Great Bull Market: Wall Street in the 1920s* (New York, 1968), pp. 120–22.
7. A. U. Romasco, *The Poverty of Abundance: Hoover, the Nation, the Depression* (New York, 1965), p. 181; G. D. Nash, "Herbert Hoover and the Origins of the Reconstruction Finance Corporation," *Mississippi Valley Historical Review*, 46 (1959): 462–65.
8. David Hamilton, "Herbert Hoover and the Great Drought of 1930," *Journal of American History* 68 (1981): 871; L. V. Chandler, *America's Greatest Depression: 1929–1941* (New York, 1970), p. 125.
9. Romasco, *Poverty of Abundance*, pp. 88, 90; Nash, "Reconstruction Finance Corporation," pp. 462–65; Herbert Hoover, *Memoirs: The Great Depression* (New York, 1952), p. 97.
10. Sidney Pollard, *The Gold Standard and Employment Policies between the Wars* (London, 1970), p. 9.
11. Skidelsky, *Politicians and the Slump*, p. 205; Susan Howson and Donald Winch, *The Economic Advisory Council, 1930–1939* (Cambridge, Engl., 1977), pp. 180–243, esp. 198, 200–201, 77–78.
12. Quoted in A. U. Romasco, *The Politics of Recovery: Roosevelt's New Deal* (New York, 1983), p. 16.
13. Skidelsky, *Politicians and the Slump*, pp. 348–49.

14. Jacques Chastenet, *Histoire de la troisième république*, vol. 5 (Paris, 1960), p. 191.
15. Quoted in David Thomson, *Democracy in France* (London, 1952), pp. 70–71.
16. Edouard Bonnefous, *Histoire politique de la troisième république*, vol. 5 (Paris, 1962), p. 103. For French budget statistics see Sauvy, *Histoire économique*, vol. 2, p. 577.
17. Sauvy, *Histoire économique*, vol. 2, p. 17.
18. H. H. Tiltman, *Slump! A Study of Stricken Europe To-day* (London, 1932), p. 217–18.
19. Andreas Dorpalen, *Hindenburg and the Weimar Republic* (Princeton, 1964), p. 196.
20. Romasco, *Poverty of Abundance*, p. 187.
21. Wilhelm Grotkopp, *Die grosse Krise* (Dusseldorf, 1954), p. 18.
22. Halperin, *Germany Tried Democracy*, p. 520.
23. Sauvy, *Histoire économique*, vol. 2, p. 49.
24. Alan Sweezy, "The Keynesians and Government Policy, 1937–1939," *American Economic Review* 62, no. 2 (1921): 121; Lauchlin Currie, "Comments and Observations," *History of Political Economy* 10 (1978):541; H. W. Richardson, *Economic Recovery in Britain* (London, 1967), p. 185.
25. H. W. Arndt, *Economic Lessons of the Nineteen-Thirties* (London, 1963), p. 129.
26. *Economist*, June 18, 1932, quoted in Richardson, *Economic Recovery*, pp. 213–14.
27. Joel Colton, *Léon Blum: Humanist in Politics* (New York, 1966), p. 80.

CHAPTER III

1. B. B. Wallace and L. R. Edminster, *International Control of Raw Materials* (Washington, 1930); League of Nations, *Raw Materials Problems and Policies* (Geneva, 1946); A. J. H. Latham, *The Depression and the Developing World, 1914–1939* (London, 1981), p. 170; Richard Cotter, "War, Boom and Depression," in James Griffin, ed., *Essays in the Economic History of Australia* (Brisbane, 1967), pp. 272–73.
2. Michael Tracy, *Agriculture in Western Europe: Crisis and Adaptation since 1880* (London, 1966), pp. 117–24, 137; Paul de Hevesy, *World*

263

Wheat Planning and Economic Planning in General (London, 1940), pp. 1, 3–4; Latham, *Developing World*, p. 176.

3. C. P. Kindleberger, *The World in Depression: 1929–1939* (Berkeley, 1973), pp. 86–91, 94–95; Theodore Saloutos, *The American Farmer and the New Deal* (Ames, 1982), pp. 5–14; V. P. Timoshenko, *World Agriculture and the Depression* (Ann Arbor, 1953); H. V. Hodson, *Economics of a Changing World* (London, 1933), pp. 1–29; Edgars Dunsdorfs, *The Australian Wheat-Growing Industry: 1788–1948* (Melbourne, 1956), pp. 204–5, 263.

4. Karl Brunner, ed., *The Great Depression Revisited* (Boston, 1981), p. 176.

5. K. E. Knorr, *World Rubber and Its Regulation* (Stanford, 1945), pp. 4–5, 23–24, 90–101; C. A. Gehlsen, *World Rubber Production and Trade* (Rome, 1940), pp. 17–19; A. Neytzell de Wilde and J. T. Moll, *The Netherlands Indies during the Great Depression* (Amsterdam, 1936), p. 26; Wallace and Edminster, *International Control of Raw Materials*, pp. 172–218, esp. pp. 174–75. For the text of the Stevenson report see ibid., pp. 401–21.

6. C. K. Warner, *The Winegrowers of France and the Government since 1875* (New York, 1960), pp. 26–30; Pierre Barral, *Les agrariens Français de Méline à Pisani* (Paris, 1968), p. 203; Gordon Wright, *Rural Revolution in France* (Stanford, 1964), pp. 37, 44.

7. Quoted in U. S. Dept. of Agriculture, *Yearbook: 1940* (Washington, 1941), pp. 309–10.

8. G. C. Fite, *George N. Peek and the Fight for Farm Parity* (Norman, Okla., 1954); Saloutos, *Farmer and the New Deal*, pp. 20–24, 27.

9. International Institute of Agriculture, *The World's Coffee* (Rome, 1947), pp. 447–48, 467–73; Celso Furtado, *The Economic Growth of Brazil* (Berkeley, 1963), pp. 193–99; J. M. Young, *The Brazilian Revolution of 1930 and the Aftermath* (New Brunswick, 1967), pp. 71–72.

10. Herbert Hoover, *Memoirs: 1920–1933*, vol. 2 (New York, 1952), p. 110; J. H. Shideler, "Herbert Hoover and the Federal Farm Bureau Project," *Mississippi Valley Historical Review* 42 (1956): 710–29; E. W. Hawley, ed., *Herbert Hoover as Secretary of Commerce: Studies in New Era Thought and Practice* (Iowa City, 1981), p. 32.

11. Edward Marcus, *Canada and the International Business Cycle* (New York, 1954), pp. 55–58, 143–44; J. W. F. Rowe, *Markets and Men* (New York, 1936), pp. 65–70; Ernest Watkins, *R. B. Bennett: A Biography* (London, 1963), pp. 183–84; W. S. Evans, "Canadian Wheat

Stabilization Operations, 1929–35," *Wheat Studies* 12 (1936): 257–59.

12. Wilfred Malenbaum, *The World Wheat Economy, 1885–1939* (Cambridge, Mass., 1953), p. 199; A. F. Wyman and J. S. Davis, "Britain's New Wheat Policy in Perspective," *Wheat Studies* 9 (1933): 327–33; Tracy, *Agriculture in Western Europe*, p. 140.

13. Kindleberger, *The World in Depression*, pp. 91–94; Lazar Volin, *A Century of Russian Agriculture* (Cambridge, Mass., 1970), p. 232; Dunsdorfs, *Australian Wheat*, pp. 267–70; C. B. Schedvin, *Australia and the Great Depression* (Sydney, 1970), pp. 146–73, 340–41; *1940 Yearbook*, pp. 312–13; Rowe, *Markets and Men*, pp. 110–12; A. U. Romasco, *The Politics of Recovery: Roosevelt's New Deal* (New York, 1983) p. 172.

14. Furtado, *Economic Growth of Brazil*, pp. 206–7; V. D. Wickizer, *Coffee, Tea, and Cocoa: An Economic and Political Analysis* (Stanford, 1951), p. 80; V. D. Wickizer, *The World Coffee Economy* (Stanford, 1943), pp. 147ff. For the details of Vargas's restructuring of coffee controls see U. S. Congress, 73:1, Senate Doc. 70, *World Trade Barriers in Relation to American Agriculture* (Washington, 1933), pp. 313–15.

15. International Institute of Agriculture, *World Cotton Production and Trade* (Rome, 1936), pp. 179, 185–90; *World Trade Barriers*, pp. 247–48, 357–58.

16. Wickizer, *Coffee, Tea, and Cocoa*, p. 191–92; V. D. Wickizer, *Tea under International Regulation* (Stanford, 1944), pp. 66–70; de Wilde and Moll, *Netherlands Indies*, pp. 31–33; W. H. Ukers, *All About Tea*, vol. 1 (New York, 1935), pp. 347–48.

17. Knorr, *World Rubber*, pp. 102–7; de Wilde and Moll, *Netherlands Indies*, p. 27; Latham, *Developing World*, pp. 162–63.

18. Rowe, *Markets and Men*, pp. 82–84; de Wilde and Moll, *Netherlands Indies*, p. 38; *World Trade Barriers*, pp. 97–99, 276–78, 338–42.

19. Barral, *Agrariens Français*, pp. 226–30; Warner, *Winegrowers*, pp. 93–112.

20. *World Trade Barriers*, pp. 352–53; *Wheat Studies* 7 (1931): 439–66.

21. League of Nations Economic Committee, *Considerations on the Present Evolution of Agricultural Protectionism* (Geneva, 1935), pp. 26, 29; J. S. Cohen, "Fascism and Agriculture in Italy: Policies and Consequences," *Economic History Review* 32 (1979): 71–73; C. L. Mowat, *Britain Between the Wars* (Boston, 1971), pp. 253, 439; Wyman and Davis, "Britain's Wheat Policy," pp. 330–32.

22. Gerhard Kroll, *Von der Weltwirtschaftskrise zur Staatskonjunktur* (Berlin, 1958), p. 525; J. E. Farquharson, *The Plough and the Swastika: The NSDAP and Agriculture in Germany 1928–45* (London, 1976), p. 27; Hugh Seton-Watson, *Eastern Europe between the Wars* (New York, 1967), pp. 100–101; Adam Rosé, et al., *Pologne: 1919–39*, vol. 2 (Neuchâtel, 1946), p. 141; E. E. Malefakis, *Agricultural Reform and Peasant Revolution in Spain: Origins of Civil War* (New Haven, 1970), p. 236n; J. Vincens Vives, "Espagne: La Crise Economique," Denise Fauvel Rouif, ed., in *Mouvements ouvriers et dépression économique* (Assen, Holland, 1976), pp. 106, 109.

23. Zbigniew Landau, "Polish Countryside in the Years 1929–1935," *Acta Poloniae Historica* 9 (1964): 44; B. R. Mitchell, *European Historical Statistics: 1750–1970* (New York, 1976), p. 260; Tracy, *Agriculture in Western Europe*, pp. 120–24, 140, 157–58; Michael Tracy, "Agriculture in the Great Depression," in Herman van der Wee, ed., *The Great Depression Revisited: Essays on the Economics of the Thirties* (The Hague, 1972), pp. 94–98, 102; I. M. Drummond, "The British Empire Economies in the Great Depression," ibid., pp. 229–30; Malenbaum, *World Wheat Economy*, pp. 161–63, 166–67.

24. Tracy, *Agriculture in Western Europe*, pp. 130, 137; *Wheat Studies* 8 (1932): 229.

25. League of Nations Economic Committee, *The Agricultural Crisis*, vol. 1 (Geneva, 1931), passim, esp. pp. 57, 60, 73–74, 81, 127, 139, 236, 264, 286–87.

26. Saloutos, *American Farmer and the New Deal*, pp. 48–49.

27. W. D. Rowley, *M. L. Wilson and the Campaign for the Domestic Allotment* (Lincoln, 1970), pp. 3–5, 48–49.

28. 72nd Congress, 2nd Session, House Committee on Agriculture, *Hearings*, December 16, 1932, pp. 141–58.

29. Mitchell, *European Historical Statistics*, p. 573; A. E. Taylor, "Economic Nationalism in Europe as Applied to Wheat," *Wheat Studies* 8 (1932): 259, 274–76; League of Nations, *Agricultural Protectionism*, pp. 15–29.

30. Wickizer, *Tea under International Agreement*, pp. 72–75; de Wilde and Moll, *Netherlands Indies*, pp. 33–35.

31. de Wilde and Moll, *Netherlands Indies*, pp. 27–31; Knorr, *World Rubber*, pp. 107–13; Galensen, *World Rubber Production and Trade*, pp. 22–27, 179–92.

32. Tracy, *Agriculture in Western Europe*, p. 147; Paul de Hevesy, *Le*

problème mondial du blé (Paris, 1934), pp. 135–36, 268–71; *Wheat Studies* 11 (1934): 141–43.

33. Malenbaum, *World Wheat Economy*, pp. 13–14; M. J. Francioni and Emilio Llorens, *Ritmo de la Economía Argentina en los últimos 30 Años* (Buenos Aires, 1941), pp. 299–300; de Hevesy, *World Wheat Planning*, p. 22n; *Wheat Studies* 11 (1934): 143, 147; Tracy, "Agriculture," pp. 99–100; Tracy, *Agriculture in Western Europe*, pp. 219–21.

34. Tracy, *Agriculture in Western Europe*, pp. 127, 159–60, 176; Sidney Pollard, *The Development of the British Economy: 1914–1967* (London, 1969), pp. 139–42; Bertil Ohlin, "Economic Recovery and Labour Market Problems in Sweden," *International Labour Review* 31 (1935): 686; Barral, *Agrariens Français*, pp. 228–29; Sauvy, *Histoire économique*, vol. 2, pp. 65–66, 382.

35. Tracy, *Agriculture in Western Europe*, pp. 202–6; Farquharson, *Plough and Swastika*, pp. 25–70; Kroll, *Weltwirtschaftskrise*, pp. 525–28.

36. Kindleberger, *World in Depression*, pp. 215, 219; Pollard, *British Economy*, p. 142; Romasco, *Politics of Recovery*, pp. 75–90; Herbert Feis, *1933: Characters in Crisis* (Boston, 1966), pp. 25, 170–71, 234, 262; J. R. Moore, "Sources of New Deal Economic Policy: The International Dimension," *Journal of American History* 61 (1974): 728–44.

37. Wickizer, *Coffee, Tea, and Cocoa*, pp. 192–207, *Tea under International Agreement*, pp. 75–79, 93–95; Knorr, *World Rubber*, pp. 113–15, 130–31.

38. *World Cotton Production*, pp. 190–99, 236, 244; Romasco, *Politics of Recovery*, p. 173; Rosemary Thorp and Geoffrey Bertram, *Peru: 1890–1977* (London, 1978), pp. 175–76; Furtado, *Economic Growth of Brazil*, p. 207; *World's Coffee*, pp. 396, 400–401.

39. Lionel Robbins, *The Great Depression* (New York, 1934), p. 67; *Wheat Studies* 11 (1934): 138, 143–44; J. S. Davis, *Wheat under International Agreement* (New York, 1945), p. 7; Donald Worster, *Dust Bowl: The Southern Plains in the 1930s* (New York, 1979), pp. 157–58; C. M. Campbell, *The Farm Bureau and the New Deal* (Urbana, 1962), p. 70; V. L. Perkins, *Crisis in Agriculture: The AAA and the New Deal: 1933* (Berkeley, 1969), pp. 128–29.

40. H. B. Neatby, *William Lloyd Mackensie King*, vol. 2 (Toronto, 1966), p. 366; *Historical Statistics*, vol. 1, pp. 511–12; Worster, *Dust Bowl*, p. 151. On the causes of the ups and downs of wheat production and prices during the depression see J. S. Davis, *et al.*, *A Guide to Wheat*

Studies of the Food Research Institute (Stanford, 1945), pp. 6–13.
41. Michel Gervais, *La fin de la France paysanne* (Paris, 1976), pp. 558–60; Barral, *Agrariens Français*, pp. 245–46; Georges Lefranc, *Histoire du Front Populaire* (Paris, 1965), pp. 344–50.
42. Wright, *Rural Revolution*, p. 64; de Hevesy, *World Wheat Planning*, p. 29.
43. C. F. Diaz Alejandro, "Latin America in Depression," Yale Economic Growth Center Discussion Paper #344 (1980), p. 5; Vera Anstey, *The Economic Development of India* (New York, 1952), pp. 497, 514; K. L. Mitchell, *Japan's Industrial Strength* (New York, 1942), pp. 20–23; E. J. Riches, "The Depression in New Zealand," *International Labour Review* 28 (1933): 617–34.
44. P. T. Ellsworth, *Chile: An Economy in Transition* (New York, 1945), pp. 3–16, 23–32; Hirschman, *Journeys toward Progress*, pp. 180–81.
45. Anstey, *Development of India*, pp. 495–99, 514, 519–29; Mitchell, *Japan's Strength*, pp. 18–25; G. C. Allen, *Japan's Economic Recovery* (London, 1958), p. 8.
46. Enrique Cárdenas, "Mexico's Industrialization during the Great Depression: Public Policy and Private Response," *Journal of Economic History* 44 (1984): 603–5; Joseph Harrison, "The Inter-War Depression and the Spanish Economy," *Journal of European Economic History* 12 (1983): 296; Juan Hernández Andreu, *Depresion Economica en España: 1925–1934* (Madrid, 1980), pp. 83–86, 170–73; Schedvin, *Australia and the Depression*, pp. 301–7, 377; Cotter, "War, Boom and Depression," p. 269; Diaz Alejandro, "Latin America in Depression," p. 38; Albert Fishlow, "Origins and Consequences of Import Substitution in Brazil," in L. E. Di Marco, ed., *International Economics and Development* (New York, 1972), pp. 326–39; Furtado, *Economic Growth of Brazil*, pp. 211–20; Young, *Brazilian Revolution*, p. 82; Warren Dean, *The Industrialization of São Paulo* (Austin, 1969), p. 112.
47. Diaz Alejandro, "Latin America in Depression," pp. 13–14, 30.
48. Perkins, *Crisis in Agriculture*, pp. 170, 175; D. E. Conrad, *The Forgotten Farmers* (Urbana, 1965), passim; W. C. Whately, "Labor for the Picking: The New Deal in the South," *Journal of Economic History* 43 (1983): 926–29; Cohen, "Fascist Agriculture," pp. 82–83, 85; Knorr, *World Rubber*, p. 122.
49. Harrison, "Spanish Depression," pp. 311–12; John Gunther, *Inside Latin America* (New York, 1941), p. 70; S. A. Mosk, *Industrial Rev-*

olution in Mexico (Berkeley, 1950), pp. 53–57; C. W. Reynolds, *The Mexican Economy: Twentieth Century Structure and Growth* (New Haven, 1970), pp. 141–42, 146; Hirschman, *Journeys toward Progress*, pp. 96, 107–11.

50. Twelve Southerners, *I'll Take My Stand* (New York, 1930), pp. 234, 243–44; Jean Giono, *Lettre aux paysans sur la pauvrété et la paix* (Paris, 1938), pp. 34–35, 41, 53, 55, 60–68.

51. R. S. and H. M. Lynd, *Middletown in Transition* (New York, 1937), pp. 192–93; Tracy, *Agriculture in Western Europe*, pp. 199–200; Farquharson, *Plough and Swastika*, pp. 107–24; J. A. Garraty, "The New Deal, National Socialism, and the Great Depression," *American Historical Review* 78 (1973): 919–20; Karl Brandt, "The German Back-to-the-Land Movement," *Land Economics* 11 (1935): 123–32; Japanese Imperial Agricultural Society, quoted in Tracy, *Agriculture in Western Europe*, pp. 129–30.

52. Garraty, "New Deal and National Socialism," pp. 919–20; Barral, *Agrariens Français*, pp. 233, 249.

53. Cohen, "Fascist Agriculture," p. 85; Brandt, "Back-to-the-Land," p. 132; Letellier, *Chômage*, pp. 318–19.

54. O. E. Baker, "Back to the Land," *World Today* 1 (October, 1933): 58; J. M. S. Careless and R. C. Brown, *The Canadians*, vol. 1 (Toronto, 1968), p. 240; Barral, *Agrariens Français*, pp. 221–34.

55. W. S. Woytinsky, *Social Consequences of the Economic Depression* (Geneva, 1936), p. 230.

CHAPTER IV

1. B. R. Mitchell, *European Economic Statistics* (New York, 1976), p. 169.

2. Sidney Pollard, "The Trade Unions and the Depression of 1929–1933," in Hans Mommsen, ed., *Industrielles System und politische Entwicklung in der Weimarer Republik* (Dusseldorf, 1974), p. 244; Sean Glynn and Alan Booth, "Unemployment in Interwar Britain: A Case for Relearning the Lessons of the 1930s?" *Economic History Review* 36 (1983): 333.

3. Irving Bernstein, *The Lean Years: A History of the American Worker, 1920–1933* (Baltimore, 1966), p. 49.

4. Denise Fauvel-Rouif, ed., *Mouvements ouvriers et dépression écon-*

omique de 1929 à 1939 (Assen, Holland, 1966), pp. 44, 124–25, 164–69, 235.

5. Philip Taft, *Organized Labor in American History* (New York, 1964), pp. 412–14.
6. Glynn and Booth, "Unemployment in Interwar Britain," p. 336.
7. D. H. Aldcroft, *The Inter-War Economy: Britain 1919–1939* (London, 1973), p. 147.
8. W. Campbell Balfour, "British Labour," in Fauvel-Rouif, *Mouvements ouvriers*, pp. 136–37; Robert Skidelsky, *Politicians and the Slump* (London, 1967), pp. 9, 395.
9. V. R. Lorwin, *The French Labor Movement* (Cambridge, Mass., 1954), pp. 71–72; Leon Jouhaux, *La C. G. T.: ce qu'elle est, ce qu'elle veut* (Paris, 1937), pp. 169–87.
10. Georges Lefranc, *Le mouvement syndicale sous la Troisième République* (Paris, 1967), p. 265; R. Dufraisse, "Mouvement ouvrier français 'rouge'," in Fauvel-Rouif, *Mouvements ouvriers*, pp. 183–85.
11. Lefranc, *Mouvement syndicale*, pp. 282–83.
12. Dufraisse, "Mouvement ouvrier français," pp. 185–87; Alfred Sauvy, *Histoire économique de la France entre les deux guerres*, vol. 3 (Paris, 1972), pp. 186–87.
13. Lefranc, *Mouvement syndicale*, p. 307.
14. Dufraisse, "Mouvement ouvrier français," p. 185.
15. W. Conze, "Mouvement ouvrier en Allemagne," in Fauvel-Rouif, *Mouvements ouvriers*, pp. 41–47.
16. Ibid., pp. 53–55.
17. W. S. Woytinsky, *Stormy Passage* (New York, 1961), passim; "Wladimir Savelievich Woytinsky," in *Dictionary of American Biography*, suppl. 6, pp. 708–10.
18. Glynn and Booth, "Unemployment in Interwar Britain," pp. 346–47.
19. David Montgomery, *Workers' Control in America* (Cambridge, Engl., 1979), p. 148.
20. Campbell Balfour, "British Labour," pp. 237, 247.

CHAPTER V

1. B. R. Mitchell, *European Historical Statistics* (New York, 1976), p. 172; Gene Smiley, "Recent Unemployment Estimates," *Journal of Economic History* 42 (1983): 487; *International Labour Review* 33 (1936): 90–91.

2. Jan Rosner, "Measures to Combat the Depression and Unemployment in Poland," *International Labour Review* 30 (1934): 160–63; J. A. Garraty, *Unemployment in History: Economic Thought and Public Policy* (New York, 1978), p. 168.
3. E. W. Bakke, *The Unemployed Man: A Social Study* (London, 1933).
4. Marie Jahoda, P. L. Lazarsfeld, and Hans Zeisel, *Marienthal: The Sociography of an Unemployed Community* (Chicago, 1971).
5. On this subject, see Garraty, *Unemployment*, pp. 174ff.
6. Ibid., pp. 174–75; Ray Broomhill, *Unemployed Workers: A Social History of the Great Depression in Adelaide* (St. Lucia, Australia, 1978), p. 89.
7. George Orwell, *The Road to Wigan Pier* (New York, 1961), pp. 84–89; Siegfried Kracauer, *Strassen in Berlin und anderswo* (Frankfurt-am-Main, 1964), p. 93; Garraty, *Unemployment*, p. 176.
8. R. S. and Helen Lynd, *Middletown in Transition* (New York, 1936), p. 391; Orwell, *Road to Wigan Pier*, p. 89.
9. Garraty, *Unemployment*, p. 177; H. H. Tiltman, *Slump! A Story of Stricken Europe To-day* (London, 1932), pp. 181–82; Broomhill, *Unemployed Workers*, p. 164; Barbara Blumberg, *The New Deal and the Unemployed: The View from New York City* (Lewisburg, Pa., 1979), p. 18.
10. Pilgrim Trust, *Men without Work* (London, 1938).
11. Bakke, *Unemployed Man*, pp. 64–67.
12. Pilgrim Trust, *Men without Work*, p. 159.
13. Lazarsfeld, *Marienthal*, pp. 52–54, 66.
14. Pilgrim Trust, *Men without Work*, pp. 149, 150; L. J. Louis and Ian Turner, eds., *The Depression of the 1930s* (Melbourne, 1968), p. 118; Walter Greenwood, *Love on the Dole* (London, 1969), p. 169; B. N. Haken *Die Ehe des Arbeitslosen Martin Krug* (Oldenburg, 1932), p. 71.
15. Kracauer, *Strassen in Berlin*, p. 74; C. Trout, *Boston, the Great Depression, and the New Deal* (New York, 1977), p. 175; W. W. Bremer, "Along the 'American Way': The New Deal's Work Relief Programs for the Unemployed," *Journal of American History* 62 (1975): 636.
16. Garraty, *Unemployment*, pp. 180–81.
17. Ibid., pp. 179–82; Broomhill, *Unemployed Workers*, p. 43.
18. G. H. Elder, Jr., *Children of the Depression* (Chicago, 1974), pp. 114, 278; Lazarsfeld, *Marienthal*, pp. 84–85.

271

19. *Vossische Zeitung*, January 18, 1931, quoted in Wilhelm Treue, ed., *Deutschland in der Weltwirtschaftskrise in Augenzeugenberichten* (Dusseldorf, 1967), pp. 245–62.
20. Clifford Kirkpatrick, *Women in Nazi Germany* (Indianapolis, 1938), p. 211; Marguerite Thibert, "The Economic Depression and the Employment of Women: II," *International Labour Review* 27 (1933): 620–23.
21. J. S. Mill, *Principles of Political Economy* (London, 1925), pp. 344–45, 362.
22. Karl Marx, *Capital: A Critique of Political Economy*, vol. 1 (Chicago, 1906), pp. 690, 694–95.
23. Lionel Robbins, *The Great Depression* (London, 1934), pp. 60–75, 188, 190.
24. Jacques Rueff, "L'assurance-chômage, cause de chômage permanent," *Revue d'économie politique* 45 (1931): 222ff.; Wilhelm Grottkopf, *Die grosse Krise* (Dusseldorf, 1954), pp. 28, 49.
25. R. F. Harrod, *The Life of John Maynard Keynes* (New York, 1971), p. 470; R. F. Kahn, "The Relation of Home Investment to Unemployment," *Economic Journal* 41 (1931): 173–98.
26. I. M. Drummond, *Imperial Economic Policy: 1917–1939* (London, 1974), pp. 43–144.
27. G. S. Cross, *Immigrant Workers in Industrial France* (Philadelphia, 1983), pp. 200–204.
28. A. O. Hirschman, *Journey toward Progress: Studies in Economic Policy-Making in Latin America* (New York, 1963), p. 101; Warren Dean, *The Industrialization of São Paulo* (Austin, 1969), p. 118; Enriques Sievers, "Unemployment in Argentina," *International Labour Review* 31 (1935): 792; Gabrielle Letellier, *Le chômage en France de 1930 à 1936* (Paris, 1938), pp. 317–19.
29. L. M. Grayson and Michael Bliss, eds., *The Wretched of Canada* (Toronto, 1971), pp. xv–xvi; Fritz Rager, "The Settlement of the Unemployed on Land in Austria," *International Labour Review* 29 (1934): 287–93; Addison of Stallingborough, *A Policy for British Agriculture* (London, 1939), pp. 242, 249–50; R. S. Kirkendall, *Social Scientists and Farm Policy in the Age of Roosevelt* (Columbia, Mo., 1966), p. 23.
30. Addison, *British Agriculture*, pp. 251, 253; Letellier, *Chômage*, p. 70.
31. Tiltman, *Slump!*, pp. 223–24; Garraty, *Unemployment*, p. 212.

CHAPTER VI

1. George Soule, *The Coming American Revolution* (New York, 1934), pp. 189, 191; Joseph Dorfman, *The Economic Mind in American Civilization*, vol. 5 (New York, 1959), p. 630.
2. Soule, *Coming Revolution*, p. 300.
3. Georges Hersent, *La bataille économique* (Paris, 1934), pp. 196, 193; Robert Wolff, "Réflections sur les crises," *Revue d'économie politique* 46 (1932): 1288–1320; Marguerite Perrot, *La monnaie et l'opinion publique en France et en Angleterre de 1924 à 1936* (Paris, 1955), p. 210.
4. A. M. Schlesinger, Jr., *The Coming of the New Deal* (Boston, 1959), p. 364.
5. A. M. Schlesinger, Jr., *The Politics of Upheaval* (Boston, 1960), pp. 113–14.
6. Gina Lombroso, *Le retour à la prosperité* (Paris, 1933), p. 201.
7. Werner Sombart, *Deutscher Sozialismus* (Berlin, 1934), pp. 7, 12–21, 31–36; Herman Lebovics, *Social Conservatism and the Middle Classes in Germany, 1914–1933* (Princeton, 1969), pp. 63–65.
8. Paul Hollander, *Political Pilgrims: Travels of Western Intellectuals to the Soviet Union, China, and Cuba* (New York, 1981), p. 93; Georges Duhamel, *Scènes de la vie future* (Paris, 1930), pp. 18, 102–10.
9. Aldous Huxley, *Jesting Pilate* (New York, 1926), p. 300.
10. Duhamel, *Vie future*, pp. 230–32.
11. C. C. Cox, "Monopoly Explanations of the Great Depression," in Karl Brunner, ed., *The Great Depression Revisited* (Boston, 1981), pp. 178, 176; Stuart Chase, *A New Deal* (New York, 1932), p. 130.
12. Enid Charles, *The Twilight of Parenthood* (London, 1934), pp. 75, 100, 105, 219; Ferdinand Fried, *Das Ende des Kapitalismus* (Jena, 1931), pp. 5–15; Lebovics, *Social Conservatism in Germany*, pp. 181–85.
13. Dorfman, *Economic Mind*, 5: 724; Alvin Hansen, "Economic Progress and Declining Population Growth," *American Economic Review* 29 (1939) :1–13; Alvin Hansen, *Full Recovery or Stagnation?* (New York, 1938), p. 29; Joan Robinson, *Introduction to the Theory of Employment* (New York, 1937), pp. 120–23; Stuart Chase, *Mexico: A Study of Two Americas* (New York, 1931), p. 315, 322.
14. Jacques Duboin, *Le grand relève des hommes par la machine* (Paris, 1932), passim; R. H. Pells, *Radical Visions and American Dreams* (New York, 1974), pp. 108–9.

15. H. V. Hodson, *Economics of a Changing World* (New York, 1933), p. 283.

16. On Technocracy, see J. G. Frederick, ed., *For and Against Technocracy* (New York, 1933); W. E. Akin, *Technocracy and the American Dream: The Technocrat Movement, 1900–1941* (Berkeley, 1977); Walter Rautenstrauch, "Technocracy," *World Today* 1 (October, 1933): 34; Dorfman, *Economic Mind*, vol. 5, pp. 647–49; G. A. Laing, *Towards Technocracy* (Los Angeles, 1933); Henry Elsner, Jr., *The Technocrats: Prophets of Automation* (Syracuse, 1967).

17. Paul Devinat, *Scientific Management in Europe* (Geneva, 1927), pp. 164–68 and passim.

18. J. A. Merkle, *Management and Ideology: The Legacy of the International Scientific Management Movement* (Berkeley, 1980), pp. 105–15, 121–23, 186–99, 227–31; C. S. Meier, "Between Taylorism and Technocracy," *Journal of Contemporary History* 5, 2 (1970): 51n, 47–49; W. A. Lewchuk, "The Role of the British Government in the Spread of Scientific Management and Fordism in the Interwar Years," *Journal of Economic History* 44 (1984): 360–61.

19. G. D. H. Cole, *Economic Planning* (New York, 1935), p. 3.

20. Ibid., p. 361.

21. C. A. Beard, *Toward Civilization* (New York, 1930), pp. 300–301; C. A. Beard, *America Faces the Future* (Boston, 1932), p. 124.

22. R. T. Ely, *Hard Times—The Way In and the Way Out* (New York, 1931), pp. 104–5, 122.

23. David Caute, *The Fellow-Travellers: A Postscript to the Enlightenment* (New York, 1973), pp. 67–70; Hollander, *Pilgrims*, pp. 77–78, 116; Julian Huxley, *A Scientist among the Soviets* (New York, 1932), p. 102; Pells, *American Visions*, p. 64; Hewlett Johnson, *The Soviet Power* (New York, 1940), pp. 63–64.

24. M. I. Cole, *Twelve Studies in Soviet Russia* (London, 1933), p. 33; Merkle, *Management and Ideology*, p. 125; P. G. Filene, *Americans and the Soviet Experiment, 1917–1933* (Cambridge, Mass., 1967), pp. 221, 241; Louis Fischer, *Men and Politics* (New York, 1941), pp. 216; Aneurin Bevan *et al.*, *What We Saw in Russia* (London, 1931), p. 9; Walter Johnson, ed., *Selected Letters of William Allen White* (New York, 1947), p. 337.

25. Andreas Dorpalen, *Hindenburg and the Weimar Republic* (Princeton, 1964), pp. 216–17; H. H. Tiltman, *Slump!: A Study of Stricken Europe To-day* (London, 1932), p. 16; H. R. Knickerbocker, *The Red Trade*

Menace (New York, 1931), pp. viii–xiii, 267, 271; André Gide, *Return from the USSR* (New York, 1937), pp. 16–18.

26. Filene, *Soviet Experiment*, pp. 196–97, 256; Beard, *America Faces the Future*, pp. 118, 397.

27. M. L. Roux, *Le socialisme de M. Henri de Man* (Paris, 1937), pp. 143–46; R. F. Kuisel, *Capitalism and the State in Modern France* (Cambridge, Engl., 1982) p. 108; Henry de Man, *L'idée socialiste* (Paris, 1935), pp. 536–42; Georges Lefranc, "Le courant planiste dans le mouvement ouvrier français," *Le mouvement social* 44 (1966): 669–89.

28. Quoted in Pierre Lucius, *Faillite du capitalisme?* (Paris, 1932), p. 8.

29. Kuisel, *Capitalism in France*, p. 102.

30. Cole, *Economic Planning*, pp. 125–26; J. P. Diggins, *Mussolini and Fascism: The View from America* (Princeton, 1972), pp. 162–65.

31. Lucius, *Faillite du capitalism?*, pp. 176, 181.

32. J. G. Frederick, ed., *The Swope Plan: Details, Criticisms, Analysis* (New York, 1931); Beard, *America Faces the Future*, pp. 117–40, 160–85; R. M. Collins, *The Business Response to Keynes* (New York, 1981), p. 27.

33. Kuisel, *Capitalism in France*, p. 75.

34. Dorfman, *Economic Mind*, vol. 5, p. 680; D. H. Bennett, *Demagogues in the Depression* (New Brunswick, 1969), pp. 34, 63, 78; Alan Brinkley, *Voices of Protest: Huey Long, Father Coughlin, and the Great Depression* (New York, 1982), p. 156–57.

35. Wilhelm Grotkopp, *Die grosse Krise* (Dusseldorf, 1954), pp. 126, 142–43.

36. Abraham Holtzman, *The Townsend Movement: A Political Study* (New York, 1975); Bennett, *Demagogues in the Depression*, pp. 151–52, 159.

37. J. M. Keynes, *The General Theory of Employment, Interest and Money* (New York, 1964), pp. 357–58; Dorfman, *Economic Mind*, vol. 55, p. 686–87.

38. J. R. Bellerby, "World Inflation," in R. L. Smyth, ed., *Essays in the Economics of Socialism and Capitalism* (London, 1964), pp. 328–37.

39. J. A. Garraty, *Unemployment in History: Economic Thought and Public Policy* (New York, 1978), pp. 154–57.

40. J. M. Keynes, *The Economic Consequences of the Peace* (New York, 1920), p. 235; J. M. Keynes, *Essays in Persuasion* (New York, 1963), p. 92; D. E. Moggridge, *John Maynard Keynes* (New York, 1976), pp. 62–63; L. J. Louis and Ian Turner, eds., *The Depression of the 1930s* (Melbourne, 1968), pp. 217–19.

41. Keynes, *Essays in Persuasion*, pp. 86–87, 103, 152.
42. Lars Jonung, "The Depression in Sweden and the United States," in Brunner, *Depression Revisited*, pp. 298–303, 309–11; J. C. Wood, ed., *John Maynard Keynes: Critical Assessments*, vol. 2 (London, 1983), p. 345n.; Donald Winch, "The Keynesian Revolution in Sweden," *Journal of Political Economy* 74 (1966): 168–69.
43. R. F. Harrod, *The Life of John Maynard Keynes* (New York, 1971), pp. 505, 514, 519; *New York Times*, June 12, December 31, 1933, June 5, 1934; Frances Perkins, *The Roosevelt I Knew* (New York, 1946), pp. 225–26.
44. Moggridge, *Keynes*, p. 108; J. R. Davis, *The New Economics and the Old Economists* (Ames, 1971), p. 39.
45. A. U. Romasco, *The Politics of Recovery* (New York, 1983), p. 236.
46. G. C. Allen, *Japan's Economic Recovery* (London, 1958), pp. 3–4; Ursula Hüllbüsch, "Die deutschen Gewerkschaften in der Weltwirtschaftskrise," in Werner Conze and Hans Raupach, eds., *Die Staats- und Wirtschaftskrise des deutschen Reichs 1929/33* (Stuttgart, 1967), pp. 136–40.
47. Garraty, *Unemployment in History*, pp. 193–94; George Garvy, "Keynes and the Economic Activists of Pre-Hitler Germany," *Journal of Political Economy* 83 (1975): 399–401.
48. Heinrich Dräger, *Arbeitsbeschaffung durch produktive Kreditschöpfung* (Dusseldorf, 1932); Arthur Schweitzer, *Big Business in the Third Reich* (Bloomington, 1964), p. 83; Garvy, "Pre-Hitler Germany," p. 402.

CHAPTER VII

1. Paul Einzig, *The World Economic Crisis: 1929–1931* (London, 1932), pp. v, 83; J. M. Keynes, *Essays in Persuasion* (New York, 1963), pp. 135–36; *New York Times*, April 13, 1931.
2. League of Nations, *World Economic Survey: 1932–33* (Geneva, 1933), pp. 11, 63; Lionel Robbins, *The Great Depression* (New York, 1934), p. 11.
3. *Fortune* (September, 1932), p. 19.
4. Malcolm Little, *The Autobiography of Malcolm X* (New York, 1966), p. 13.
5. J. B. Priestley, *English Journey* (New York, 1934), p. 136.
6. Marie Jahoda, P. F. Lazarsfeld, and Hans Zeisel, *Marienthal: The*

Sociography of an Unemployed Community (Chicago, 1971), p. 33; Wilhelm Treue, ed., *Deutschland in der Weltwirtschaftskrise in Augenzeugenberichten* (Dusseldorf, 1967) pp. 348–49.

7. Ministry of Labour, *The Unemployment Problem in Germany* (London, 1931), p. 9; A. M. Schlesinger, Jr., *The Crisis of the Old Order* (Boston, 1954), p. 256; Eugen Varga, *The Great Crisis and Its Political Consequences* (New York, 1934), p. 9.

8. A. J. P. Taylor, *English History: 1914–1945* (London, 1976), pp. 404, 406; Irving Bernstein, *Turbulent Years: A History of the American Worker, 1933–1941* (Boston, 1971), pp. 236–46, 272–85.

9. Matthew Josephson, *Infidel in the Temple* (New York, 1967), p. 96.

10. John Strachey, *The Coming Struggle for Power* (New York, 1933), pp. 131, 175, 354, 357, 374, 396, and passim; Hugh Thomas, *John Strachey* (London, 1973), pp. 114, 130, 140.

11. R. H. Pells, *Radical Visions and American Dreams* (New York, 1974), pp. 62, 67.

12. Hans Fallada, *Little Man, What Now?* (New York, 1933), pp. 319, 370; Maxence van der Meersch, *Quand les sirènes se taisent* (Paris, 1933), p. 213.

13. Priestley, *English Journey*, pp. 161, 224; Theodore Dreiser, *Tragic America* (New York, 1931), pp. 201, 296.

14. Ferdinand Fried, *Das Ende des Kapitalismus* (Jena, 1931), pp. 62–81; Matthew Josephson, *The Robber Barons* (New York, 1934), pp. 452–53; Augustin Hamon, *Les Maîtres de la France*, vol. 2 (Paris, 1936–38), p. 341.

15. Alan Brinkley, *Voices of Protest: Huey Long, Father Coughlin, and the Great Depression* (New York, 1982), pp. 72–73, 149; T. H. Williams, *Huey Long: A Biography* (New York, 1969), pp. 692–96.

16. Strachey, *Coming Struggle for Power*, p. 132n; W. R. Garside, "The Failure of the 'Radical Alternative': Public Works, Deficit Finance, and British Interwar Unemployment," *Journal of European Economic History* 14 (1985): 539.

17. Ibid., p. 300; Robert Skidelsky, *Politicians and the Slump* (London, 1967), pp. 217, 287.

18. Erich Matthias, "Social Democracy," in *The Road to Dictatorship: Germany 1918–1933* (London, 1964), p. 62; K. D. Bracher, *The German Dictatorship* (New York, 1970), p. 171.

19. Josephson, *Infidel*, p. 81; E. H. Sutherland and H. J. Locke, *Twenty*

Thousand Homeless Men: A Study of Unemployed Men in Chicago Shelters (Chicago, 1936), pp. 160–61.

20. L. J. Louis and Ian Turner, *The Depression of the 1930s* (Melbourne, 1968), p. 5; Josephson, *Infidel*, p. 80.

21. J. A. Garraty, *Unemployment in History: Economic Thought and Public Policy* (New York, 1978), pp. 183–85.

22. Ibid., pp. 183–85; C. H. Trout, *Boston, the Great Depression, and the New Deal* (New York, 1977), p. 84.

23. Walter Greenwood, *There Was a Time* (London, 1967), pp. 150–52; C. Vannutelli, "Les conditions de vie des travailleurs italiens," in Denise Fauvel-Rouif, ed., *Mouvements ouvriers et dépression économique de 1929 à 1939* (Assen, Holland, 1966), p. 318.

24. Robert Graves and Alan Hodge, *The Long Week-End: A Social History of Great Britain, 1918–1939* (New York, 1963), p. 316.

25. Trout, *Boston*, pp. 59–60, 93–95.

26. W. S. Allen, *The Nazi Seizure of Power: The Experience of a Single German Town* (Chicago, 1965), pp. 67–68.

27. Louis and Turner, *Depression of the 1930s*, p. 113.

CHAPTER VIII

1. A. U. Romasco, *The Poverty of Abundance: Hoover, the Nation, and the Depression* (New York, 1965), pp. 202, 213.

2. Andreas Dorpalen, *Hindenburg and the Weimar Republic* (Princeton, 1964), pp. 216–17.

3. Ibid., p. 332; Gustav Stolper, *The German Economy: 1870 to the Present* (London, 1967), p. 121.

4. Walter Lippmann, *Interpretations: 1931–1932* (New York, 1932), p. 262.

5. Max Domarus, ed., *Hitler: Reden und Proklamationen*, vol. 1 (Munich, 1965), p. 192.

6. W. E. Leuchtenburg, *Franklin D. Roosevelt and the New Deal* (New York, 1963), p. 44.

7. J. C. Fest, *The Face of the Third Reich* (New York, 1970), pp. 61, 63; Albert Speer, *Inside the Third Reich: Memoirs* (New York, 1971), pp. 44–45.

8. J. M. Burns, *Roosevelt: The Lion and the Fox* (New York, 1956), pp. 371–75; K. D. Bracher, *The German Dictatorship* (New York,

1970), p. 212; Wolfram Fischer, *Deutsche Wirtschaftspolitik: 1819–1945* (Opladen, 1968), p. 77.

9. J. C. Wood, *John Maynard Keynes: Critical Assessments*, vol. 2 (London, 1983), p. 344; R. J. Overy, "Cars, Roads, and Economic Recovery in Germany, 1932–8," *Economic History Review* 28 (1975): 466–76, and "The German *Motorisierung* and Rearmament: A Reply," ibid. 32 (1979): 110.

10. S. I. Rosenman, ed., *The Public Papers and Addresses of Franklin D. Roosevelt*, vol. 1 (New York, 1938), p. 82; Domarus, *Hitler*, p. 321.

11. J. A. Salmond, *The Civilian Conservation Corps, 1933–1942: A New Deal Case Study* (Durham, 1967), p. 221 and passim; C. W. Johnson, "The Army and the Civilian Conservation Corps, 1933–42," *Prologue* 4 (1972): 139–56.

12. David Schoenbaum, *Hitler's Social Revolution: Class and Status in Nazi Germany, 1933–1939* (New York, 1967), pp. 123–24.

13. Herbert Hoover, *The Memoirs of Herbert Hoover: The Great Depression, 1929–1941* (New York, 1952), pp. 334, 420; Nicholas Halasz, *Roosevelt through Foreign Eyes* (Princeton, 1961), p. 47; J. P. Diggins, *Mussolini and Fascism: The View from America* (Princeton, 1972), p. 281; Rosenman, *Roosevelt Papers*, vol. 2, p. 447.

14. E. W. Hawley, *The New Deal and the Problem of Monopoly: A Study in Economic Ambivalence* (Princeton, 1966), pp. 470, 476.

15. Taylor Cole, "Corporate Organization of the Third Reich," *Review of Politics* 2 (1940): 449; T. W. Mason, "The Primacy of Politics—Politics and Economics in National Socialist Germany," in S. J. Woolf, ed., *The Nature of Fascism* (New York, 1968), pp. 173–74.

16. David Brody, "Labor and the Great Depression: The Interpretive Prospects," *Labor History* 13 (1972): 235.

17. Schoenbaum, *Hitler's Social Revolution*, p. 90.

18. Overy, "Cars," pp. 475–76.

19. F. D. Roosevelt, "Back to the Land," *Review of Reviews* 84 (October, 1931): 63–64; State of New York, *Public Papers of Governor Franklin D. Roosevelt* (Albany, 1937), pp. 752–59, 780–82.

20. Domarus, *Hitler*, vol. 1, pp. 174, 234–35, 304; Martin Busse, "Bauer und Boden," in Otto Mönckmeier, ed. *Jahrbuch für nationalsozialistische Wirtschaft* (Stuttgart, 1935), pp. 65–66; Schoenbaum, *Hitler's Social Revolution*, pp. 156–57; J. E. Farquharson, *The Plough and the Swastika: The NSDAP and Agriculture in Germany, 1928–45* (London, 1976), p. 63.

21. Hans-Jürgen Schröder, *Deutschland und die Vereinigten Staaten, 1933–1939* (Wiesbaden, 1970), pp. 88, 91.
22. D. E. Kaiser, *Economic Diplomacy and the Origins of the Second World War* (Princeton, 1980), pp. 74–80, 157, 161–67, 319.
23. H. S. Johnson, *The Blue Eagle from Egg to Earth* (New York, 1935), pp. 255–58, 264; Rosenman, *Roosevelt Papers*, vol. 2, p. 310.
24. W. E. Leuchtenburg, "The New Deal and the Analogue of War," in John Braeman et al., eds., *Change and Continuity in Twentieth-Century America* (Columbus, 1964), pp. 132–34.
25. Rosenman, *Roosevelt Papers*, vol. 2, pp. 12, 14–15; J. P. Lash, *Eleanor and Franklin: The Story of Their Relationship Based on Eleanor Roosevelt's Private Papers* (New York, 1971), p. 360.
26. Arnold Offner, *American Appeasement* (Cambridge, Mass., 1969), p. 14; G. L. Weinberg, "Hitler's Image of the United States," *American Historical Review* 69 (1964): 1008–9; *New York Times*, July 10, 1933; Schröder, *Deutschland und die Vereinigten Staaten*, p. 113.
27. Helmut Magers, *Roosevelt: Ein Revolutionär aus Common Sense* (Leipzig, 1934), pp. 5, 10, and passim; Robert Dallek, *Democrat and Diplomat: The Life of William E. Dodd* (New York, 1968), pp. 196–211.
28. Schröder, *Deutschland und die Vereinigten Staaten*, pp. 118–19; *Foreign Relations of the United States: Diplomatic Papers, 1934*, vol. 2 (Washington, 1951), p. 419; *Völkische Beobachter*, November 9, 1934.
29. H. W. Arndt, *The Economic Lessons of the Nineteen-Thirties* (London, 1944), p. 174.
30. Anders Stephanson, "The CPUSA Conception of the Rooseveltian State," *Radical History Review* 24 (1980): 161–76; A. M. Schlesinger, Jr., *The Politics of Upheaval* (Boston, 1960), p. 80.
31. Schlesinger, *Politics of Upheaval*, p. 77.

CHAPTER IX

1. Robert Skidelsky, *Oswald Mosley* (New York, 1975), p. 296; John Strachey, *The Coming Struggle for Power* (New York, 1936), pp. vi, 398; Nicholas Halasz, *Roosevelt through Foreign Eyes*, (Princton, 1961), p. 53.
2. Editors of *The Economist*, *The New Deal: An Analysis and Appraisal* (New York, 1937), pp. viii, 13–14, 46, 55, 145, 149.
3. D. H. Aldcroft, *The Inter-War Economy: Britain, 1919–1939* (London,

1970), p. 364; B. B. Gilbert, *British Social Policy, 1914–1939* (Ithaca, 1970), p. 308.

4. Keith Feiling, *The Life of Neville Chamberlain* (London, 1947), pp. 242–43; H. W. Richardson, *Economic Recovery in Britain, 1932–9* (London, 1967), p. 21.

5. Skidelsky, *Mosley*, pp. 200–201.

6. Robert Skidelsky, "Great Britain," in S. J. Woolf, ed., *European Fascism* (New York, 1969), p. 248; Colin Cross, *The Fascists in Britain* (London, 1961), p. 53.

7. Cross, *Fascists in Britain*, p. 58, Skidelsky, *Mosley*, p. 284.

8. F. D. Pingeon, "French Opinion of Roosevelt and the New Deal," Master's Thesis, Columbia University, pp. 3–4; David Strauss, "The Roosevelt Revolution: French Observers and the New Deal," *American Studies* 14 (Fall,1973): 33.

9. Pingeon, "French Opinion," p. 12; Strauss, "Roosevelt Revolution," pp. 27–28, 34–35; Halasz, *Roosevelt through Foreign Eyes*, p. 38.

10. Halasz, *Roosevelt through Foreign Eyes*, p. 97; Pingeon, "French Opinion," p. 43.

11. Georges Lefranc, *Histoire du Front Populaire* (Paris, 1965), p. 139.

12. J. A. Garraty, "The New Deal, National Socialism, and the Great Depression," *American Historical Review* 78 (1973): 939n.

13. Ibid., p. 941n.

14. Joel Colton, *Léon Blum: Humanist in Politics* (New York, 1966), p. 161n; H. W. Arndt, *The Economic Lessons of the Nineteen-Thirties* (London, 1963), p. 144n.

15. Colton, *Blum*, p. 140.

16. Lefranc, *Front Populaire*, pp. 145, 164.

17. G. S. Cross, *Immigrant Workers in Industrial France: The Making of a New Laboring Class* (Philadelphia, 1983), pp. 208–9; Simone de Beauvoir, *La force de l'age* (Paris, 1960), p. 273.

18. Alexander Werth, *The Destiny of France* (London, 1937), pp. 326–27.

19. Lefranc, *Front Populaire*, p. 339.

20. A. Dauphin-Meunier, *La Banque de France* (Paris, 1936), pp. 222–24.

21. Alfred Sauvy, *Histoire économique de la France entre les deux guerres*, vol. 2 (Paris, 1967) pp. 267, 303; R. F. Kuisel, *Capitalism and the State in Modern France* (Cambridge, Engl., 1983), p. 124.

22. Colton, *Blum*, p. 187; Kuisel, *Capitalism and the State*, pp. 122, 304; Sauvy, *Histoire économique*, vol. 2, pp. 254–55.

23. Kuisel, *Capitalism and the State*, pp. 114, 116; Lefranc, *Front Populaire*, pp. 450–52.

24. Colton, *Blum*, p. 181; Léon Blum, *L'histoire jugera* (Paris, 1945), p. 282; Daniel Guérin, *Front Populaire: révolution manquée* (Paris, 1963), p. 114; Cahiers de la Fondation Nationale des Sciences Politiques, *Léon Blum: chef du gouvernement, 1936–1937* (Paris, 1967), p. 90.
25. Fondation Nationale des Sciences Politiques, *Blum*, pp. 92, 169.
26. Georges Lefranc, "Le courant planiste dans le mouvement ouvrier français de 1933 à 1936," *Le Mouvement Social* 54 (1966): 89.
27. Colton, *Blum*, p. 89; Lefranc, *Front Populaire*, p. 289.
28. Colton, *Blum*, p. 303.
29. Lefranc, *Front Populaire*, p. 96.
30. Colton, *Blum*, pp. 284, 305.

CHAPTER X

1. *Political Science Quarterly* 51 (1936): 600–603; Wilhelm Grotkopp, *Die grosse Krise* (Dusseldorf, 1954), p. 238; *Weltwirtschaftlisches Archiv* 45 (1937): 493–522; *Economica* 3 (1936): 132.
2. J. M. Keynes, *The General Theory of Employment, Interest, and Money* (New York, 1964), p. 32; C. B. Turner, *An Analysis of Soviet Views on John Maynard Keynes* (Durham, N.C., 1969), pp. 23–27, 62–63.
3. Georges Lefranc, *Histoire du Front Populaire* (Paris, 1965), pp. 275–76.
4. Lauchlin Currie, "Comments and Observations," *History of Political Economy* 10 (1978): 543; B. L. Jones, "Lauchlin Currie and the Causes of the 1937 Recession," ibid. 12 (1980): 304–5; National Industrial Conference Board, *The Economic Doctrines of John Maynard Keynes* (New York, 1938), pp. 15–27; Marriner Eccles, *Beckoning Frontiers: Public and Personal Recollections* (New York, 1951), pp. 131–32.
5. League of Nations, *World Economic Survey 1936/37* (Geneva, 1937), p. 42.
6. Jones, "Currie and the Recession," p. 303–4; E. G. Nourse et al., *Three Years of the Agricultural Adjustment Administration* (Washington, 1937), p. 462; H. S. Dennison, et al., *Toward Full Employment* (New York, 1938), p. 1; R. M. Collins, *Business Response to Keynes* (New York, 1981), pp. 64–65; Jules Romains, *Visite aux Américans* (Paris, 1936), pp. 132–33.
7. G. C. Peden, "Keynes, the Treasury and Unemployment in the Later

Nineteen-Thirties," in J. C. Wood, ed., *John Maynard Keynes: Critical Assessments*, vol. 1 (London, 1983), p. 571.

8. Ibid., p. 564.
9. Susan Howson and Donald Winch, *The Economic Advisory Council: 1930–1939* (Cambridge, 1977), pp. 106–8, 346–47, 350–51.
10. Eccles, *Beckoning Frontiers*, pp. 293, 296–97.
11. Ibid., p. 296; Herbert Stein, *The Fiscal Revolution in America* (Chicago, 1969), p. 92.
12. K. D. Roose, *The Economics of Recession and Revival: An Interpretation of 1937–38* (New Haven, 1954), p. 237.
13. C. P. Kindleberger, *The World in Depression: 1929–1939* (Berkeley, 1973), p. 278.
14. J. M. Keynes to F. D. Roosevelt, February 1, 1938, Roosevelt Papers, Hyde Park, N.Y.
15. J. M. Blum, ed., *From the Morgenthau Diaries: Years of Crisis, 1928–1938* (Boston, 1959), pp. 420–21.
16. Joel Colton, *Léon Blum: Humanist in Politics* (New York, 1966), p. 303.
17. L. V. Chandler, *America's Greatest Depression* (New York, 1970), pp. 241–45; J. K. Galbraith, *The Great Crash: 1929* (Boston, 1961), p. 198.
18. Galbraith, *Great Crash*, pp. 187–88.
19. J. W. F. Rowe, *Markets and Men* (New York, 1936), p. 6; P. W. Martin, "The Present Status of Economic Planning," *International Labour Review* 35 (1937): 195.
20. J. M. Keynes, *Essays in Persuasion* (New York, 1963), p. 197; Keynes, *General Theory*, pp. 271, 307.
21. Quoted in J. A. Garraty, *Unemployment in History: Economic Thought and Public Policy* (New York, 1978), p. 242.
22. Keynes, *General Theory*, p. 378.

INDEX

Einzig, Paul, 10, 162
Elder, Glenn, Jr., 113, 114
Ely, Richard T., 142–43
Employed, the, 86, 96–98
Employment: full, 249–50
Evans, Walker, 204

Fallada, Hans, 169, 172
Farquharson, J. E., 200
Fascism, 148, 177, 209–11, 218–21
Fechner, Robert, 189
Feder, Gottfried, 160, 192
Federal Reserve Board (U.S.),
   4, 14–15, 22–23, 35, 242–43,
   245
Feis, Herbert, 71
Fest, Joachim, 186
Films, 204
Finland, 64, 150
Fischer, Louis, 143
Fischer, Wolfram, 187
Fisher, Irving, 154
Flandin, Pierre-Etienne, 40,
   223–24
Ford, Henry, 140, 188n.
Foster, William Trufant, 16
France: fiscal policies of, 16,
   21–22, 28, 30, 46, 121, 151;
   Depression in, 39–41;
   agriculture in, 55, 60–62, 68,
   73–74; unemployment in, 83,
   101, 105–7, 122, 124–26
Fried, Ferdinand, 134, 135, 170,
   172
Friedman, Milton, 14
Furtado, Celso, 77

Galbraith, John Kenneth, 31, 108,
   241, 247–48
Game, Philip (Sir), 179
Garside, W. R., 173
*General Theory of Employment,
   Interest, and Money* (Keynes),
   157, 238–41, 256n.
Germany: collapse of banks in, 4,
   15, 43; hyperinflation in, 22, 28,
   150; Depression in, 30–31,
   41–46; agricultural policies in,
   81–82; labor unions in, 88,
   94–96; and unemployment, 106,
   121, 125, 153, 159–60, 167;
   women in, 116–17, 188;
   compared to U.S., 182–211;
   Four-Year Plan (1936), 194, 202,
   241. *See also* Nazi Party; War
   reparations
Gide, André, 144–45
Gilbert, Bentley B., 216–17
Giono, Jean, 80–81, 84
Gold standard, 251–52; and Great
   Britain, 10, 15, 21, 23, 37–39,
   41, 47, 156, 216; and U.S., 70,
   221, 222
Göring, Hermann, 194
Government regulation, 11–13,
   20
Grapes of Wrath, The (Steinbeck),
   169
Great War: and Depression, 1, 12,
   52–53
Greenwood, Walter, 111, 176–77
Great Britain: Depression in,
   29–30, 35–39, 46; agricultural
   policies in, 60–62, 66, 68;
   workers in, 88, 89, 97, 141;

291